BOOKS BY

GEORGE ARLISS

UP THE YEARS FROM BLOOMSBURY

MY TEN YEARS IN THE STUDIOS

Mr. and Mrs. George Arliss

GEORGE ARLISS

My
Ten Years
in the
Studios

WITH ILLUSTRATIONS

LITTLE, BROWN AND COMPANY · BOSTON

1940

TO

FLO

*In Recognition of a Brave Deed
off Harley Street*

Illustrations

Mr. and Mrs. George Arliss, *Frontispiece*

Scenes from "The Green Goddess"

"East Meets West"

The author in "The Last Gentleman"

George Arliss as Shylock

The author in "Old English"

Darryl Zanuck, Joseph M. Schenck, George Arliss, Samuel Goldwyn

The author being received by Queen Mary at the première of one of his pictures

Scenes from "The Iron Duke"

Filming "The Iron Duke"

Scene from "The Guv'nor"

The author in "The Guv'nor"

George Arliss in "A Successful Calamity"

THE COVER WAS PRINTED IN OFFSET FROM A PHOTOGRAPH BY PACH BROTHERS, NEW YORK CITY.

Warning

THE instinct of self-preservation leads us to pause when we are directed to "Read carefully the instructions before taking the medicine." This admonition printed on the label shows a kindly consideration on the part of the vendor. It is with the same generous spirit of warning that is shown by the purveyor of poisonous drugs that I recommend you to read these preliminary lines. If there should be a paper "jacket" on the cover of this book, do not be misled by it. The "blurb" is probably written by someone whose motives are purely mercenary. It is dangerous at any time to be too trusting.

You have no doubt read in your fan magazine that Miss Blank (who is probably your favorite movie actress) has become "poison at the box office." What a shock that is — and what a lesson! Miss Blank, so charming, so clever, so delightful to listen to — and yet she is poison at the box office. It just shows that you can't trust anybody. How much more probable is it that your hitherto faithful movie star shall prove poison in the library — and if he should, how much more dangerous! To be poison at the box office really means that the mass of the audience will not take you. Presumably they have taken you many times without knowing you are poison. They have felt certain discomfort but they put it down to something else — the play or the story perhaps. Then when they take you again and again, always with a recurrence of the pain, they conclude that you are poison, and they don't take you any more. You see that is a cumulative poison which brings no sudden shock to the system and its ill effects are perhaps alleviated by the fact that it is more or less shared with a number of other people.

But poison in the library is much more deadly. You get the entire shot, — unshared, — undiluted by the sympathy of your neighbor.

By this time I am afraid you will think I am apologizing for having stepped into print at all. I am not. I am merely trying to be honest with you. I am writing these lines as sort of preface, so that you may not be misled as to the kind of book this is. I might have got someone else to write a preface — some writer of distinction — Mr. Bernard Shaw for instance. I don't think he would have done it, but I could have asked him. I once asked him to write a play for me about Voltaire and he replied by asking me how old I thought he was. He looked fresh and vigorous but glancing at his beard and not knowing whether I ought to bet on the high or low field I hedged with "What difference does that make?" He implied that he had enough work in hand to last him comfortably to the end of his life. I said I thought it a pity that there should be no play written about Voltaire, one of the greatest figures in history. I told him that he was the one man in the world to do it. What an opportunity! He said he was not looking for opportunities. This was a just rebuke for my unguarded remark and I lost confidence. Finally he said, "Besides I'm quite the wrong man to write a play about Voltaire." I asked him why, and Mr. Shaw, with his customary modesty, said: "I'm too much like him."

But if I had got a distinguished author to write a preface, would he have told you the truth? Does the writer of a preface to another man's work ever say what he really thinks about it? The reason those prefaces are so beautifully written is that the gifted author who is thus brought in as an added attraction is using all his powers as a creative writer to avoid saying what he really thinks. The consequence is there is great danger that the contrast in style between the preface and what follows may be greatly to the disadvantage of the accredited author of the book.

In case you should think I am modest, let me say at once that I should highly commend this volume to my friends, who may feel it their duty to read it, if I could declare boldly that it contains even a reasonable proportion of those sparkling stories of life in Hollywood which any reader would be quite justified in expecting. But it is in this aspect of comedy that the chief weakness of my efforts will be apparent. I cannot hope to arouse the deep, delightful chuckles of the isolated reader, or those screams of merriment from the family circle, at the sidesplitting mistakes made by the great picture magnates when confronted with the superior intelligence of the author. I am aware that that should be the comic relief in any book written about the movies. I am probably lacking in what my Uncle Charlie always regarded as God's exclusive gift to him and his immediate family — a sense of humor. I feel bound to arrive at this conclusion for although I have met many directors and managers, and executives and men who have made millions out of pictures, they have seldom said anything that has made me laugh up my sleeve. I can laugh with the rest at the misfortunes of other people. But I do not count it as a misfortune that the picture magnate has not had the Higher Education. At any rate, it doesn't amuse me. His mispronunciation of a word or his lack of knowledge of historical figures and "standard authors" does not make him, to me, a figure of fun. I do not expect any man to be blessed with a million of money together with a university education unless he has been able to pick both off the family tree. When I wanted to do Voltaire and had to "sell" the idea to my managers, I didn't think it so frightfully funny when one of them said "It ought to be good. I've read the book." He had read a good "Life," and Voltaire remained in his mind as the central figure of a novel or a story. After all, why should he know anything about Voltaire? How much does the average man know? Little more than the fact that he was an atheist — which he wasn't.

I cannot read with patience the stories of the colossal ignorance of the Hollywood producers. They are men drawn from divers countries, and therefore many of them speak broken English. But I can hardly believe that inability to speak perfect English is an infallible sign of imbecility. I should like to make it clear, however, to those readers who, like my Uncle Charlie, have a sense of humor, that I have no objection to their laughing at a man's broken English, but I am impatient when they conclude that because he speaks like that he cannot produce a good moving picture.

You have been warned.

MY TEN YEARS IN THE STUDIOS

Chapter 1

IN ORDER to get a full appreciation of the influence of the movies on the theatre and of the influence of the theatre on the movies, I feel that it is necessary to review for a moment the condition of the stage immediately before the arrival of the silent pictures. Just as the automobile has succeeded in forcing the horse off the road, so the moving pictures have gradually eliminated the second- and third-rate touring companies, and with them has gone, except for a few faded remnants, a certain type of actor that was familiar in my early days. I refer to the aging actors and actresses whom we have never heard of, but who nevertheless have "had their day," whose past successes are remembered by no one but themselves, and are recorded only on scraps of yellowing newspaper preserved and guarded as carefully as though they were the family jewels (as indeed they are). These have always seemed to me pathetic figures. And there are the men who have grown gray in the service of the theatre and have never arrived at the dignity of a press notice except in the chilly environment of "Other parts were well taken by . . ." or "Amongst those who gave a good account of themselves may be mentioned . . ." or "We must not omit a word of praise to . . ." always followed by a list of names

3

which nobody ever reads. Men who all their lives have made only shadowy appearances as lawyers, and doctors; inevitable fathers; dignified priests and butlers — seen for a fleeting moment and then *"Exit, slowly."* And how slowly those actors will exit, in an effort to make their parts as long as possible!

In my early days in the English "provinces" I knew this class well. Many had started with great promise, and then for some reason or other had dropped out. Others just went on from one second-rate company to another, year after year, the safe, dependable actors, playing all sorts of parts, but never getting out of the rut. Flo's uncle, Brander Matthews, used to call these "the Jevversees," because in conversation with other actors they could so frequently be heard to say "Jevversee me as the First Gravedigger?" or Sir Peter Teazle, or Tony Lumpkin, or some other of their cherished memories — and this was an excellent opening for the production of the press notices. Good actors, many of them. They always seemed hopeful of "getting their chance," at any rate they kept a stiff upper lip. But I am afraid if we could look deep enough we should find that hope had died years ago. The character man would say brightly "I see Irving's going to put on 'Hamlet'; I've written in for my old part — First Gravedigger. Well, you never know." But deep down he really knew there wasn't a chance in the world for him. The women did not arouse my sympathy to quite the same extent, because for the most part they had entered the profession by way of the Established Church; a very worthy beginning, and at any rate one definite step in their progress was accomplished — they were married. Their

4

ambition was henceforth usually centered on their husbands; the wife's faith in her husband's ability to make a hit if he only got his chance was strong and abiding. In the companies of which I am speaking a married couple was engaged by the manager at an upset price. Considerable reduction was expected in taking a quantity. Whereas an actor, for his unaided services, might be worth thirty shillings a week, a married couple could hardly expect to get more than forty shillings the pair, or at most forty-five shillings. The wife, to put it harshly, was thrown in, for a small consideration. Of course the manager was a reasonable human being. He did not expect her to be superlative. Often his own domestic experience had taught him that a sprinkling of the marriage service over a lady who is holding the hand of a dependable actor does not necessarily mean that she will emerge a dependable actress; but somebody has to go on for bits, and she can do that.

The financial position of these brave, hard-working actors and actresses was not improved when the silent pictures made their appearance and the cinema encroached upon the field of the theatre. Gradually these actors were pushed further and further into obscurity. I have often wondered what became of them all. I expect the wives rose to the emergency and developed ability in other directions, such as the keeping of lodging-houses or other business ventures in which the services of the husbands were thrown in and the dependable actor became a less dependable odd man.

The silent pictures as I recall them had very little use for the "has-beens" of the stage. For the most part the early pictures were a primitive entertainment and enlisted the services of youth whenever possible. The selection of a cast for the silent pictures was on a very different basis from that of its immediate predecessor, the theatre. The most important person for the success of the picture was the director. He was a conjurer who could often make the most astonishing silk purses out of synthetic material. If I tell you later how he did it, my disclosure need not be regarded as secret and confidential, because, with the coming of the talkies, his bag of tricks, effective only in the silent pictures, became obsolete, and was relegated to the deeper silence of the attic.

The actors that I have described belonged to the cheaper provincial companies in England, a class of company which, as I have said, has now passed away. As you mounted higher into the more rarefied atmosphere of the "West End companies," — those companies that perform in London theatres, — you found, and still find, another very definite class of actor. He is what is known as the "supporting" actor, and holds much the same relative position in the West End company as the bit-actor in the provinces. But there is one striking difference between them. Whereas you know at once that the established actor of small parts in the provinces could never succeed in a large part even if he had the chance, the supporting actor in London is frequently a very good actor and you are continually surprised that he goes on year after year supporting instead of being supported. He seems to us, sitting in front, to be just as good as the star, and even might outshine him if he only had the chance. Why he doesn't rise, is, to the average audience, one of the mysteries of the stage that they cannot explain. I don't know that I can explain it either. It's puzzling but I think there must be a reason. I am of opinion that in the field of the drama there is seldom a light hidden under a bushel. I believe that given, say, ten years on the stage all these people have had their chance and have failed to seize it — not from any fault of their own. They may be sober, hard-working, clever, intelligent; they know their business from A to Z, and yet they cannot support the weight of a leading part. The same audience that found them stimulating during a brief appearance discovers that they are unaccountably dull on closer acquaintance.

It is as difficult to ascribe a reason for this as to give a satisfactory definition of personality. It may be that small parts are more easy to sustain; or that we are not expecting so much from the supporting player and are therefore easily satisfied. It may be that, although he is a sound actor, he lacks imagination. In nearly all leading parts — so-called "star" parts — the actor finds moments when the author has let him down: dull moments — a scene here and there out of key with the character as already developed. The star frequently has this to contend with, and has to exert all his ingenuity to disguise these lapses from the audience. To arrive at a leading position and to hold it, it is, I believe, necessary for an actor to have the faculty of being able to deliver to an audience something more than the author has set down. There may be many instances in which he falls short, in which he fails to develop the possibilities in the script; but in looking through the career of an actor who during many years of varied productions has had to "carry the play," as we say — if he has come through

7

successfully and maintains his position, I believe it will be found that he has frequently displayed a power to raise a mediocre play above the level of mediocrity and to make a good play appear a little better than it really is. Perhaps that is why the supporting actor remains just where he is; perhaps he can be ever faithful to an author, without being able to help him in an emergency.

(I hope it is not a sign of madness to hear voices of people who are not present. I can distinctly hear voices of authors saying "Listen to George Arliss talking about helping the authors. Oh, my hat!")

As soon as it became apparent that the audience who had once seen a talking picture was no longer satisfied with a silent one, there was a tremendous rush and scramble to produce talkies at lightning speed. It was then that there came to the producer an unhappy revelation. It was brought home to him (I think much to his surprise) that there is a great deal more in acting than meets the eye; that, in point of fact, a large percentage of the actors who were quite satisfactory in the silent films were, in reality, not actors at all. You may think it strange that this fact had been hidden from him until then, but the truth is that the producers (by which I mean the men who find the money to establish picture companies), although they are vitally interested in results, are frequently innocent of how those results are attained; those producers of silent pictures realized that the director was all-important, but they didn't know how often he could make a bad actor seem like a good one. Producers, however, are almost unbelievably active and intelligent in the face of difficulties. As soon as they were told (presumably by the long-suffering directors)

8

that actors with theatrical experience were what was needed for the talkies, they started to snap up all the available good actors of the living theatre; sometimes they snapped up some bad ones, but a large army was needed at short notice, and almost any stage actor of experience was better for the talkies than the rank and file of the silent brigade. I was leading up to this when I dwelt upon the different grades of actors in the theatres. The established actors of some distinction still looked upon the movies with a certain contempt.

The stage actors, of whom I was one, were very snobbish when it came to a question of "our profession." We were very superior people. And so, in spite of the temptation of vulgar money, many of us held aloof. The London actor was a particularly uppish person. I was in America, so I was no longer a London actor, but I had been one and the snobbishness of my compatriots still clung to me. We were the actors who appeared before the Best People. It was for us to uphold the honor of our Profession. Once we stepped down into movies, we should lose prestige and the best people would never again accept us as superior actors. So we either boldly refused these Hollywood offers, or we hesitated. This reluctance of one class gave to another a tremendous opportunity. Small-part actors, whose "profession" was in the habit of neglecting them for periods of six to nine months at a stretch, came to the conclusion that honor was likely to get a trifle tarnished if it wasn't polished up with a little butcher's meat every now and then; so they rushed in where angels disdained to tread and many of them were actually sitting on the right hand when eventually the angels, with wings rather damaged,

9

arrived at the gates. In the history of the stage there never was such a time for the aging actors and actresses, those who all their lives had had to fight for a living. They now found themselves actually in demand.

In a short time they were receiving salaries such as they could not have believed possible in their wildest flights of imagination. While the "superior" actor was holding back, these pioneers were going forward and many of them were able to dig themselves into assured positions which they could never have reached if the superior class had been a little closer at their heels. It has always given me a great deal of satisfaction to see these members of my own profession making a good substantial income and living in comfort. No one knows much better than I do the struggle they have had in the theatre, and how richly they deserve any good luck that comes their way. If they haven't made a success it is not because they haven't tried — and tried hard. And don't believe those stories about the improvident actor. If the average actor did not save during his good times he could not exist throughout those long, dreary disengaged periods that are always waiting round the corner.

Chapter 2

THE fact that I got into the talkies so early was not due on my part to any special foresight of their future development. I was pursued by a man who believed in me. He firmly believed that I was *the* actor of all others to be seen in the talkies! He was not in any way connected with the business; he was interested in newspapers and was afterwards Secretary of the Commonwealth of Pennsylvania, and if he is not at this moment a Senator he ought to be. He is an Irishman of considerable girth and even wider general knowledge; he chuckles and laughs his way through life. If he attacks a problem he solves it, and no possible argument is proof against his decision. If you go to him for advice your troubles disappear with his first words of welcome and life becomes one melodious song. If he believes in a man you soon become convinced that there is no other man in the world to compare. He drinks little, but sitting over a glass of lemonade he can develop all the mellowness of a three-bottle man. If Dickens had drawn him he would have looked for a name to fit him, and with that never-failing gift for picking the right one he would have called him Beamish. And strange to say that is in reality his name — Richard Beamish.

It happened that at this time the Warner Brothers

were thinking of me. I don't wish to imply that all the Warner Brothers were sitting up at night thinking of me. But speaking of them as a unit, I had jumped into their mind in connection with an experiment; the Warner Brothers were always trying new experiments — it was their persistent efforts that had convinced the world that talking pictures had come to stay, destined to supersede all other kinds of entertainment in their appeal to the great public. The idea that the Warners now had in mind was to give the public a different kind of picture. By comparison with the pictures that were being made at this early period (1928), I believe that the plays I was doing in the theatre might be looked upon as "high-brow," and I was regarded as an actor devoted to that exalted plane of the drama. This was the time when everybody didn't go to the movies — the prehistoric days when these new talking pictures were called movie-tones. (Can you believe that's little more than ten years ago?) There is no doubt that a considerable percentage of the people that came to see me in the theatre never went to the movie-tones at all. That was an entertainment a trifle beneath them; very good for the masses, but not for the intelligentsia. The Warner Brothers realized that these lost sheep must be collected and brought into the fold. They could not be hounded in — there must be no bloodshed; they must be coaxed. And that was why they came to think of me, Harry Warner told me afterwards. (Harry Warner is the one who spends a great deal of time in New York, and as far as I am able to judge, never goes to sleep. His eyes are permanently open; his most sensitive finger he places on the pulse of the picture-going public and keeps it

there. A pulse of a hundred and six gives him great satisfaction; but if ever it goes to normal he is alarmed and
there is a hurried consultation with the Brothers. But
he also has a finger in a great many pies; if he sees a pie
that he thinks his brothers might like, he puts his finger
in it and doesn't take it out again unless he finds it's too
hot — in which case he doesn't whistle, but withdraws it
noiselessly. His whistling is reserved for the time when
his brother Jack, in Hollywood, telephones that some
large sum is required to finance a few million dollar
pictures that are to be made; and then Harry strolls into
the fertile fields of Wall Street and whistles the money
off the trees.) Well — Harry Warner told me that
when he decided to do "Disraeli" he did not expect it
to pay, but he was using me as an expensive bait to hook
people into the cinema who had never been there before.

Just how it was that Beamish was in touch with the
Warners I cannot remember, and perhaps I never knew,
but I realize now that even if I had sworn a solemn oath
never to be a talkie actor, these combined master-minds
would have overpowered me.

I certainly had no idea of "deserting the stage" at this
time. I had just finished a season in America as Shylock,
with Peggy Wood as Portia (and incidentally Romney
Brent as the best Young Gobbo ever seen), and was arranging for a London production of "The Merchant of
Venice" to open in September (1928). I am not a
Shakespearean actor, but I was tremendously interested
in "The Merchant of Venice." I have always believed
that it would make a magnificent movie. It would be an
expensive production and could not be done as I should
like to see it unless both the American and the English

13

markets were open to it. Unfortunately the Jews don't like it, and as they are great supporters of the cinema and the theatre in the United States, the American producer doesn't care to hurt their feelings — or his own. I don't understand the Jewish attitude towards the play. The Gentiles might object to it with good reason, for a greater collection of dishonorable cads than Antonio and his set it would be difficult to find. Shylock is the only gentleman in the play. Perhaps I felt this rather too strongly and must have expressed it to the detriment of my performance, because a New York critic headed his notice of the play *"SHYLOCK GOES SLUM–MING."*

Leon M. Lion was at this time the Lessee of Wyndham's Theatre. He and I had had two or three of those long luncheons which are likely to be observed hopefully and reported to the out-of-work actor. We had measured the stage of Wyndham's and found that it was too small to take my scenery. Winthrop Ames had given me a very beautiful production in New York and the suggestion was to form a partnership between Ames and Lion, and bring over all the original scenery.

For the benefit of those who do not know where Wyndham's Theatre stands, I might inform them that it is in Charing Cross Road not far from Piccadilly Circus and three thousand miles from where Richard Beamish lives. Having said "Good-by" to Leon M. Lion and turned into Charing Cross Road, I was considerably surprised to see Richard puffing towards me (he always puffs a little) wearing a brilliant tie, and looking to me rather like a newly decorated pleasure-steamer that had puffed its way across the Atlantic, through to Piccadilly

14

Circus, and never stopped until it found me in Charing Cross Road. Resistance was useless. The sun came out; the birds began to sing, the Richard Beamish weighed anchor, took me aboard — kidnaped me — and that was the beginning of the end of my career on the stage.

We now cut to the Park Lane Hotel and come to a close-up of three men sitting at a table at the far end of a long lounge. The men were Beamish, myself and Mr. Hazen. Beamish was now in close harmony with the Warner Brothers who had deputed their lawyer, Mr. Hazen, to come to terms with me. I didn't want to come to terms — I belonged to the theatre and I loved it. But Beamish was so insistent that he became serious, and when Beamish is serious one almost bursts into tears. "This is the moment! You are free!" — which was true. I had not made any promises to Leon M. Lion, and Winthrop Ames was really too ill to attend to business and was coming into the London venture merely out of friendship for me. Mr. Hazen with all modesty confessed that Shakespeare at present did not seem to him like a "paying proposition." And Richard broke into violent laughter at the idea of my doing "The Merchant" in London in preference to signing a contract for the movie-tones.

It was not entirely due to my native weakness of mind that I decided at last to consider a contract. I had sense enough to know that I was in most things too Victorian in my outlook. I remembered that I continued to take hansom cabs and even "growlers" in London long after my more sporting friends were dashing about in taxis. I realized that no invention as remarkable as talking pictures could possibly stand still; that by its intro-

15

duction the gulf between the silent pictures and the stage had undoubtedly become narrower, and that this was probably the moment for me to take the plunge.

So I said "Yes" and we all shook hands, and Mr. Hazen smiled and Beamish chuckled and there was nothing left to be done but to sign the contract.

Let us now cut to my solicitor's office in Gray's Inn Square, and come to a medium shot of four men — Mr. Hazen, Mr. Beamish, myself and my solicitor. Mr. Hazen, being an American lawyer on a short visit to London, was unfamiliar with many of our English manners and customs. In New York his office would be spacious and immaculate, with a flashing mahogany table bearing a handsome leather-bound blotter surrounded by all the things that the user of a handsome leather-bound blotter might conceivably require, *en suite* — a complete set, such as you would give as a Christmas present to a rich uncle. There was some excuse, therefore, for a certain bewilderment on the part of Mr. Hazen, as he followed Beamish and me into the private office in which this very important and rather expensive contract was to be signed. Of course I was quite familiar with the office, so I knew at once where I could put my hat; by edging round the table I could reach a pile of papers which only partially obscured the window; on the top of this pile my hat would be safe from disturbance, if necessary for many years. The resourceful Richard solved the question of his hat by deftly hanging it on the back of his own head. His stomach he steered due east, although a southerly course would have been more convenient for the interview if there had been room. There was no place left for Mr. Hazen's hat but the inside of a large iron safe that stood open and was never closed. Law papers of all shades clustered round the iron safe like ivy round an ancient church, so the opening and shutting of its massive door would be a long and arduous process; it was therefore obviously much more convenient, when once it was open, to leave it open. As it requires superhuman courage to put your hat inside a man's iron safe, Mr. Hazen held his in his hand. There was only one small chair and part of another one visible. There was, in fact, a huge armchair out of all proportion to the room, but only a few of the very old clients were aware of its existence. The spot is now marked by a mysterious eruption of documents done up with red tape. I can remember the time when the faint outline of the great chair was still to be seen, but that was many years ago.

Well, this was the office of Bolton and Mote, my solicitors — that is to say, not really Bolton and Mote, because Mr. Bolton had died some fifty years before and there had been no Bolton since, and Mr. Mote of Bolton and Mote had died even earlier than Mr. Bolton, so the entire control of the business was taken over about fifty years ago by Mr. Mote Junior — who is of course Mr. Mote Senior, there being at this present date another Mr. Mote Junior, in fact, two. But it is still Bolton and Mote, mainly because no favorable opportunity has presented itself of having the plate on the door changed. Nothing has been changed in my time, except in so far as the passing of years causes a more solid outer crust to form on the walls, the ceiling and the furniture. Yes — there was one change, about thirty years ago. There used to be a rickety staircase running from the outer office to a small room above, which room was occupied by Mr. Mote's head clerk; but the ceiling above Mr. Mote began to take on strange shapes and it became obvious that there was great danger of Mr. Mote's head clerk coming through the ceiling on to Mr. Mote's head, so the room above was shut up and the staircase was swept away — I use the term advisedly.

Having gone into particulars about the office it is only fair that I should tell you about Mr. Mote. As Mr. Mote Jr. he was tall and fair and terribly good-looking, at least my wife used to say so. As Mr. Mote Sr. he is tall and fair and terribly good-looking. He has never changed except that, like his surroundings, his outer crust is a little more solid. It would be mysterious if he had changed. It would seem strange to see a man change as he sat writing at his desk, or as he stepped into a cab to take him home, or as he stepped out of a cab having come back again. A man may change through illness, but Mr. Mote has never had time for illness. Sudden shock may change a man, but nothing could shock Mr. Mote except perhaps if a female client showed signs of being forward when alone with him in the office. And there is no such female. He has always arrived half an hour earlier than any client would expect to be able to see him, and has remained until all legal businesses are closed. Nobody has ever heard that "Mr. Mote has gone to lunch" or that "Mr. Mote is on his holidays." Nobody ever questions Mr. Mote's decisions — or his accounts. Judges accept his word without question. He is so honest he bends backwards, as my American friends would say. He has only two weaknesses; one is stamp collecting, which he carries on in the middle of the night so as not to interfere with business; the other is buying things he doesn't want from poor clients who need the money. This last is partially responsible for the lack of room, because once anything is brought into the office it remains there and becomes part of the interior. If a client is facing Mr. Mote on the other side of the table, he becomes conscious of the presence of a large dog-kennel, some aged musical instruments, many brown-paper parcels, books tied up with string, innumerable pictures turned face to the wall — all behind Mr. Mote's chair, and mellowing into the landscape. I ventured at one time to ask if we might hope for a dog to fit into the kennel and was surprised to find that it was not a kennel at all, but a huge and hideous cigar-case.

You may think that I have taken up an unreasonable amount of your time in describing my solicitor and his office, but I have done so because I do not want you to be misled as to Mr. Mote's character. You will not be shocked now, and perhaps not even surprised, when I tell you that he doesn't trust American lawyers — or any Americans. He has a kindly feeling towards them but he realizes that an entirely new combination of individuals such as make up the United States cannot be trusted when it comes to points of law, in fact cannot be trusted at all. I have a great and enduring regard for Mr. Mote and I don't wish to give a wrong impression. On consideration I think I have been guilty of exaggeration. Perhaps the only Americans that he is greatly suspicious of are those who wish to do business with his clients. He does not actually regard them as thieves, but he has a deep-rooted conviction that they would not

19

go to all this trouble about an Englishman unless they intended in some way to get the better of him. Mr. Hazen of course didn't know this, as Mr. Mote has a very pleasing if noncommittal way of saying "How do you do?" Mr. Hazen had "signed-up" many picture stars with very little more trouble than presenting the printed contract of the firm he represented, and pointing to the dotted line. He therefore said it was quite all right, please don't trouble, when Mr. Mote rang and instructed a clerk to bring another chair. (This chair is no longer in the office as it had to be removed to allow Richard to get out.) So Mr. Hazen was really surprised when Mr. Mote produced the printed contract that had been sent to him to read overnight, and said, "Of course I couldn't allow my client to sign a thing like this." Mr. Hazen said quietly, "Oh, what's the matter with it?" "Everything," said Mr. Mote. "Why, if I allowed a client of mine to agree to some of these clauses . . ." He proceeded to draw a picture of me, if I had signed a thing like that, finding myself an outcast in a strange country, practically begging for bread. . . .

"But," said Mr. Hazen, "we want Mr. Arliss; it is to our interest to treat him with the utmost consideration. We need his special services. What are you afraid of?"

"I'm afraid of a good many things." [Mr. Mote now became kindly but cunning.] "This may be all right for America — I daresay it is. But if my client comes to me and says 'What is your opinion of this?' I say 'It's nonsense — ' (*getting severe*) 'perfectly ridiculous.' If my client comes to me and says 'Do you advise me to sign that?' I say: 'No — I don't. Not unless you're an idiot.' "

Mr. Beamish, who has pulled down his waistcoat several times (a sign of agitation) during the last few minutes, considers this a good opening for ringing laughter, which he successfully employs to break the tension. We now all smile and Mr. Mote becomes very agile and businesslike. "However," he says, "we need not trouble any more about this." (*Throws aside the printed contract with gentlemanly contempt.*) "I have drawn out a contract which I am willing to recommend my client to sign."

And he now produced about twenty-five pages of foolscap, written in longhand. He had written this in the small hours of the night, in time borrowed from his stamp classifying, in order to be ready for this American invasion in the morning. He settled himself comfortably in his chair and started off brightly with a civilized British "*Whereas . . .*" Mr. Hazen sighed and no longer hesitated to sit down, in fact he went so far as to lean his arms upon the table (or rather, upon the upper crust of legal papers which formed the surface), thereby I'm afraid disturbing some ghosts of clients of Bolton and Mote reposing beneath.

Mr. Mote was now in his glory. He had drawn out twenty-five pages of clauses that gave me legal protection against everything except death. As he read on, it was more and more obvious that this was a contract between me and a band of brigands. Mr. Hazen, representing the band, was a pleasant friendly man and seemed quite unaware of the dangers that can beset an Englishman in the wilds of California. I too was surprised. I had no idea until then of the risks I had been running for many years in America, making friendly contracts with American managers. Beamish, as my agent, felt it incumbent upon him to uphold Mr. Mote, but there were moments when I had a horrible suspicion that Beamish blushed. It was in vain for Mr. Hazen to protest that he and his associates had a great respect for Mr. Arliss, that he would be the Star and could have anything he asked for.

"That's all very well," said Mr. Mote. "You have a great respect for him and so have I and so no doubt has Mr. Beamish." (*Beamish in an effort to brighten things up says he would like to take legal opinion about that.*) "That's all very well while we're in England," says Mr. Mote, "but suppose when my client finds himself in California he suddenly discovers . . ." And then comes some remote possibility fished out of the fertile brain of Mr. Mote. Presently Mr. Hazen jumps up and makes a firm stand against a clause that might have driven Warner Brothers into bankruptcy. After a legal battle, that item is at last disposed of, and Mr. Mote proceeds; and this goes on hour after hour. Beamish takes a hand now and then when he feels an umpire is needed, but I try to keep out of it. It is nothing to me. All this argument about "my client" and a certain "Mr. Arliss" gets very tiresome. I feel rather like a figure in a waxwork show — everybody crowding round and talking about it. I can't help thinking how surprised they would be if the figure suddenly came to life. But I had to keep quiet. I have a most inconvenient way of seeing the other man's point of view. I found myself continually siding with Mr. Hazen, not because I thought Mr. Mote was legally wrong but because I could not bring myself to believe that the Warner Brothers were brigands who sent a representative across the Atlantic to procure English-men merely that they might ruin them and humble Great Britain to the dust. It did seem to me much more likely that they wanted to make pictures and that they were collecting the men that could be most useful to them. So Mr. Hazen had to fight every point and Beam-ish, who was really there to protect the wax figure, finding that Mr. Mote was before him every time, re-lapsed into silence.

As time went on both Mr. Hazen and Mr. Beamish began furtively to consult their watches; they knew that whatever deadlock might be reached, it must soon be relieved by the arrival of lunchtime. The English-man's lunchtime is a standing joke amongst American businessmen. They believe that he begins to brush his silk hat and reach for his umbrella about a quarter to one and, having been placed in a taxi at one o'clock by a clerk, does not return until shortly before the end of office-hours. This of course is an exaggeration — a slight exaggeration. The lunch of the American business-man is, on the other hand, a very hasty and unimportant affair — at least that is how he himself regards it. In spite of that I have never known him to miss it. Regu-larly as lunchtime comes round, he has got to have something. He either invites you to the restaurant which is up on the roof, or down in the basement, or just next door — never far enough away to make it necessary to take a silk hat, or an umbrella; or if business is very urgent the boy is sent for a sandwich and a cup of coffee — always a cup of coffee.

At the time when Mr. Mote was expounding his twenty-five points, I was not a slave to lunch; I was still a theatre actor and while I was acting in the theatre, I took my dinner at 4 P.M. and, of course, no lunch. Mr. Mote never thought of food at any specified time during the twenty-four hours. Mr. Hazen was also a lawyer, it is true, and a good one, but he was likewise a healthy human being — and as for Richard, you had only to look at him to see for yourself. So as one o'clock came and went there was a feeling of uneasiness in the American section, — two o'clock, dismay, — three o'clock, bitter resentment, — four o'clock, a giving up of the ghost. And Mr. Mote, clear and determined and blissfully unconscious of the passing of time, went on and on. If ever there was a case of victory of matter over mind it was here. Mr. Hazen knew that the contract must be signed and it was gradually being revealed to him that the English solicitor was superhuman; that he could go on all through the night without being ruffled or disturbed or hungry. There was nothing for Mr. Hazen to do but to break down or to give in. And so at last when the distant tinkling of teacups could be heard, coming probably from the clerk's office, the contract was signed. Mr. Mote rose from his seat, with the freshness of a young man who had just had a shave and a haircut, said "Good-by" brightly and simply — not at all with an air of victory, but merely as one whose mission it is to protect British actors from Hollywood producers, and who has done his duty. And we three men tottered out with stiff eyes and necks and a feeling of strangeness with the outside world. And yet how much worse it must have been in olden times for those people who were confined in the Tower of London in little tiny dungeons year in and year out.

I was afraid that as a result of this long and painful conference Mr. Hazen would feel that he had sacrificed his reputation, and that I should be regarded with suspicion by my future employers. But it didn't come out that way at all. I am given to understand that in the inner circle of producers that contract is a great curiosity and the subject of much admiration. I would not say that it will come down side by side with the Magna Charta — but more on a level with the signing of the Treaty of Versailles. I was many times congratulated by those high up in the movie world who had been permitted to read it. They said in effect: "That's a great lawyer of yours. I certainly must hand it to you as a good picker." Mr. Hazen was completely exonerated. It was at once conceded that no ordinary lawyer could stand against one with the imagination of Mr. Mote.

As a matter of fact I might just as well have signed the printed contract, — right on the dotted line, — because I never took advantage of any power I had that was contrary to custom. And the people with whom I worked were so ready to defer to my wishes that I am quite sure that I could have done without any contract at all. But although throughout my association with the Warner Brothers I practically never needed to refer to my contract, Mr. Mote was right; with some other group of producers I might not have been treated with the same consideration. My advice to actors entering into engagements both at home and abroad is always to have a cast-iron contract, especially with corporations. If you are dealing with an *individual* whom you know by long experience to be a gentleman — I mean the type of man who would not fail to do the decent thing under any circumstances — you may be better off without a contract at all. I am speaking for the moment of stars. The Actors' Equity Association protects the actor today, but hard-and-fast clauses can only apply to minimum conditions. Contracts for stars must necessarily be special documents. My contracts with Winthrop Ames consisted of half a sheet of note paper on which I jotted down, in consultation with him, the date of the opening of the season, the season's approximate length, how much salary I was to get, and how much percentage. He would read it and nod, and that was all. We neither of us signed anything. But he was the sole manager, responsible for everything, and he was a rare character. I have known several instances of his insisting on giving more than he bargained for, but I have never heard of his attempting to give less. But with corporations, be severe. Corporations are robots — power, but no heart and no soul. The pleasant, conscientious people who are in power when you sign your contract may be replaced by quite a different set by the time it comes into force.

Chapter 3

WELL, the ambition of Richard Beamish was so far achieved; he had wrested me from the stage and I was now to be a movie-tone actor. I had no intention of making this anything but a brief adjournment of my work in the theatre. I suppose most of the actors who were being signed up at this time, and have since taken residence in Hollywood, had no idea that they were closing the stage-door behind them forever — that they would never return to the theatre. They didn't know, and I didn't know, to what extent the foundations of the stage had been weakened. We still thought of the stage as the unshakable Temple of the Drama, and of the movie-tones as a sort of rival to be reckoned with, but something that would never be taken up by the best people. England had not seriously entered into the business of making pictures; a great many serious workers were making the effort but they had not succeeded in making a really good English picture.

I had signed to make three pictures, "Disraeli," "The Green Goddess," and one other; this would consume a year of my time, and I reckoned that was not long enough for me to be entirely forgotten in the theatre. My youngest brother, who is the most Victorian person I know — except Tony Pullin — shook his head sorrowfully when he heard I was going into the movie-tones; he thought it a great pity that with one stroke of the pen, as it were, I should give up all my high ideals, all the quality and virtue of the stage that I had for years so jealously guarded. I had a number of friends like that, many of whom found it hard to restrain their tears — until at last I began to think it would have been better had Richard Beamish never been born — and that was a selfish thought, because he has such a nice wife and daughter, which under those circumstances he could never have had.

I think now we had better have a series of "dissolves." First some wheels going round very rapidly — train wheels; you know what that means — that I am leaving London. Then the unmistakable hoot of the departing ship; then a flash of a liner at sea — in case the hoot wasn't so unmistakable; then things falling off the wall which turn out to be leaves of a calendar, to show the passing of time; then a flash of the Statue of Liberty; then more train wheels to show I am off the boat; then quite a long time with nothing but train wheels going round, to show that I am going a long way without stopping; then birds singing, and carrier pigeons or doves with white envelopes in their mouths, which cleverly turn into notebooks held in the hands of press men who are meeting me at Hollywood. Of course my arrival in Hollywood is sensational news — not really, you know, but it is the business of Warner Brothers' Press Department to make it appear so. I have never quite understood why the producers go to so much trouble to get headlines in the Los Angeles papers about the enormous importance of their stars. I suppose it is because the Eastern papers know nothing about Hollywood except what they learn by reading the reports of their Western contemporaries. Only two world-staggering events ever happen in California: one is an earthquake and the other is the arrival of a new picture star in Hollywood. The effect on the population of the arrival of the star is generally greatly exaggerated in the press, while that of the earthquake is discreetly diminished.

As a matter of fact, neither event has any lasting effect on the community. Of the two, the interest in the star may last a little longer, but not much. Hollywood is one of the few places in the world in which a popular picture actor can stroll about in comfort. The natives soon become used to mixing with these live animals which the rest of the world see only in pictures. Although the familiarity by no means breeds contempt, it relieves the star of the distress of being followed about and examined as though he were a museum piece — his admirers so close at his heels that they might be trying to read the label. That is what happens in all other towns. If he stops to look in a shop window, in a moment he feels at his elbow some adventurous collector, apparently making a minute inventory of his wardrobe; or should he be with his wife, at once there is a purveyor of tittle-tattle, all ears to catch something that can be developed and then repeated. The people who are shopping or strolling on Hollywood Boulevard are mostly men and women connected with the studios. To them the star is no longer a curiosity. He is left unmolested, except that sometimes they will come up to him and ask if there is likely to be anything for them in his next

picture (they have different methods of approach —
timid — respectful — earnest — hopeful); in my case
there is the man who insists he is an old friend, and
that I know him intimately. He generally opens from
a distance with a ringing "George" of welcome. I have
a good ear for voices; this one sounds strange to me and
if it is behind me I do not turn round. Again "Hullo,
George!" comes, even more joyful than before. I still
remain untouched by this note of appeal. Then I hear
hurrying footsteps and I stop; the man comes panting
and with outstretched hand. As I suspected, his face is
quite strange to me. This time he says "Why, hullo!"
Having come face-to-face with me he drops the George,
sensing perhaps that that was overdoing it. But he is
surprised that I do not take him in my arms. He says
with great warmth "You remember me — Franklin P.
Wilson — you remember!!" There have been hundreds
of extra-gentlemen in my pictures; this might have been
one. I might even have spoken to him at some time. So
I take the easiest course and say vaguely, "Oh — yes —
how are you?"

"Fine!" and shakes me lovingly by the hand. "Well,
I stopped you because I thought you'd like to know.
You remember Alfred Langdale — an Englishman —
you must remember him — been over here for years.
You remember, Alf Langdale."

Again I take the easiest way. "Oh yes, I think I remember the name."

"Well, he died the day before yesterday. I thought
you'd like to know. Well, you're going to do a picture
I suppose — any little character bit, you know. I'm
just as good as ever — you remember me — the old re-

liable — used to be known as One-Take Wilson . . ."
until I break away.

My experience of the world is limited (and Flo did
so want to go to China) but I don't think there can be
any such pleasant hotel accommodation anywhere as in
Hollywood and Los Angeles. You can go to any one of
a number of first-class hotels, with their magnificent
dining rooms, and drawing rooms, and ballroom, and
you can book a bedroom or a suite just as in any other
big city. But in this same hotel you can take what is
called a "housekeeping apartment," which in addition
to the usual bedroom and bathroom accommodation,
has a sitting room, a small dining room and a kitchen —
a kitchen which has everything in it that any woman
could ask for, and half a dozen things that the average
British housewife has always wanted without having any
idea that they exist. Although there would naturally be
extra profit to the hotel if you ordered things from the
dining room, every incentive is given you to remain entirely independent of the public service. How far you
take advantage of these opportunities is for you to decide, but it gives one a pleasant feeling of seclusion and
security.

There is one other method of hotel service of which
I have had no experience except in California, and that
is the private bungalow. In the grounds of the hotel
there are many bungalows consisting of the same accommodation as the housekeeping apartment I have described (or more extensive if needed). You can have
your own service or everything can be served from the
hotel. There is a certain charm about being in your own
detached cottage, with your grapefruit growing outside

31

your front door — and yet with the advantage of being able to get anything you want by pressing a button. It is possible that this method of hotelkeeping exists in other parts of the world, but I have not met it. Flo, however, is never quite happy unless she is severely "keeping house," so after a few weeks we decided to take a house.

Up to this time we had had very little experience in hunting furnished houses, because we had always kept our own headquarters both in London and New York. I had supposed that you spent several weary days seeing impossible places recommended by the house-agent. We were therefore pleasantly surprised when the agent (a woman) said, "I think I know just the place to suit you — if you will get into my car I will drive you there." Everybody in Hollywood has a car waiting — day and night, it seems to me. You can't live in Hollywood without a car: the standard of distances there cannot be gauged by the mileage in other cities; the roads are wide and straight and comparatively unobstructed. You don't "settle yourself" for a five- or ten-mile drive when you go to have a cup of tea with a friend; you just jump in and jump out. We rather expected that the agent might be taking us to a pleasant little place that would do very well for the time we needed it. But we had not then got used to Hollywood standards. In any other city the house to which she took us would be described as a mansion; it was really luxurious — two stories high, wide and spacious. There is much more excuse than you imagine for those enormous bedrooms that you see in the movies — not every excuse but a certain amount, because the Hollywood bedrooms if allowed to grow a little would be rather like that.

My first impression of Hollywood was space — always room for expansion; an enormous village stretching for miles and miles with no building more than two stories high. This is not actually fact; there are some high hotels and towering stores, but they are few and far between and the general effect is long ranges of low buildings — photographic shops, teashops, antiques, "art" (of all kinds), dry goods stores, restaurants, English pipes and tobacco, stationery, hot dogs, drugstores (at every corner). Nearly every one of these places is a personal venture, I mean it is run by a man or a woman who is making an earnest effort to get a living by it. And everything looks temporary. All the shops seem to be saying "Wait and see! Wait till we rebuild, we'll show you something!" But Hollywood goes on — it can't wait to rebuild. Another real estate company puts up another quarter of a mile of shops, which are at once occupied by more antiques, transformed into more beauty parlors, — more stationery, — more drugstores, — and on again for miles and miles. But not a factory or a railway within sight or hearing. . . . As far as I know, nothing is ever made here except moving pictures. Everything has been brought in from some other part of the United States, even the trees. A mighty desert that once defied man and the elements is now tamed to do tricks and lie side by side with the hot dog. . . . At night if you drive in the mountains which form a silent and magnificent frame to this strange Hollywood, you see beneath you an immense carpet of sparkling lights; impossible to believe that that is a village — all those miles and miles of lights: twenty — twenty-five —

miles; no village was ever so vast; it must be some great fairyland with every fairy bearing a starry wand. It is disturbed only at times by a powerful shaft of light which tells you there be mortals there and that a Grand Opening may be seen tonight.

If you are a lover of the desert, if the desert fascinates you, then you must regard this making of Hollywood as sacrilege. Personally, I find the desert dull. I have driven through hundreds of miles of nothing but sand and brushwood with no sign of habitation, except an occasional wooden shack erected to supply an ice-cream soda, without which no traveler in the American desert could exist — even the camels, if they traversed this country, would I am sure stop and buy one. There are in my opinion very few spots upon the earth settled by man and not defiled. I have no use for civilization and improvements. I suppose trees have to come under the axe, but I hate to watch the execution. The sight of our English country being raided and plundered and turned into rows of thin, uniform, impersonal homes for the working classes who have hitherto enjoyed the privilege of living in nice warm slums in their beloved London depresses me. But Hollywood is the exception. I have spoken of the shopping sections as having a temporary aspect. But the residential parts are quite different. The houses are for the most part attractive and picturesque. Every house has a character of its own. There are no "rows of houses" — every structure is different from the one next door. There may be some instances of a builder having put up two or three houses alike but if so I have never noticed them. The gardens are mostly large and perfectly kept. One hardly ever sees a neglected garden. This is partly due to the fact that continual watering is necessary to maintain any kind of growth, so nothing can be left to chance. You pay a gardener so much a week or month and he is responsible for your garden. But he is not exclusively *your* gardener; he undertakes the same responsibility for a number of other residents. These gardeners all seem to be Japanese. How many gardens one man takes care of I don't know, but he works diligently and silently all day with the most satisfactory results. The act of watering is made simple for him. He does not have to walk round with a hose or a can. He turns on a tap and behold all over your lawn, at intervals of about six feet, jets of water spray up. I have no inside information as to how much water is allowed by law to be used, but there seems to be no limit. (I know that if I adopted the same method at my cottage in Kent, the bills from the local water supply company would be quite prohibitive.) There are beautiful side-roads bordered with handsome pines, or shaded with pepper trees. If you are of an adventurous nature, and fond of walking, you may be beguiled into exploring one of these roads, which has every indication of leading you into remote wooded country and then to the mountains; you set out for a long constitutional. You go through handsome avenues; you admire the houses with their well-kept gardens, the palms, the orange trees and lemon groves; on through lovely shady roads — and in the space of about fifteen minutes you find yourself back in Hollywood Boulevard about a hundred yards from where you started. The explanation of this is that some land developing company has bought a large tract of unattractive land and has transformed it into this very beautiful residential colony.

Apart from the magnificence of the embracing mountains, the beauty of Hollywood is due entirely to the hand of man. For once man has not brought destruction, but grace and charm where there was nothing but waste. You must stand amazed at the tremendous labor and determined effort that have made Hollywood what it is today; at the fine broad motor roads running clear through to the sea — not with chalk-lines to regulate the traffic but often with broad ribbons of green, and with flowers running down the center, which gives one a joyous holiday feeling as one drives along; and you must be amazed at the unbelievable amount of work that has been expended in grading the mountains, making it possible for us to enjoy the exhilaration of driving higher and higher into the rarefied air, without the unpleasant anticipation of meeting death at every turn (a peculiar fascination of mountaineering which never appealed to me). And everywhere an abundance of water. . . . I don't want to sell Hollywood to you; I own no property there; but I wish you to know that it is not just a large, barren place where people do nothing but hold conferences in studios and mutilate the English language.

Well, we took the house and settled down.

We will now dissolve. You know what that means, of course: it implies the passing of time, whereas a cut shows something immediately connected with the present scene; we will dissolve to the Studio.

Chapter 4

MY great difficulty throughout my career in pictures has been to find the right story. The "story" means the subject or the plot on which to hang the picture. This difficulty did not present itself during my first contract with Warner Brothers because, as theatrical successes were always considered a good gamble for the screen, it was obvious that "The Green Goddess" and "Disraeli" should be the first selections.

"Disraeli" I played on the stage for five years, throughout the length and breadth of the United States, "The Green Goddess" for three years including a year at the St. James's Theatre, London. "Old English" was ruled out because Galsworthy had no use for the movies. It was decided that "The Green Goddess" had the greatest picture possibility. There were a murder, airplanes, threatening natives, secret wireless, British officers in danger, and the lovely lady desired by the wicked Rajah. What more could you ask for? Well, the play had to be given to the "writers" whose business it was to prepare it for the screen. When the screen version was submitted to me, I was very much disappointed to find that many of my pet scenes had been cut out. Of course I had had no experience of the talkies (I forget how long the term "movie-tones" survived — certainly not very long) and I had not realized that the limit of time for a picture was eighty minutes, whereas the play had run from about eight-thirty to eleven. Even allowing for entr'actes, it was obvious that the original script was too long. Pictures have lately been allowed to run to a hundred minutes — or even to two hours, or more; but the most popular length is still under an hour and a half.

So when it was seen I was not satisfied there was a great deal of discussion as to how much might be replaced in order to make me feel happier. It was explained to me by the experts that, in pictures, action is of more vital importance than dialogue, and I am afraid that this is an argument that cannot be disproved. So we cut where we could without destroying the situation. We sacrificed dialogue and kept in the thrills. But when I saw the finished article it seemed to me that the thrills were not nearly as thrilling as they had been in the play. It was nobody's fault. The fact is that what made William Archer's play an unusually good melodrama — what had given it its popularity — was not the story, but the way he told it. It is probably fairly easy to cut a play in which the central figure is a handsome square-jawed young fellow who saves the lady by following the rules of the cave-man system. But you cannot cut to the bone the part of a subtle Rajah with varying moods for which an audience must be more or less prepared if his character is to be understood.

Unfortunately the scenes that lifted Archer's play above the level of the ordinary melodrama were those that could be most easily cut out without interfering with the action. I think my advisers would admit today

38

that we were a little hasty in cutting the cackle and coming too baldly to the bombs and airplanes.

Of course everything was done on a scale of great magnificence. I have seldom known an instance in the making of my pictures in which the management has not been willing to go to any reasonable expense to gain an effect. Having grown up in the theatre where we depend almost entirely on canvas and paint for our illusions, I never cease to be impressed by the unlimited resources of the studios. Houses are built that are almost good enough to live in — churches that inspire you to think seriously of other people's sins — castles that conjure up magnificent ancestors to whom you have no claim. It should be easy to act in such surroundings.

I once met Joseph Jefferson, the famous actor who is remembered in two continents for his performance of Rip Van Winkle. I asked him if he thought that acting was better in his day than in mine. He thought for a moment and then said that in his day it perhaps required more imagination, because, he said, when he was young you had to feel like a king as you sat on a soapbox covered with red cloth, while today you were sitting on a real throne, or something very like it. I often thought of this when I was playing the Rajah for the screen, and being carried in my palanquin through real rocky Californian country, surrounded by real natives, with real sunshine and a real blue sky.

"The Green Goddess" was my first experience of the talkies, and to me it was not only interesting, but restful. People think it must be tedious, when they see us go through the same scene over and over again before it is finally shot. They think it is so different from the living theatre. They do not realize that when we are rehearsing a play in which we have to appear before the public we spend many weeks going over the same scenes time and time again before we arrive at a state that seems as near perfection as we can get it. I do not speak of the performances that follow the first night in the theatre — a year, two years, perhaps five, according to the success of the play. I do not count these, because then it is not mere repetition: the presence of the audience causes new light to be thrown upon a scene almost every night. But in the movies, when a scene is finally shot it is finished, done with, — "in the can" as we say, — and you have probably repeated it less often than if you had been rehearsing a play. More patience is required in the studio than in the theatre, because you are constrained by mechanical contrivances, but the process of reaching for perfection is the same.

In the studio you may not learn how to act or to make up, or to cook, or to be a good wife and mother, but you inevitably learn patience. If you are an extra, you come to work at 7:30 A.M. and make your first appearance on the screen at 7:30 P.M. — perhaps. If you are a bit-actor you are elaborately made-up soon after sunrise and you sit about until, having earned a night's repose by attempting nothing and doing nothing, you take off your make-up and go home and come back again at sunrise the next day. If you are the star you are dressed at 9:30 A.M. as usual; but if the director is not ready for you, you are allowed to stay in your dressing room until you are called.

So for a couple of hours you smoke, and try to read the newspaper, and try to write some letters which you would give anything to get off your mind — but you can't; you can't do anything useful, because your mind is on the big scene that is before you. At long intervals you send your dresser to see how they are getting on, and he always comes back with the same answer: "They'll be ready for you in about ten minutes, but they'll give you a call." And finally you are called and you go on the set and everything is ready for you; the main lighting effects have all been rehearsed with your stand-in. You run through for lines and to make sure of the lights. And then comes your further test of patience; the cameraman didn't know that you were going to look up in that scene; so "If you don't mind doing that again, Mr. Arliss — that — where you look up," and then there are directions and corrections, and directions again to invisible men in the upper ether to kill Number Five, and to bring up Number Eight, and to kill the baby — all because I looked up. At last I say, "Never mind, I won't look up; it doesn't much matter."

But by this time the cameraman has got thoroughly interested in this unexpected diversion, and nothing can stop him. So after he has said "Do you mind just looking up again?" at intervals during the next twenty minutes, and I have been all ready to go, half a dozen times, all is really ready. Once more I am all keyed-up; the director is all ready to say "Shoot." I square my shoulders, tighten all my muscles, become perfectly unnatural, because I have been natural so often during the past twenty minutes that I can't be natural naturally any more — when the script girl with an eagle eye swoops down upon me and pecks a piece of cotton off my sleeve and swoops back again. I sigh, and tighten up again, more

41

unnaturally than ever, when the director (if it is Adolphi) dashes forward with surprising alacrity and pulls my coat upward from behind, so that it shall cling closely and immaculately to my collar. (Adolphi always lacked confidence in my English tailors.)

I say if you are a movie actor you have learned patience. You do not throw your eyes and your arms towards the heavens; you do not say "Go away all of you! How can I be expected to have imagination? How can I play my great scene with you all hopping about me? Leave me alone! I am an artiste!" No, you do not say that; you have patience; the director says "Shoot," and you play your scene. You are a movie actor.

I say acting for the screen is restful to me, because in the studio I am not burdened with the presence of an audience; this absence of an audience is a very bad thing for acting as an art, but it is a great relief to the nervous actor. All my life on the stage I have suffered from nervousness. Every night when it comes near the time to go to the theatre my heart behaves in a most unpleasant way; and when I am made up, as the overture begins, I am seized with a fit of the greatest depression. Once I am on the stage the tension is relaxed, but always, throughout the evening, I feel that I am in the presence of a powerful creature that must never be allowed to become aware of its strength — that must be watched and humored, never flogged; that I must never relax for a moment or it will overwhelm me. I do not mean that I necessarily remain George Arliss, the careful and meticulous actor, throughout the evening. I believe I have the capacity of taking on the skin of the character I am playing, but the character has to take over the reins from George Arliss and hold the audience in check. This nervousness can be very terrifying. I have walked round and round a theatre for half an hour, not daring to go through the stage door. I have stood at the side-wing waiting for my cue and knowing that I was going to create a sensation within the next few minutes by entirely forgetting my lines and hopelessly collapsing on the stage. I have conjured up the headlines in the local newspaper of the next morning reporting the horrible details; and I have known that if that happened I was down and out for good — that I should never be able to face an audience again. Of course it never did happen, because there are angels watching over actors — not in the daytime, but at night — in the theatre, nice experienced angels, ready and willing to get actors out of the most frightful difficulties.

In case you should think after what I have told you about my nervous condition that I imagine myself a strange and unusual creature, let me hasten to inform you that a surprising number of actors have the same symptoms. Some suffer more than others; it depends on their power of resistance. But there are very few who do not have recurring seizures of stage fright in some form or other. If it is a mark of genius to forget your audience, then acting for the genius must be fairly easy. But should an actor forget his audience? Is the genius making the greatest effect upon his listeners when he is unconscious of them? My friend Brander Matthews told me that he once went to see Edwin Booth, the great American tragedian, play one of his favorite roles. Brander sat in front with Booth's daughter, who had seen her father play the part a hundred times. On this particular night Booth was so carried away in his emotional scene that he was overcome and wept — really wept, without restraint. When he went off he felt that he had never played the part so effectively; but the audience didn't respond, and after the play his daughter said, "What was the matter with you in that scene? I've never known it miss fire before." Booth that night had been too much of the genius and not enough of the artist.

I am acutely conscious of the presence of an audience. I am conscious even of the quality of their varying degrees of silence: the silence that steals over them when they are approaching boredom and conveys itself to the actor and takes his very soul out of him; and again that breathless silence of acute interest which inspires him and lifts him to heights he never thought himself capable of reaching. There are many kinds of audiences: there are those that are with you from the start, and there are tantalizing ones that you can "never get hold of."

It is this variety of reception that teaches the actor his business; there are many Schools of Acting, but there is only one almighty teacher — and that is an audience that has paid to come in. It is for this reason that, when called upon, I feel it incumbent upon me to give fatherly and unwelcome advice to the young people who are eager to "go into pictures." They are very discouraged at the thought of wasting two or three years in stock and touring companies (which is what I advise), when they might be stars by that time if they went straight into the movies. I sometimes repeat to them a remark that W. S. Penley (of "Charley's

Aunt" fame) made to me when I was a beginner. He said, "It may be easy, with luck, to get to the top of the tree, but the difficulty is, dear boy, to stay there." If the aspiring amateur goes at once to the screen he probably remains an amateur always. The luckier he is at the beginning, the worse it may be for him in the end. His early success leads to his being entrusted with important work for which he is unprepared; he disappoints his audience and his managers: and once he falls, he is going to find it very difficult to get up again.

It is because of the large part played by the audience that the really good actor is seldom if ever seen at his best on the screen. However good an actor may be the audience makes him better. There is hardly a night when the good actor does not learn something from his audience. I say "good actor" because there are cast-iron actors who are entirely unreceptive, who cannot be inspired either by their fellow actors or their director or their audience — who remain on a dead level of mediocrity. But it is the audience which tells the actor of imagination just how far to go in the expression of an emotion. It is his audience which causes to jump into his head effective bits of business and new and better readings. It is that magnetism which on occasion will lift an actor above himself and cause him to achieve a great moment which he may never be able to repeat. He is uplifted by his audience and inspired by his art. He may lose *himself*, but in my opinion he must never lose consciousness of the presence of his audience; and he must never forget his technique or he is in danger of becoming ineffective. It is good to hold the mirror up to nature, but you must be sure you get the right light on the mirror. I have said that the actor is seldom seen at his best on the screen, but perhaps on the whole there is some compensation, because he is seldom seen at his worst. When he is in front of the camera he is making an effort to uphold his reputation, and although he does not give an inspired performance, he may give a very good one. This performance is registered on the screen and remains at the same level, unchanged by temperament, repetition or fatigue.

I hope I have made it clear that the reason I am at the moment avoiding contact with an audience is not because I have not the utmost respect for audiences, not because they have ever failed to be exceedingly patient with me, but merely because I want a holiday. And the making of pictures after a great many years in the theatre is to me a holiday. I cannot imagine anything much pleasanter than what is called "location" work — that is, scenes that are shot in the open country. To be out all day in the pure air and sunshine of California, and to be paid for it, is an aspect of work which seems too good to be true.

In transferring to the screen those plays in which I had for years been appearing on the stage, I naturally felt a great personal responsibility, for no matter how competent a director may be he cannot be expected to have as deep an insight into the story as one who has lived with it for several seasons. If the scenes were shot in sequence, it would be much easier for the directors and for the actors. But for many reasons this is impracticable. Some actor of distinction may be in the first sequence and then not appear again until the last. If the scenes were shot in their regular order it is likely that the lapse of time between the shooting of these scenes would run into four or five weeks or longer. It is often impossible to hold an actor for that length of time. Or it may be a question of space in the studio: some enormous set may be placed in the story at long intervals. It is necessary, then, to shoot those scenes occurring with it as background one immediately after the other, in order that this expansive structure may be scrapped and room made for other sets. So, as a rule, the story has to be rather ruthlessly shuffled and then pieced together afterwards. It requires the most careful watching on the part of the director as well as the actor, that the mood of the character may be maintained, unbroken by these abrupt interferences. Sometimes we see an actor on the screen play a scene in a temperament that is entirely out of key with what we suppose his state of mind would be, judging by what has just previously passed. This is not always the fault of the actor; it is sometimes due to the fact that changes have been made in the script at the last moment, or that the story was not actually completed when the shooting began. The actor becomes confused as to what is really expected of him, and the writers have frequently got themselves so entangled that they are more than a trifle uncertain of what they mean themselves.

There is danger, too, of a director allowing himself to fall into the error of getting a sure laugh or a dramatic climax without due consideration of its effect on the story as a whole. I was relieved of the possibility of any such lapses by the presence of Maude Howell, who has been my stage manager since 1920. She knew every line of my plays and the correct mental attitude of every actor at any given moment in the story. I could therefore leave the set when I was not actually taking part in a scene, with the full assurance that none of the values of the original play was lost. She remembered everything I ever did in the development of a character on the stage, and would frequently remind me of some little trick that had slipped my memory.

This filming of "The Green Goddess" was particularly interesting to me because it was my first experience in pictures since my short excursion into the business in the silent days. I could not help being impressed by the great strides made in the industry in the few years that had passed since then. As I have said, the standard of acting became considerably higher with the introduction of sound. There were many good actors in the silent days, but there were also many in prominent positions who were chosen merely because they screened well. A lady might be cast for an important part because her portrait, advertising somebody's furs, had attracted the attention of the producer. Having had no experience on the stage, these people acted almost entirely on their emotions — which of course is not the way to act — and these emotions were stirred partly by the playing of emotional music during the action of the scene, but more particularly by the efforts of the director, who was able to talk to the leading lady through a megaphone during the actual shooting of a scene; to tell her to take out her handkerchief and cry. "Cry a little more! . . . Oh, my dear, you're leaving your home forever! Fine! . . . Not too much: just cry gently — feel for the door — now look at the painting of your old father — your dear old father — never mind about shutting the door — Fine!" And for the moment she very likely was fine. The director gave her the uplift which an actor in the theatre gets from his audience, and which the talking-picture actor never gets.

Where are all those silent-picture actors today? Those young men and women whose prospects seemed so bright; who, because they had "picture faces," were carried out of their proper environment and found themselves side by side with the pioneer movie actors who had seized their opportunity and were making fortunes in Hollywood! Where are those favorites of the silent screen to whom fame and fortune came so rapidly that they lost all sense of values? They have nearly all faded into obscurity. Some who had business capacity were clever enough to transfer their energies from acting to the executive end of production and became very rich. The majority are heaven knows where. Sadly enough some are to be found today amongst the supers. Often in the studio someone will say to me in a whisper, "Do you know who that is and do you know who that is?" — pointing from one to another and giving names that movie fans even with comparatively short memories will remember as names to conjure with. It is pathetic to see with what courage these old-timers (who are not themselves old) accept defeat. They never ask for sympathy — all they want is work, and that is the hardest thing to find for them.

On the whole the directors are kindly and considerate towards them, but apparently these silent actors cannot be entrusted with characters that talk. They have been tried and found wanting. We of the talking pictures are warned that our time may be short, that the talent and the industry and the amazing patience of Mr. Walt Disney are showing the way to an entirely mechanized actor — an actor that is manufactured in the studio by a thousand hands, that can be controlled in every movement, that can demand nothing, that will require no examination by doctors, that cannot die because it never lived. However unlikely this may seem we are bound to admit that nothing now, in this machine-made world, is impossible. Personally I have no fear of it because although scientists claim that they can manufacture life, maintain the beating of the heart that has been released from the body, and other amazing tricks, I believe they have no hope of constructing brains, and brains are photographed on the screen through the eye; the eye mirrors the thought behind. An actor may be able to juggle with both his hands, but he cannot juggle with his eyes; they refuse to be drawn into any conspiracy of deceit. If there is nothing behind them they admit it. So the emptiness of the machine-made man would at once be revealed.

The supers (or extra people as they are now generally called) are drawn from all nationalities and nearly all classes. I do not wish to be unjust to a group of people so necessary to the making of pictures, but it is my opinion that most of those who work in this capacity have enlisted because they regard it as an easy way of making a living. Perhaps we have no right to blame a man for taking the easiest way, but it seems rather a pity that one should continue along a road that leads nowhere. Supering in the films leads only to supering in the films; it seems to unfit a man for any other occupation, so if he has no supering, he has no living. There is in Hollywood a British contingent (a fairly large one) amongst the twenty-two thousand, five hundred men and women registered as extras at the studios; they are mostly English, and so English and so proud of being English that your heart warms to them if you are English — and if you like that sort of Englishman. You cannot help wondering how and why they ever arrived in Hollywood, which is six thousand miles from the British Isles. Some of them perhaps came for their health — the clean mountain air; others may be a remnant of the silent picture colony; and there is probably a fair sprinkling of the fraternity of remittance-men. There is also a certain complacent, well-dressed, well-fed American group. These are the fortunate ones who have a small income and have taken up extra-work in order to be able to buy luxuries or extra comforts that would otherwise be beyond their means.

As a place of residence Hollywood can be the cheapest and the most expensive of any city in the United States. The best hotels are perhaps a little dearer than the same class in other towns, and of course you can build and live just as extravagantly as you could elsewhere. On the other hand if you want to live cheaply you can get more for your money in Hollywood than in any town I know in America. You can get a pleasant apartment with all modern conveniences at a very low rent. Life is comparatively easy in an equable, reliable climate where there are no snow, no severe frosts and a great deal of sunshine. If you can once get your relatives to raise the money to send you out there, and give you a little for furniture, then you can live in comparative comfort on a very small income. Of course it costs your family a lot of money for your fare, but on the other hand it is such a long way from home that you will probably never be able to come back again; and you'll have hot and cold water all the time and perhaps even a refrigerator; so it's really nice for everybody.

There is an interesting volume of short stories to be written about almost any half-dozen of this crowd telling what led to their landing as extras in Hollywood. When I am watching my director handling the confusion and perplexities of a great drawing-room scene, or a royal reception or some such tremendous affair, and an impressive but apologetic extra gentleman edges up to me, and draws my attention to the fact that the director is instructing a military super on some technical point — when the impressive extra gentleman whispers in my ear, "No captain of the Guards would ever do that, sir," I know that I am in the presence of a retired British officer. And if an elderly lady ventures, in a low voice, "No lady of the Court would ever dare to do that in the presence of Her Majesty," I am not very much surprised to find that she was at one time something-or-other in Buckingham Palace; and when a tall and solicitous extra says, "Excuse me, sir, but reely somebody ought to tell the director that no well-trained servant . . ." I am bound to be a little impressed to find that I am getting expert advice from one who was once a valet to a noble English lord.

The advice of these well-meaning people cannot be accepted without verification, because it is frequently incorrect. It is generally believed that all matters of etiquette are left to the discretion of the director, but as a matter of fact in the making of important pictures technical advisers are carefully chosen to watch every scene that is likely to need special knowledge. When I was making "Richelieu" I was so impressed with my priestly advisers that I became terribly good and truthful; when I went up in my lines, instead of attributing the cause to the furniture or my costume, or the carpet, or somebody looking at me strangely from behind the camera, I was in danger of confessing that it was my fault, that I had really forgotten my words — an admission that no self-respecting and dignified star should be reduced to.

By the time I had finished "The Green Goddess" I began to know a little more about the picture business. I was gradually breaking myself of thinking in acts — Act I, Act II, Act III, Act IV — the habit of years on the stage, but I still found it disconcerting to have to act the scenes out of their proper sequence. Al Green, who was then my director, was a most understanding man; he made every effort to help me in this respect, and, with a view of making me feel happy, a very great deal of the picture was shot in its proper relative position in the story. I was always grateful to Al Green for saying, in reply to my question about something I wished to do: "Mr. Arliss, whatever you did on the stage we can do on the screen; just say what you want to do and we'll do it!"

There are directors who believe that the stage offers opportunity for only a primitive manner of expression compared with the screen, directors who are always inclined to elaborate out of all proportion to the importance of the scene. It was largely due to simple and straightforward direction that the effects that we had made on the stage were so faithfully maintained when transferred to the screen. Al Green believed in telling the story clearly and unbrokenly, not cluttering it up with extraneous shots introduced to exploit the director at the expense of the story. The possibilities of photography are so amazing that I suppose it is difficult to refrain from doing things because you can do them. On the stage we have very definite limitations — on the screen almost anything is possible.

Al Green was a soft-spoken, quiet man. I never heard him shout at a super. He never assumed the airs of a great producer, although he had more excuse for doing so than many others. Even when the great bosses looked in he never tried to appear intelligent or impressive — he was far more likely genially to offer them a cigar which was designed to discharge a shower of sparks at the most unexpected moment, or to place under the visitor's chair a sort of time fuse which would bring about some similar convulsion. Nobody ever seemed to resent these little pleasantries and they brightened the lives of the actors and the staff. Having formed your estimate of his intelligence by watching him perform a few of these tricks, you were considerably surprised to find that he had for years collected good and rare books and now owned a most valuable library.

Many directors are careful to explain to actors whose experience has been gained entirely in the theatre that the technique of screen-acting is entirely different from that of the stage; that it is a different medium and a thing apart. If this is so I have failed to realize it. The only difference I have ever made is to subdue in some cases the climaxes of what we call our "big scenes." But this is merely an accentuation of the difference we make in the rendering of scenes in large and small theatres. One of the things an actor has to learn in a living theatre is how to reach his audience. His technique is always the same, but his method of expression may be broadened for a large theatre in order to conform to the physical conditions of the building. The employment of this elasticity becomes practically automatic with an experienced actor. The mechanical devices of the cinema bring the audience quite close to the actor, so that the broad manner of the large theatre would be an over-accentuation. But the actor does not have to discard anything that he has learnt on the stage: his technique remains the same; it is merely a matter of how to employ it. If you are acting for the screen you say to yourself: "Here is my audience, in the front row; they can see my most fleeting expression and my slightest movement. I need not force anything upon their notice"; but you use all the art you have learned from the stage — it is merely a matter of degree. That, at any rate, is my opinion, based on my own experiences. There are many in the business who will disagree with me, and will probably hold the conviction that if I had forgotten a little more of my stage technique it would have been all the better for my pictures.

It is a most unfortunate thing that in a book of this kind one is drawn into giving an opinion on stage and screen acting and how it is done. It lays one open to criticism which is likely to be quite unanswerable. It is dangerous to voice one's opinion about anything without grave consideration. I once gave my opinion in

Hyde Park. It was about eating meat. It was years ago, but I cannot forget it. It was before I appeared in pictures; those happy, carefree days when I could stroll about and examine things in shop windows without the consciousness of being myself examined at close quarters by some bright-eyed follower. I was in the habit of occupying periods of leisure in the simple and harmless practice of joining the crowd at Hyde Park Corner and listening to those reformers who hold forth on a variety of subjects from inexpensive platforms, those altars of free speech — the outlet for smoldering anger against rulers and governments, against real and fancied oppression; the vent for religious fanaticism, for a hundred grievances which the London Police so wisely permit to be dissipated into free air. I had listened for some time to a coffee-colored, bearded man who tried to convince me and a small number of other people that money and worldly possessions meant nothing if you would only follow his religion — whatever it was. And then I had moved on to a larger crowd who were being told that poor people could never be happy until they had taken away the money from the rich. And then I was attracted by a man who was talking about the humane slaughter of animals — a subject which held for me considerable interest.

There are generally a few hecklers in these crowds, those who like to make witty remarks at the expense of the lecturer. There was one large and particularly aggressive man who kept on interrupting with remarks about meat. What were we going to do without meat? He liked meat. He failed to realize that this was beside the subject of the lecture, and he got more and more angry. At last he said, "What I want to know is, can a man live without meat?" There was considerable discussion about this between various sections of the crowd, and I was surprised that a collection of men could be so ignorant on the subject.

I believe I am a very modest man when it comes to public speaking. I have been kept away from many pleasant gatherings by the fear of being called upon to speak. But as I listened to this argument I felt a strange, unnatural emotion overcoming me. It was borne in upon me that I was a man and an Englishman and a friend of the animals, and that I had something to say that these unenlightened people should hear. I was not an impressive figure. I was thin and pale and nervous, but it had to be done. There was a moment's pause and I did it. I said: "Well, it may interest you all to know that I haven't eaten meat or birds for more than thirty years." There was another moment's pause as the aggressive man turned a withering glance upon me and said: "Yes. And look at you!" That was a criticism that was quite unanswerable, and I withdrew defeated amidst victorious laughter from the crowd.

CAST

The Green Goddess

The Rajah . . .	GEORGE ARLISS
Lucilla	ALICE JOYCE
Major Crespin . . .	H. B. WARNER
Dr. Traherne . . .	RALPH FORBES
The High Priest . .	DAVID TEARLE
Lieutenant Cardew . .	REGINALD SHEFFIELD
The Temple Priest . .	NIGEL DE BRULIES
Ayah	BETTY BOYD
Watkins	IVAN SIMPSON

ৰূপ

Director	ALFRED E. GREEN
Story	WILLIAM ARCHER
Adaptation . . .	JULIAN JOSEPHSON AND MAUDE T. HOWELL
Camera	JAMES VAN TREES

Chapter 5

I HAVE said that my experience in making "The Green Goddess" had taught me to think in picture formula instead of in play construction, but I still clung rather obstinately to my theatre habits regarding make-up. In an earlier book of reminiscences I think I mentioned that in the beginning of my career at the Elephant & Castle Theatre on the Surrey side (a district in which some of the pleasantest-smelling hot fried fish could be bought, and was bought by the patrons of the gallery to comfort them between the acts), I had given a great deal of study to the art of make-up. My parts consisting chiefly of "Omnes," the only distinction I could hope for was a purely physical one. As I was very young, I always made up very old, hoping I suppose that the effect which reached the audience might at least be a happy medium. Grease paint was comparatively cheap and a yard of crepe hair could be bought for eight-pence. I am not absolutely sure of the exact number of whiskers that could be made from a yard of crepe hair, but roughly speaking I should say a hundred — fifty pairs. Although actually whiskers had begun to go out rather earlier, the news of this impending reform had not yet reached the Elephant & Castle. At any rate, all our old men had to have whiskers. A great deal of character can be got with whiskers, especially the mutton-chop variety; they should be full on the cheeks for instance for farmers, and much closer and thinner for the collectors of rates and taxes. So I got very proficient in putting them on. Our theatre was lighted by gas, a soft and pleasant light and not too hard on the whiskers; in fact, when a quick change was required, I had no hesitation in wearing one of those wire confections which carry both mustache and beard in one instantaneous effect, and which I believe are now almost exclusively used by the Salvation Army at Christmas-time to promote an illusion of warmth and happiness at cold street-corners.

As I progressed in my profession, and as the lighting of theatres became more exacting with the introduction of electricity, I made up with greater care and greater proficiency. There was no such person as a professional make-up man in any theatre in England and neither is there today, as far as I know — either in England or America. It has always been part of the business of the actor to know how to make himself up (that is a perfectly good technical expression, although it may not look it). If he does it well, so much the better. If he is careless or unskilled, so much the worse. In these days when so great an amount of money is spent on producing plays in the theatre, it seems a strangely hit-or-miss arrangement that so important a part of the production should be left to chance. Fortunately an audience easily adjusts itself to the effects of the theatre, so they seldom resent the obvious wig, or even the dab of powder on the side of the hair, placed there to establish the fact that the character is a man of the world. I am not familiar with the stage in Germany, but I understand it is the custom there to have attached to every theatre an expert make-up man who is responsible for uniform excellence in his department. This seems to be the obvious reason why so many of the make-up men in the films are Germans.

As making up is not seriously regarded as an art in either the English or the American theatre, there were of course no specialists, and so, when with the coming of pictures experts were needed, they were drawn from Germany. Strange to say, however, the pioneers of better make-up for the films were an English family. The Westmores, father and sons, established themselves in Hollywood, and became and still remain the leaders in the art of wig-making and facial disguises. I believe that it was they who first recommended the importing of German experts to keep pace with the growing requirements of the studios.

Both in "The Green Goddess" and in "Disraeli," although I was anxious to have advice, I could not consent to place myself unreservedly in the hands of a make-up man. That was the sort of thing that the English actor always associated with amateur theatricals. So I was allowed to make myself up. I soon realized, however, that making up was an art that I had never really learnt, and that what was good enough for the theatre was generally impossible for the screen. I have grown to have a great admiration for the make-up men in the studios. Many of them may justly be called artists. When I played a dual role of two brothers who, in the working out of the story, had to be mistaken one for the other, Mr. Heidfelt, who had learned his art in the German theatre, was responsible for many clever touches in my make-up designed to make this mistaken identity possible and at the same time to prevent confusion in the minds of the audience. I am of opinion that the make-up department does not get sufficient screen credit. Much of the illusion that we get in pictures could easily be spoiled if it were not for the extreme cleverness of these artists.

Great strides have been made of late years in the art of make-up, and this is due largely to the efforts of these men, who are not content with results as they are but who are continually experimenting in an effort to do better. There are some who spend long hours of unpaid time working on new ideas and new effects. I have, however, one serious complaint to make against them, and that is the way they paint the ladies. They can make you a charwoman, or an Indian, or a bogey-man or any variety of man or character woman with the greatest success. But to them, apparently, a lady is just a lady, always a lady, and nothing but a lady — and always the same kind of lady. I have sometimes rehearsed with a beautiful creature, and thought how fortunate I was to have as my leading woman one who had such expressive features — that sensitive mouth — large, but how expressive and how exactly right — and those brows — how individual! Well, I expect you know what I am going to say. When she appears before me made-up, everything that was most attractive in her has been wiped out. She is just another one of those girls. Her lips are a perfect bow — oh, how perfect — and her brows would do credit to the most fastidious shopgirl.

Why will these clever make-up men do it? I don't know. This has happened to me so often that of late years as the periods of rehearsals came to a close I have taken the girl aside and in the persuasive tones of an elderly guardian — guardian angel I mean — I have begged her not to allow the make-up department to take all the character out of her face; and she has always smiled sweetly in reply. And yet — Well, it's hard to say why they persist in doing it. I am rather afraid that the girls like it. When the man has finished doing their face, they gaze at themselves in the mirror, and are surprised to see how beautiful they look. And they go back on me; they don't say a word to their destroyer.

"Disraeli" followed "The Green Goddess" after a very short breathing space. One of the advantages of earning your living in Hollywood is that during the periods between pictures, I mean that time when you are not earning your living, you can spend all your days out of doors. Flo loves to be on the top of a mountain, and my Favorite Occupation is Walking, — as numerous questionnaires will testify, — so with as little delay as possible after "The Green Goddess" was finished we betook ourselves to Keen's Camp, which is at the very highest point of Mt. Tauquitz, and secured one of those hidden wooden bungalows that carry with them such an air of mystery. At least that is how they impress me.

I have spent my life in cosmopolitan cities, so a shack in the mountains is to me the center of adventure; and when I am collecting logs for the fire, — it is always chilly at night, — if a dog-bird swoops down on my head and pulls out a few roots, I do not complain: he is probably making a hair-mattress for the children, so let him have it. One may go to Ritzes and night clubs and be bored, but I defy you to sit at night in front of one of those enormous fireplaces with the wood blazing and crackling and nothing else in the world happening, and not feel that you are having an exciting time. Here we stayed, feeling very woolly and Western, until we were called back to work.

With Al Green as director, the filming of "Disraeli" was almost too easy. I had appeared in the play for five consecutive years, so the only lines I had to memorize were those occasional scenes which were added in order to clarify the story. I played the part exactly as I had acted it in the theatre, with certain obvious concessions to the requirements of the screen. Flo, of course, played her old part of Lady Beaconsfield. I don't think we lost any of the values that we had discovered in the theatre. Dudley Digges had been my stage manager at the time the play was first produced in 1911 and remained with me throughout our many seasons with the play — and long after. Everybody likes to be able to say "I told you so." I did tell Dudley so, or at any rate I told Moya. Do you remember, Dudley, nigh on thirty years ago (you and Moya hadn't been married so very long) when you came to the theatre one night with a flashing gold tooth, and I was horrified; and you said it didn't matter because you were only a stage manager, not an actor, and nobody would see you, and, besides, they lasted longer; and then I spoke to Moya and told her that you were going to be far too good an actor to have a gold tooth; and she made you change it for a white one? And you are. Well, luckily for me at the time I was making the picture Dudley was in Hollywood, and although he had now come into his own and was acknowledged to be one of the best character actors in the United States, he found time to come to my rehearsals and remind me of some valuable points that had escaped my memory.

It took us until the end of July to finish the film, the only summer period that Flo and I have ever spent in Hollywood. Residents in Hollywood will tell you that the summers are just lovely and really not too hot. I will not contest the point; in fact I will concede that they are lovely, but I feel bound to record that at Busch's Gardens, where we did the Garden Party scene, I often had to change my linen three or four times in a morning in order to be faithful to Disraeli's reputation for punctilious dressing. Busch's Gardens were at this time the private property of the Busch family, and were not open to the public. There is a very good system in America which, if it is not already followed in England, might be adopted with some advantage. Owners of beautiful gardens are willing to let their grounds to movie companies, for a period of one day or one week or whatever length of time it takes to shoot the scene. The leasing of these gardens is placed in the hands of one very able woman, who not only makes all the business arrangements, but is present throughout the whole period of shooting to prevent any sort of destruction. The money so obtained is pooled for the benefit of some national charity. I have received much kindness from many of these generous people, particularly from Mrs. Jewett of Pasadena and from Mr. and Mrs. Bell of Bel Air.

"Disraeli" was now finished and "The Green Goddess" had not yet been shown. At the last moment, owing perhaps partly to my persuasion, it was decided that

"Disraeli" should be shown in advance of "The Green Goddess." As it was advisable that my first appearance in the talkies should make a good impression on the movie public, this decision turned out to be a wise one. "Disraeli" was the better picture and proved to be popular with all classes.

There are many stories told of remarks overheard since the production of the picture, some of them true and some just inventions. The young American lady who said "My, what a lovely statue of George Arliss!" when she saw the monument to Disraeli in Westminster Abbey is probably true; but the story of a visitor to the house of a nobleman who had a fine collection of pictures, including one of Disraeli, — the report that the visitor said, "I see you're broad-minded; you're not above having the portrait of a picture star amongst your collection," — does not bear the stamp of truth.

There was one story I had from a hospital nurse in America which I think is too good to have been invented. One of the patients in the ward under the care of the nurse was a young business girl — a waitress I think in a teashop. The nurse had a book under her arm as she came towards her patient's bed.

"What are you reading, Sister?" the girl said.

"Oh, just historical," said the nurse. "I don't think it would interest you."

"Who's it about?" said the girl.

"It's about Disraeli," said the nurse. "I don't suppose you've ever heard of him."

"Oh, yes I have," said the girl. "Wasn't he a great British statesman who afterwards went into the movies?"

During the filming of "Disraeli" there was a good deal

of unrest in the studios due to a proposal that the Actors' Equity Association, which for many years had controlled the actors of the theatre, should absorb the movie actors so that the rules made for the benefit of all actors should be under one administration. This movement was vigorously opposed by the great producing companies, who very naturally preferred to make their own laws. I suppose all unions, and associations established to protect the rights of the workers, are formed almost entirely for the good of the rank and file. If they are fairly conducted they generally benefit the employer also. But they are as a rule of no actual value to the workers who are far above the minimum conditions — the higher-ups. In Hollywood, the stars were in an uncomfortable position; they were mostly on terms of friendship with the producers, and in the event of a strike they had nothing to gain and everything to lose. But every one of them, I think without exception, was ready to throw in his lot with the little man. That to me is a very pleasant reflection. There are many misconceptions about actors as a class — one of them, very deeply rooted, is that they cannot hang together. This is one of the die-hard traditions. It has survived the long hair and the fur collar, but it really belongs to that period. I submit that it is an entirely false accusation; it has been proved that in emergency they can be depended upon to make sacrifices and that they were in fact the first branch of the theatrical business to establish an enduring and trustworthy representative body. Having paid the actor this pleasing compliment, I will now throw a bouquet at Jack Warner, a manager. When I was confronted by the executives of the studio and asked what line I was going to take in the crisis,

67

Jack Warner cut in with "Of course he must stand by his association," which was sporting of him, considering that the winning over of the stars would have given the producers immediate victory. The result of the quarrel was a strengthening of the Screen Actors' Guild and a better understanding all round.

My contract with Warner Brothers being finished, Flo and I now turned our faces towards England by way of New York. I had to arrange my next season in the theatre. Of course I should do nothing without consulting Winthrop Ames. He and I had been closely associated since 1920 — a partnership which I hoped would long continue. Winthrop owned the Booth Theatre in New York; the theatre was his business and his hobby. I believe he hardly ever produced a play because he considered it a sure thing. He loved the gamble of doing something which did not necessarily have all the elements of success, but which he thought was worth trying. On a certain anniversary he said to Mrs. Ames, "Shall I buy you a pearl necklace, or shall we produce 'The Merchant of Venice'?" and Lucy Ames, who knew that these adventures were the breath of life to him, chose "The Merchant." This was a brave decision for a woman to make, but Lucy did many brave things for Winthrop.

You often hear a member of a theatrical company say "We are like one big family," and if you come to know the company intimately you may find this is entirely true because they are continually squabbling. But in my long experience with the Ames management I never sensed the existence of anything but a friendly relationship, not only between the actors, but also amongst the staff in front of the theatre. Winthrop Ames had the faculty of gaining and holding the very real affection of the people he employed. Men and women stayed with him year in and year out — his secretaries, his manager, his press representative, his box-office people. They respected him because he was in reality a good businessman and they loved him because he so often gave way to generous impulses that no good businessman should be guilty of.

Edna Ferber in her autobiography draws a picture of Winthrop Ames that is vivid and true. I remember that at the end of one of my seasons at the Booth Theatre he gave the use of the theatre, free of all charges, to his executive staff, and offered to produce for them any play they selected. This was to be a present to them for their loyalty and their work. He stipulated, however, that his name should not appear on the bills. They selected a comedy and invented a fictitious name as the "Presenter." I cannot remember the name, but I remember an incident in connection with it.

Let us say that the name was James Hickory-Taylor — it was that kind of name. I had asked who this James Hickory-Taylor was, and was let into the secret that it was a purely imaginary person. Winthrop, true to his word, was hard at work rehearsing the company engaged, and I was just about to sail for England, but I found time to drop into a costumier's and hire a suit of the kind that might belong to a small-town man. I made up, very carefully, with a rather ginger mustache and little side-whiskers. I looked strange but not at all impossible. I then went to the box office of the Booth and with a voice and a method of delivery that was not my own, I demanded with some heat to see the manager. They told me that the manager could not be seen at the box office, and tried to get rid of me. I was very gentlemanly, but very angry and insistent, and at last they said the manager was rehearsing the company on the stage: I had better go to the stage door. After insisting on careful directions as to where the stage door was, I darted out, highly satisfied that these women at the box office, who had known me for years, had failed to recognize me. I went round to the stage door, and as it was a new company and mostly strange people, I got past the doorkeeper unchallenged. It was about noon; as usual at rehearsals the stage was not brightly lighted and the wings were in semidarkness. I assumed an air of one who is entirely unaware of any etiquette of the stage and asked anyone I saw if he was the manager. I kept discreetly in the shadow, but my voice was rather high-pitched and my manner aggressive, and Winthrop and everyone on the stage soon became aware that something was happening in the wings. Mr. Shaw, who had been Winthrop's manager for years, came hurriedly towards me, and in a hushed voice asked me what I wanted. I asked him if he were the manager of the company, and with a little hesitation he said he was. I then went on to say it was disgraceful, — I didn't speak roughly, I was evidently a man of good breeding, but a very angry man, — I said that my mother was turned eighty and the shock had been considerable and dangerous. By this time Ray Henderson had joined us and asked me to follow him; I declined to move without an assurance that all this would be stopped. Then Winthrop, who had been listening, came forward and said, "Who are you?" I said, "My name is James Hickory-Taylor" (*sensation*); that my grandfather was the Reverend

70

James Hickory-Taylor, and that my mother, who was in poor health, had discovered that the name of James Hickory-Taylor was plastered all over New York as the producer of a stage play and that I must insist on an assurance that everything would be immediately stopped. Ray Henderson now began to act in a manner that seemed to me suspicious; I saw that he was gradually edging the party nearer and nearer to the light; I caught his eye, and I knew that he was on to me. Ray was not the man to give me away; he was just then having too good a time, but I lost confidence in myself and in a moment my little joke was exploded. Winthrop was delighted; the more so because he knew that I was not by nature a practical joker. For years after, he told the story with embellishments of his own, and he threatened in all seriousness to have a play written for me round the character of James Hickory-Taylor.

When Winthrop Ames retired and the "Ames Office" was dispersed, the individual success of those people who had worked together for so many years proved that Winthrop surrounded himself with men of more than average ability. His assistant in production, Guthrie McClintic (who married Katharine Cornell), is now one of New York's most successful producers. He has never allowed himself to be seduced by the vulgarity of the "up-to-date" play and in this I trace the influence of his association with Ames. Johnson Briscoe, the casting director with a more amazing memory than any of his colleagues, has now a thriving theatrical agency on Fifth Avenue; many of the secretaries and assistants have been absorbed by Guthrie McClintic.

Ray Henderson — poor Ray, who recently met with

such a tragic death — was the press representative, and was always detailed to work for me. When I was on the road, he went ahead of the company and was responsible for all the preliminary advertising. And I always felt secure. I was never afraid of reading those paragraphs that are known as "squibs," and which are generally of the type of "A funny thing happened to Mr. Arliss the other night when he was playing 'Shylock' . . ." and then some absurd manufactured story without point or humor. I have suffered from such press agents, in common with most other actors. When I get a string of letters from schoolgirls asking whether it is true that I prefer the old-fashioned snap purse to the modern wallet, or one from a dealer saying "I see you have a collection of two thousand walking-sticks. I have in my possession one that belonged to . . ." then I know that the active mind of my press representative has been at work.

Nothing of that kind ever happened when Ray Henderson was with me. I believe he is acknowledged by all newspapermen to have been the best press agent of his day. He had taste and judgment. He could write interesting articles and write them well. He did not load me with adjectives and then hurl me in the teeth of the public. He fed me to them in pleasant doses. If I was in Shakespeare he could write entertainingly about Shakespeare; when I was playing "Old English" he had a fund of information about Galsworthy. I was introduced without effort, like a sugar-coated pill. These newspaper articles were by way of preparation for more definite allusion to his star later on. He had the confidence and respect of the editors of all leading papers — and he had a great regard for me. I don't think I exaggerate when I say it was a severe blow to him when I signed my first contract with Warner Brothers; and until the last he never ceased to urge me to go back to the theatre.

It seemed almost inevitable that when Ames retired, Ray Henderson should come under the management of Guthrie McClintic. As time went on, Guthrie and Katharine Cornell relied more and more upon his judgment and advice. In 1937, Miss Cornell conceived the idea of doing a World Tour and Ray was sent away to cover the proposed route and to report on its possibilities. He was on his way home when the 'plane in which he was traveling from Cairo to Athens crashed, and no one survived. Ray was one of those rare characters whose place can never be filled in the lives of those who worked with him. Katharine Cornell dedicated to him her recent autobiography, as a tribute to his memory. And the press men of New York caused a tablet to be placed in his memory as a mark of their appreciation of his work.

When I reached New York I went straight to Ames. I knew that he would be chafing at the bit to be off on a new production. We neither of us had anything definite in mind. Booth Tarkington had suggested writing a play for me about Aaron Burr. I had been to see Tarkington at his home in Kennebunkport to talk over the possibilities of this idea; I had not met him since I played "Poldikin" in 1920. During our rehearsals I used to watch him writing bits of scenes on little scraps of paper, smoking cigarettes continually (large ones), bending close over his paper, and coughing as the smoke choked him. I did not realize that he was shortsighted at that time, but I often wondered how he could see to write through the clouds of smoke that were getting into his

73

eyes. But the more he choked and coughed the more he chuckled and the more he seemed to be enjoying himself.

When I called on him at Kennebunkport the chuckle was still there to greet me, the alert mind, the keen interest in his work, but the cigarette was gone and his sight was almost completely lost. His courage, however, was unbelievable. He brushed aside my allusion to his blindness as though it were a most trivial matter. And when he did speak of it, he tried to persuade me that he considered it the finest thing that had ever happened to him. He told me of the pleasure he got out of dictating instead of writing, of how much keener his imagination was, of half a dozen of the advantages of not seeing that he wouldn't have missed for anything. Of course he was just being brave, but he never let on. Eventually he wrote "Aaron Burr" for me, but by that time I was unable to produce it.

I had a number of plays under consideration. One was "Jew Süss," the central idea of which attracted me, but I felt that the last act as it stood would kill the play. Lion Feuchtwanger, the author, wrote that I might make any change that I liked, but as I could suggest nothing better, I decided against it.

At this time I would have given anything for a long holiday, but my experience has taught me that in the theatre, from a business point of view, an actor should never take a holiday and should never appear tired. If you are an actor you must either keep on or keep off. You cannot play fast and loose with the theatre. I reflected, however, that my two pictures would shortly be shown so that if I did go home for six months I shouldn't entirely drop out. I should not be in the

74

theatre, it is true, but my public would very likely see me on the screen. But there was Winthrop and I couldn't let him down.

When we met he had a hundred questions to ask me about the "movie-tones," of the technical side, of which he knew nothing; and then we talked over our next season in the theatre. He was most enthusiastic about this — something must be found that we could do — wouldn't it be grand to be working together again? How soon could I get back from England? Didn't I feel happy about coming back to the stage — didn't we have a grand time doing "The Merchant" — and what did I think about doing "Much Ado" — or what about a perfectly grand revival of "Rip Van Winkle"? My hopes for a lazy holiday faded away as I listened to him and I envied this restless impatience for work coming from a man who was far from well.

I knew Winthrop Ames very intimately, perhaps better than most people, and gradually I began to suspect that this exhibition of exuberance was not quite real.

These vague suggestions of possible productions didn't sound like Ames, who, when it came to business, was always most definite in his ideas. And it suddenly came to me that he was acting, and that he wasn't a very good actor either — that he was a tired man and needed rest, but that he would rather die than go back on a friend. So I said, "Winthrop, I don't want to do anything next season; I want to loaf. Would it upset your arrangements terribly if we didn't produce a play at all?" When anything happened to make Winthrop Ames very happy, he at once rang for whisky and soda; not that he particularly wanted a drink, but when any sudden good fortune or happiness came to him he must have a "party" and a party for him was to do everything the doctors had told him he mustn't do. I had lifted a great weight from his shoulders. He confessed that he was aching to retire from work and that his association with me was all that was keeping him in the business. So we had a party. He could work on occasions for days and nights almost without ceasing. But he had a great capacity for play. I am always sorry for people who don't know how to play or forget how as they grow old. Winthrop Ames never grew old because he never forgot how to play.

CAST

Disraeli

Disraeli	GEORGE ARLISS
Lady Clarissa Pevensey .	JOAN BENNETT
Lady Beaconsfield .	FLORENCE ARLISS
Charles, Lord Deeford .	ANTHONY BUSHELL
Lord Probert . .	DAVID TORRENCE
Hugh Myers . .	IVAN SIMPSON
Mrs. Travers . .	DORIS LLOYD
Duchess of Glastonbury	GWENDOLEN LOGAN
Potter	CHARLES E. EVANS
Mr. Terle . . .	KYRLE BELLEW
Bascot . . .	JACK DEERY
Count Bosrinov . .	MICHAEL VISAROFF
Foljambe . . .	NORMAN CANNON
Duke of Glastonbury .	HENRY CARVILL
Dr. Williams . .	SHAYLE GARDNER
Flookes . . .	POWELL YORK
Queen Victoria . .	MARGARET MANN

ↄ

Author . . .	LOUIS N. PARKER
Director . . .	ALFRED E. GREEN
Scenarist . . .	JULIAN JOSEPHSON
Camera . . .	LEE GARMES
Director Advertising and Publicity . . .	A. P. WAXMAN

Chapter 6

So Flo and I stepped aboard the first boat bound for England, with a feeling of freedom from responsibility that we had not experienced for many years — if ever before. It now seemed a little strange to me to find the silent pictures still being shown on the Atlantic liners — the sound apparatus not having yet been installed. I was very grateful when pictures were introduced on the boats, because they displaced the old ship's concert, an entertainment composed of vocal efforts dispensed by the passengers, reinforced by talent supplied by the crew, the performance derived from either source being of uncertain quality. As an actor I was supposed to be able to speak with authority on the subject of the Sailors' Home, and I was generally approached by the purser, who in his most ingratiating way would ask me to take the chair. As public speaking has always been an effort to me I was much relieved when the pictures rendered the concert and the speech obsolete. During my last voyage, however, I was alarmed by a recurrence of the kindly attitude of the purser. Ever since pictures were introduced and the chairman and the speech no longer needed, the purser had retired to his office, had become very exclusive, and did merely whatever a purser does in the purser's office. So when he once more emerged and became anxious about my comfort, approaching me in a brotherly way, I suspected the worst. And I was right. A speech was wanted.

Permit me to suggest, fellow actor, that, if you are caught in the toils and have to make the speech, instead of throwing bouquets to the sailors and to the directors of the Sailors' Home, you seize the opportunity to deliver some gentle criticism of the Directors of the Magnificent British Liner on which you are traveling. It is not only easier, but the sympathy of the audience is with you from the start. Of course, fellow actor, it requires courage, but afterwards you will find that you are tremendously popular with the passengers.

"I am hoping," you can say, "that the time may come when the imagination of the Directors will give out — when they will be unable to think of any more embellishments to these floating palaces and when these Directors will realize that the majority of the passengers don't live in palaces and don't want to, and that they would welcome a little bit of home from home, commencing with a reasonably comfortable bedroom (can somebody tell me why it was ever called a stateroom?). Or perhaps the Directors might vote to send one of the board on an expedition to travel in one of these boats and see what it is like when it's all built. And if they did and if I met him on the grand staircase, I would take him into my bedroom and ask him on his oath as a gentleman whether he thought it was a nice room and if he would like to pay two hundred pounds for it, and then if he began to tell me about the ballroom and the swimming pool, I would say to him, "*Listen,* there's a ballroom in every

Main Street in the world today — including Piccadilly and Broadway. Swimming pools can be found in every city and are becoming more and more common — not only in connection with private houses but in public houses; also gymnasiums" — I should go on like this for some time and then I should say, "Don't you think that people when they are crossing the ocean could do without these so-called luxuries for a few days? And that they would be glad to do without them in exchange for a fair-sized — a good-sized — comfortable bedroom, something that is not a hallway with a bed in it, but a room of comfortable dimensions at a reasonable price?" And I should leave him stunned by my oratory and earnestness, and I should then mingle with the crowd and be lost in the ballroom or the lounge.

Very well, gentle reader, if you insist, I will leave this subject. But what is the use of living to a ripe old age if you are not to be allowed to give advice to your fellow actor?

At the time we were crossing — 1929 — America was at the very peak of prosperity. Prices were up — everything was on the up-grade. Stocks and shares were soaring to heights that we now know were far above their actual value. It is strange that so many of America's veteran financiers lost all sense of proportion and allowed themselves to be swept into the current with the great unthinking public. We were in Paris in October when the crash came. I have always been interested in watching people — the effect upon them of any great emotional issues — I suppose it is part of my business. During this crisis I used to go with Edwin Milliken into an American broker's office in Paris. Edwin is a wizard.

He knows the market by heart. He had foreseen the crash and prepared for it — the only person I know that came out on the right side. This office remained open at night until the closing of Wall Street and of course all the rich Americans were there watching the ghostly figures as they were conjured up on a board by those apathetic magicians who walk up and down and seem to pick numbers out of the air and stick them on the wall. The millionaires sat or stood and watched their millions stalking away from them, a step at a time but always down, down, downhill to what seemed then almost impossible obscurity. I have never regarded Americans as being phlegmatic — that is supposed to be an essentially British attribute — but as I studied these men, I never once saw any evidence of violent emotion; they chewed their cigars more vigorously at one moment than another, but there was no sound, no ejaculation even; they took it like gentlemen. And yet many of them during those hours were ruined, wiped out, and their fortunes were never recovered.

Meanwhile Richard Beamish in America was puffing through the channels of Movieland, probably with a compass on his watch chain, mapping out my future career. I had no idea of giving up the theatre for the cinema, but at the moment I felt rather lost at the prospect of the possible definite retirement of Winthrop Ames. Beamish had pulled down his waistcoat and expressed his determination that I should be henceforth a movie actor and nothing else. And when Richard spoke, he spoke for the entire United States. When he came to a decision he knew he had right on his side and that no great and enlightened people could ever disagree with him. So throughout my retreat to England, wires and cables were kept hot (at least, in these days of wireless, I suppose it is the air that is hot) with suggestions from Richard. Village telephone exchanges were startled to find themselves interrupted at teatime or bedtime with mysterious calls from America. Village policemen got secret information from village telegraph offices about such messages as "SHALL I FIX DEVIL?" and "OLD ENGLISH HELD UP" until I was regarded with considerable suspicion by the minions of the law. Of course Beamish got his way; and it was decided that I should make another picture with Warners and that, if arrangements could be made with Galsworthy, it was to be "Old English." This was in reality a very obvious selection, because I had done it as a play for so long on the stage that it was reasonable to suppose there was a public for it on the screen. Although Galsworthy was weakening in his stand against pictures, he was not an easy man to deal with because he would not permit, without considerable resistance, the slightest change to be made in his plays. I knew that it was impossible to make a play into a picture unless someone had authority to make cuts and even occasionally to introduce a few words in order to carry on the sequence of the story. So I thought it quite likely the contract would never be signed.

In order to show Galsworthy's resentment of any changes it may perhaps be of some interest if I go back three years to the time when I first did "Old English" on the New York stage. I was then under the management of Winthrop Ames, who had produced several of Galsworthy's earlier plays. I was physically unsuited to Old English as he was drawn, but in spite of that Galsworthy agreed to my playing the part and Ames took up the American rights. Lyall Swete, a man of great ability, had produced the play in London, with Norman McKinnell in the part. Galsworthy made it a condition of the contract that Swete should go to America and duplicate the London production. I was in London at the time the contract was made, and when I came to a careful study of the part, I found that I needed a few minor changes in order to adjust it to my own capabilities. As Swete was to have entire control of the production I thought I had better find out before we both left England how far he would be allowed to use his discretion in such changes. Swete had caught a chill and was being kept in bed, so I had to write. This is his reply: —

Nov. 31st, 1924 [*sic*].

Dear Arliss,

J. G. does not easily alter. I have been thinking over the suggested alterations (all of which I think admirable) and I am uneasy. . . . The alteration affecting you with Phyllis . . . I feel must be put before him for his authorization. I do not know what his contract is with Ames in so far as alteration of text is concerned, but certainly I have no authority to alter. His evident unwillingness . . . to alter far less debatable matter convinces me that he would regard any such consent on my part as treachery. . . . My position is difficult. I am engaged to go out because he himself cannot go, which means he is absolutely relying on me to see that no serious alterations are made. In his letter, which I do not enclose, he says, "I can't have the play mauled about over there to get what they think will suit the Yanks." That's

83

pretty definite isn't it? I believe in this major and all minor alterations, which clarify the text. . . . I can explain it to J. G. and beg him not to oppose the *actor* in this. I will do my utmost to get it carried. . . .

Yours ever,

TEDDIE SWETE.

The upshot was that Swete and I lunched with Galsworthy by invitation. It was not a jolly lunch; in fact it was rather depressing. I felt very like an upper servant who had come to ask for an increase in wages. However, I was helped by the strong backing of Lyall Swete, and finally Galsworthy grudgingly gave his consent. I do not blame him for his evident hostility in this matter. Everything he wrote had been long and carefully considered, and nobody has a greater admiration for his literary genius than I.

Lyall Swete came over to New York and we produced the play in December 1924, and I played it for three consecutive years. It was a long time before Galsworthy visited America; but when at last he did arrive he came to see the play and brought Mrs. Galsworthy.

Having taken up your time with this rather long story about "Old English" in the theatre, I should like to have had some dramatic situation to offer you — something with heart interest. I should like to be able to tell you that after seeing my performance he dashed round, joyfully embraced me, said I was marvelous and admitted that he was sorry ever to have doubted me for a moment. That would have been a pleasing scene. But it didn't happen. He did come round. We shook hands. We exchanged a few well-chosen words. He made no complaints. We shook hands again in a very English manner (it was March and no doubt chilly in England) and that was that. Mrs. Galsworthy put a little heart into me when she stepped back and whispered that she liked it better than the London production.

And now comes the real climax. There is a lapse of five years. We are back in London and the Warner Brothers are all trying to persuade Galsworthy to allow "Old English" to be filmed; they offer him a large sum because they know of his objection to the movies. Dissolve to me, receiving an invitation to tea — an invitation from Mr. Galsworthy to take tea at his house in Hampstead. This surprised me considerably, but there was a greater surprise in store for me. When I arrived there and got my tea, Galsworthy told me of the Warners' offer and that he had replied that he would let them do the play on one condition only — that no change or cut should be made without first being submitted to me, that I was to have complete control in this respect, and that he had perfect confidence in my judgment. This, as I have intimated, took me quite by surprise. I accepted the responsibility, without asking questions — one can't ask questions at tea; it isn't like being asked to dinner, when you can become intimate. But I began to think I must have been quite wrong about his attitude at Indianapolis when he saw the play: I began to think that he really liked my performance but forgot to say so, or that perhaps he did say so but did not express himself strongly enough to satisfy my vanity. In any case I was glad to know of his confidence in me, not only because he was a great author, but because I had had so much pleasure in playing "Old English."

I never admit a favorite part or a favorite play, on either the stage or the screen, but I do not hesitate to say Sylvanus Heythorp (Old English) is the best-drawn character that I have ever played. He is a perfect character for the theatre, but is never for a moment theatrical; he is real and human from beginning to end. I hardly ever hear the play discussed without someone saying "Isn't he like Grandfather?" — or "Uncle," or "Old Mr. So-and-so" — always somebody they know intimately; that is the great test of character drawing. This was the last time I was to see John Galsworthy, and it is a happy recollection. He did not express to me any special dislike for the movies, but when I had finished my tea, he asked me if I thought it possible that the sound could be regulated so that the voice might seem to be coming naturally from the spot at which the character was placed. He said that the voice coming from a man with his back to the audience should not be precisely the same pitch as from one who is facing them. He said he noticed on the screen that words coming from the very back of a deep scene were just as loud and blatant as those spoken in the front. I didn't know what could be done about this, but I said I was glad he'd mentioned it. So the contract was signed and everyone was satisfied.

Winthrop Ames was so interested that he transported himself and his family to Hollywood and took a bungalow next to ours in the grounds of the Beverly Hills Hotel (Bung One and Bung Two we christened them) and made a "party" of it. A very happy time. . . . He came often to the studio and watched the shooting. Some of the directors were rather afraid that he was there to learn the business of picture directing, and that I should once more become his property. But he had no such idea. He was interested in the mechanics of picture making and in everything with which I was connected. I got some valuable suggestions from him (as I knew I should), but they were always for my private ear; he never interfered. If he had had his health and could have been persuaded to desert the theatre, I think he would have been one of the greatest of all picture directors. With Maude Howell and Ames both with me, and both knowing every line and every point in the play, and with Al Green directing, I felt secure. I was fortunate in having Ivan Simpson once more in the part that he had so successfully played in the theatre.

The five weeks spent in making "Old English" was a happy period for me, mainly because of the visit of the Ameses. Lucy Ames I had long admired because of her devotion to Winthrop at all times. In work or play she gave herself wholeheartedly to his mood. And when he became an invalid, she was his constant companion, with no thought of any life that had no place for him. But at this time, although he was far from well, and looking taller and thinner and more ascetic than ever, Winthrop never spoke of giving up. We talked of plans for next year. Our idea was that we should produce two plays on the stage during the coming season, and then that I should do them in pictures the following year. I still clung to the desire to get a verdict from the public before putting anything on the screen. We also discussed the possibility of doing "Old English" in London during the London Season. At the back of his brain I think he knew he would not be able to do these things,

87

but he was always brave and hated to give way. And so we had a very pleasant time in our bungalows.

I suppose there is no place in the world where so many unexpected people drop in on you as in Hollywood. You don't even know that Cyril Maude is in America; but *tap, tap* at your bungalow door and there are Mr. and Mrs. Cyril Maude, both looking blooming and ready to swap stories of adventure. *Tap, tap,* and there are Mr. and Mrs. Otis Skinner, just arrived from or just leaving for New York. Then comes Fred Latham, with Cynthia and Babs — Fred Latham, who was at Drury Lane when I first met him (shades of Sir Augustus Harris) and afterwards at the Adelphi (shades of the Brothers Gatti) and was also one of my first managers in the English provinces. Swish! And in comes Mrs. Patrick Campbell — not quite as willowy as when she and I first reached the shores of America in 1901, but with the same remarkable enunciation of words — words that poured forth as effervescent and unguarded and vulnerable as ever. Then Robert Cronin, the proprietor and editor of the *Vancouver Sun,* with Lewis Browne who writes of and for the Jews as no other author since Zangwill. If Hollywood were close to anywhere these unexpected visitors would not be so surprising, but it is six thousand miles from London and three thousand from New York. I am refraining from mentioning everybody that blows through Hollywood because — well — I recently had an advertisement sent me of some actor's reminiscences — it was a large and important notice and in red letters it said "You Are in This" — an appeal to one's pride; and then in larger black letters "Price Four Dollars" — an appeal to one's purse. I do not believe that either of my veteran publishers, in London or in Boston, would be guilty of such methods, but you never know. And as most of my best friends are not very well off, I do not wish them to be subjected to such temptation.

When the time came for "Old English" to be shown I was back in London. A new cinema was to be opened, a great and magnificent cinema, and "Old English" was to be the first attraction. Not only were Flo and I asked to be present but I was asked to open the cinema formally. I am not fond of being on exhibition, but I knew this was a very great honor and I consented. This London opening is impressed on my memory because it marks the last time I have been present at a first night of one of my pictures. There is a reason.

Reader, have you ever seen a gold key — I mean a really gold key — a large gold key? Well, perhaps you have. But have you ever been handed a large gold key on a purple cushion, and been directed to unlock a door, which swings open helpfully under your trembling fingers and discloses a magnificent interior that cost millions? No, I cannot believe that you ever have. When the King of England drives in state from Westminster down the Strand, he has to halt at the Law Courts — or some spot where Temple Bar once stood — and he is handed on a purple cushion a large gold key — or a gold mace, or a pearl-handled sword or something terribly expensive — which opens to him the whole of the City of London. But during this ceremony men in uniform are watching him, and almost before he can turn round they take this expensive thing away from him again; and when the King goes home, he has to go home without it. Not so me. When I went to Westminster and unlocked the door of the new cinema with a key of gold, I kept the key, and no effort was made to wrest it from me: for when, after what I considered a safe length of time, I looked at it, furtively, hoping it might have been forgotten, and wondering, subconsciously, whether I could get away with it, there was my name — engraved upon it in finely chiseled letters.

Flo and I were escorted by a committee, fifteen minutes ahead of the audience, in order that we might examine the theatre undisturbed. As we passed through the door I was amazed at the splendor of the decorations. Magnificent figures of Neptune seemed to be presiding: suggesting, I thought at first, the close proximity of the river Thames, but the committee pointed out that the whole scheme of the upholstery was to create an effect of rippling water, with Neptune coming out of it. It was most ingenious — all the seats being designed to look, in perspective, like gentle waves. I confess it seemed to me that in order to appreciate this illusion you had to go down to the front row and stand with your back to the screen; and if you were to see the effect of rippling waves, the house had to be empty. But perhaps I was mistaken about this.

It was a great occasion, this opening night. It was not to be an ordinary audience, except for the cheaper parts; it was what is known as a hand-picked audience — that is what the press agent told me. All the elite of first-nighters were there by invitation. All those people that fill an actor with uneasiness and melancholy. . . . And Flo and I were given beautiful seats right in the middle of them. As it was a great occasion they came in good time so as to be able to look at the new theatre before settling down to enjoy "John Galsworthy's first moving picture, 'Old English,' with George Arliss." And the Ladies and Gentlemen bustled in, merry and bright, and I was shaken hands with, and wished luck, and then the music burst forth and all these very superior people settled themselves for a nice Galsworthy evening. But this was a very expensive theatre; I believe the ground alone cost about half a million pounds. You couldn't have a theatre costing all that money and just give "Old English." There had to be some added attractions: the best of course; something in keeping with the occasion. I think we started with some elephants; I am not quite sure — my memory is rather confused: it might have been camels, but I know we started off with something big. It was a lovely surprise. This was about eight o'clock — I expect it was a little later. Then we had a perfectly delightful lot of acrobats; they lasted quite a long time. Then the stage opened and the most amazing gigantic figures came up from the bowels of the stage and other things came down from the flies, and we were all very much impressed with the amount of money this must have cost. And then you had hardly got your breath, when suddenly the stage was filled with what seemed to be literally hundreds of most beautiful girls. And they danced and danced and the gigantic figures did the most amazing things with their eyes and their arms. It was evident that no expense had been spared to make "Old English" a success. It was now about nine-thirty. I glanced round from my front seat in the circle and found that all the Galsworthy followers were still there — smiling — a little wanly perhaps, but smiling.

And on went the show. My memory becomes more and more confused as I try to recall all the tremendous items that followed. I think there were performing dogs. And then I'm almost sure there were more acrobats. About ten-thirty I began to have an uncomfortable feeling that perhaps "Old English" had been forgotten, or that it was going to be replaced by something with more pep in it. Incredible as it may seem I almost believed that the attention of the Galsworthy groups was being distracted by thoughts of supper, and although I was still sitting in their full view, their interest in me, George Arliss in person, seemed to be gradually diminishing. About ten-thirty-five there was a great deal of noise and activity on the stage which I afterwards realized was a tremendous climax; for lo! in a moment the stage was clear — nothing was to be seen; there was an ominous, a holy calm; a religious light filled the theatre; a distant organ could be heard; and there seemed to be little doubt that we were going to hear the funeral service read over the bodies of the acrobats and the pretty chorus-girls. But I noticed a slight revival of interest in me, in person; some encouraging glances were directed towards me; and then I began to understand that this atmosphere of depression was brought about to prepare us for "Old English," and that the screen was at last to be brought into action. The Galsworthy groups once more dug themselves into their seats, and I saw that they meant to behave like Ladies and Gentlemen, no matter how thirsty they were. . . . But it turned out not to be "Old English" after all. It was another added attraction. It was a news-reel, and so interesting. It told us all about everything happening in China and Japan and the House of Lords, and Lords Cricket Ground, and all the principal centers of the world. Certainly the management was doing everything to make "Old English" a success. There was, however, a limit to their resources; the newsreel exhausted the added attractions, and it was really followed by "Old English."

But how dull it seemed! Dull, dull — after all the exciting things we had been having. I knew what I was in for. You can't advertise your star and then bring him on at bedtime. My experience of the theatre told me that "Old English" was going to fall flat. I watched it painfully for the first ten minutes. I saw that an old gentleman of eighty-odd, shuffling about on the screen, could not compete with elephants. My stanch supporters, who had held up bravely since eight o'clock, began to wilt; when suddenly, there upon the screen, appeared a novel and unexpected comic interlude. The sound entirely ceased, but the movements of the figures continued.

You have no doubt amused the children by doubling your thumb inwards and clenching your fingers over it, so that the thumb and forefinger become a funny mouth. It used rather to frighten me when I was a child because it looked so real, and yet no sound came from it. This flashed across my mind as I watched the figures on the screen. They, all of a sudden, became all mouth: you looked at nothing but the mouth. In a moment every character on the screen became a gibbering idiot. The audience behaved beautifully; not merely the specially selected hothouse ones around me, but the common or garden variety in the front. They realized

93

that there was a breakdown in the machinery, and they were sympathetic. This went on for what seemed to me an interminable time, when, in a most startling manner, the sound came back — but it hadn't caught up with the action; the sound started from the spot where it left off, while the action was ten good lengths ahead. Consequently the mouths and the words were doing the most marvelous conjuring tricks on the screen. This was too much for the audience; they let themselves go and screamed with laughter. Even the Galsworthy groups gave up being Ladies and Gentlemen and shook with delight. I, alone, sat with a dour and awful expression that would have been worth money to me if ever I could have done it on the stage. I sat rigid and no doubt purple and pale alternately, feeling like the prisoner in the dock with the scene of the crime being enacted in the courtroom, or like someone in the dentist's chair, with the one consolation that however awful it is, it can't last long. But it did — it went on and on, with all the brightness and assurance of an added attraction. When I had had as much as I could endure, I almost literally leapt from my seat in person and fled up the steep steps of the circle, down the marble stairs beyond, past marble pillars, down more marble stairways, the vastness of which you can never know unless you find yourself alone, flying through marble distances with not another soul in sight. Not a soul. What recked it that I had the golden key of the great mansion in my trousers pocket at the moment, if I couldn't find some way of stopping myself from making an idiot of myself on the screen beyond.

Well — gentle reader — we mustn't be too hard

upon them. After all it was a great occasion! As I have told you, the land alone cost half a million pounds; and on a night like this — of course there must be a number of heads of departments, and then the press was there; and it had started at eight o'clock and it was now about eleven. And through all those hours (except the last fifteen minutes) they had stuck to their posts; they had seen the ship launched and bravely away on a prosperous voyage; they had never left the bridge, as you might say, until all the livestock had made its appearance, and been safely battened down (if we continue to be nautical) and had never ceased to keep a sharp look-out until they had seen the Silver Sheet run up, or unfurled; then and not till then did they for a moment turn their backs, confident that the trusty sheet would, under the eyes of the magnificent Neptunes, wave or flap, or bulge or bend defiantly to the elements. All of which it was now doing. Well, the whole secret was, there was champagne. You must have champagne on such a special occasion, and as everything was going so beautifully, this was the time to have it, in a little private room far from the madding star. My entrance into this private room was a surprise, not a joyful one for it broke up the party and eventually resulted in the race between the sound and the action being disallowed; the contestants started again from scratch, and I'm not sure that the catastrophe didn't save the situation. It woke everybody up, put them in a good humor; Flo says they stayed to the end, and applauded. I wasn't there because I didn't go back, and have never been to a first night since. I went once lately when Queen Mary had graciously consented to receive me at the end of the picture, but I waited in a private room until the show was over.

If I return to the stage I shall probably revive "Old English." As time goes on, many parts of the play may become dated, but the character of Old Heythorp fifty years from now will ring as true as ever.

CAST

Old English

Old Heythorp	. .	GEORGE ARLISS
Joe Pillin	. .	IVAN SIMPSON
Charles Ventnor	. .	MURRAY KINNELL
Meller	. . .	HENRY MORRALL
Mrs. Larne	. .	DORIS LLOYD
Phyllis Larne	. .	BETTY LAWFORD
Adela Heythorp	. .	ETHEL GRIFFIES
Bob Pillin	. .	REGINALD SHEFFIELD
Molly	. . .	JOAN MCLAIN
Jock	. . .	LEON JANNEY
Westgate	. .	H. COOPER
Winkley	. .	C. MORGAN
Budgeon	. .	JOHN ROGERS
Mr. Brownbee	. .	M. BUNSTON
Appleby	. .	CHARLES E. EVANS
Letty	. . .	HENRIETTA GOODWIN
Clerks	. . .	LARRY WINTON AND POWELL YORK
Farney	. .	HARRINGTON REYNOLDS

∽

Director	. .	ALFRED E. GREEN
Play and Dialogue	.	JOHN GALSWORTHY
Adaptation	. .	WALTER ANTHONY AND MAUDE T. HOWELL
Camera	. .	JAMES VAN TREES

Chapter 7

HAVING signed still another contract with Warner Brothers, and "Disraeli," "The Green Goddess" and "Old English" having been disposed of, it became necessary to decide on what was to be my next picture. Many people believe that it is quite easy for me to find a subject to suit me. They say: "Not very difficult for you — whole field of historical characters never been touched — Richard the Third and that sort of thing, I mean." If I thought I were capable of playing all the parts that my most faithful followers believe I can play, life in the studio would be a great deal easier for me; but sometimes even actors are conscious of their limitations: they are not always right; perhaps they are frequently wrong. A star, however, who has to carry the play or picture must be guided by his own judgment. If he decides that he is incapable of giving a convincing performance of a part, I think his opinion is more likely to be right than wrong. Briefly, it is my belief that an actor is likely to be right in avoiding a part that is antagonistic to his own personality or one that offends his intelligence. Of course it is not necessary to be in sympathy with the behavior of a character in order to feel that you can make that character your own. The actor himself may be a person of most exemplary reputation and yet he may be tremendously attracted by the most villainous villains.

As a matter of fact, when I think back to the men I have known whose line of business was what we call "heavies" — that is, the villains — and compare them with the "leading men" of my acquaintance — the heroes, those clean-cut fellows with firm jaws and wonderful shoulders, those chaps who look so well in tweeds — comparing the two classes, I have to admit that for reliability, moral backbone and pleasant companionship, the balance is in favor of the villain. Perhaps I am prejudiced because in the Victorian Era I used to play heavies myself; "gentlemanly heavies" they were called and, my gracious, how gentlemanly they were! None of your two-gun men, mere purloiners of pearls and bonds — things out of iron safes; the "gentlemanly heavy" desired one thing only — the lady. He lived and worked and strived for only one thing — to possess the lady. He was a villain it is true, but only because he was obsessed with this absorbing passion. I am sorry for all lovers of the drama who have had no opportunity of becoming acquainted with the Victorian villain. I do not hold with evil practices; I am a law-abiding person; but I cannot help feeling a certain admiration for the gentlemanly heavy. The hero of course was admirable and of course he loved the heroine (the lady) — that goes without saying; but did he ever take the risks, or make the sacrifices for her, that the villain made? It isn't as though the gentlemanly heavy was ugly or misshapen; he was quite beautiful to look at, with his well-fitting clothes and his well-groomed hair and his graceful mustache. But from the beginning, even before they knew he was the villain, he was never treated fairly by either the hero or the heroine. At his very first entrance (to music) the heroine would direct her right shoulder towards him, rest her chin upon it, and open fire upon him with her eyes and her tongue. I suppose we have to admit that her woman's instinct warned her that he was about to make proposals of an intimate nature, proposals that did not definitely include the marriage service. But we soon find out that this is only his way. Just a sort of acid test. As soon as he discovers that she is not that kind of woman (which I confess he might have known from the first) he offers to marry her immediately. No gentleman could say fairer than that. I cannot recall any villain of the Victorian drama who was not willing to do the honest thing by the lady if you only gave him time — by Act III let us say, or at latest Act IV. And how tremendously he loves her! The hero is supposed to be in love with her, but he is always thinking of getting an honest living, saving enough money to get a home together — a nest; he will even accept work that takes him hundreds of miles away. Does the villain do things like that? As soon as he has fallen thoroughly in love, he gives up work completely and devotes himself entirely to the lady. And he is willing to take terrible chances in order to get her. I have known him to steal the jewels, not because he wanted them, but just so that he could put them in the hero's coat pocket and blacken him in the eyes of the lady. You see, he is enormously attracted by a good and beautiful woman as soon as he meets one. That shows he is not really a bad man. It always seemed to me that such intense devotion should be rewarded with some measure of success; there is no particular credit due to the hero for being good; he has known the heroine from childhood and he has always been nicely brought up — nice parents to guide him. Has anybody ever heard of a villain having parents? Never! These were the admirable villains of the last century. But as time went on and Queen Victoria passed away and heroines became less easily shocked and more and more forgiving — as the virtue of the villain was gradually revealed to a more indulgent public — authors began to merge the society hero and the gentlemanly heavy into one composite character; and as I never could play heroes, my day as a specialist in villains was over. As soon as the villain began to show the appalling bad taste of caring more for the pearls than for the lady, I washed my hands of him.

I hope I may be forgiven if now and then I stray back into the old days of the theatre. I am well aware that those good old days were not entirely good. The drama was artificial. But it had form; writing for the theatre was acknowledged to be a definite branch of literature apart from the mere capability of writing dialogue. Today we are far less bound by convention, and for that reason our theatre is better, but many writers for the stage would do well to study some of the old-established rules of construction, not necessarily to follow them blindly, but to learn why those rules were laid down, and to be guided by the principles that have stood the test of time.

In my search for a worth-while picture I may hit on a character that appeals to me, but I may not be allowed to play it. When I have quite decided that I want to do Richard III for instance, I may be told by the producer that the public is tired of historical plays. At certain periods that seem to come in cycles, the word goes through the entire industry that "They don't want costume pictures any more" ("They" always means the public) or "They don't want historical pictures," or "They don't want any more Negro pictures."

All producers seem to get this message at the same moment: a certain kind of story that was once popular now spells ruin. This condition of the public taste seems to be regarded, by producers and theatrical managers alike, as a disease which has suddenly and unaccountably seized the entire theatregoing public. I do not pretend to know as much about the public taste as those producers who have made large fortunes by their successful choice of subjects, but I am convinced that there is only one definition of "what the public wants" and that is — something really good. The public doesn't know what it wants until it gets it. Why don't they want historical pictures? The reason seems to me obvious. After a surfeit of, let us say, gangster stories, some astute producer brings out a fine historical picture which is a great success. Instantly the word goes round, "This is what the public wants," and out from the studios go research parties with shovels and picks; they dig up all the old bodies in Westminster Abbey, sort out those who look the freshest, and make a frantic effort at resuscitation — a great many historical stories are quickly written to order, some of them good, but most of them much inferior to the original success. When the public have seen a succession of poor imitations, they cease to go, and historical films become poison at the box office. People didn't flock to the first one because it was an historical film, but because it was a good picture. They stayed away from the others because they were *not* good pictures. The public happens to be an amazingly fine judge, and it seldom fails to appreciate anything good, whether Negro, costume, or gangster.

As I believe I have made it clear that it is difficult for me to find a subject for a picture, you will I hope realize that it was necessary for me at this moment to do a good deal of thinking, before I finally came to a decision. Now if there is one place better than another to think in, it is St. Margaret's-at-Cliffe. Flo and I have had a cottage there for more years than she would like me to mention. I won't tell you how invigorating the air is either; or how you are rejuvenated the moment you set foot in the place, because I don't want anybody else to come there. At present I own the entire territory south to Dover and north to Kingsdown. That is, I don't actually own it, but it is as good as mine. I can walk on the cliffs and inhale the wonderful air — all of it — nobody else is using it. I can look across the downs for miles, and not see a soul; cows and sheep, but no man, woman or child. Who milks them (the cows) I don't know. Somebody must, because we have all the milk we want. I suppose they do it before I'm up. I don't know much about farming or how things grow out of the earth (Flo won't let me do any gardening since I tried my hand at weeding and made a few little mistakes) but I am bound to believe that the soil must be very paying stuff to grow things in. Here are acres and acres — six hundred and forty to the square mile, you know — with things growing everywhere — corn and beets and cabbages and potatoes, and not a soul watching them. Apparently you can just sow these things and then go quietly home and play bridge until the autumn, or whenever they want cutting. Not a man within sight or hearing. It's so different from the studios. Occasionally in the summer a few other human beings discover my walks. Now and then I meet fifty or sixty boy or girl scouts each armed with a knife, a first-aid outfit and an autograph book, and eyes that pierce all disguises. But now I'm on to them, and when I see them coming I drop to earth, and crawl on my stomach to cover, and remain hidden until the danger is past. But generally the downs are empty of people and the world is mine.

If you love walking for the sake of walking, there is no open space to compare with this. And what a place to think in! Of course you have to be careful to remember to think. I fully understand the mentality of the old countryman who said "Sometimes I sits and thinks and sometimes I just sits." I frequently come to the end of a six- or seven-mile walk and wake up to the fact that I have forgotten to think about anything. This is very reprehensible if one has come all the way from Hollywood to this particular spot, far from the haunts of men, in order to reach some momentous decision. Even if you thoroughly make up your mind to think, and determine to take no interest in sea gulls (who are always terribly annoyed at seeing you) — even then, you have to be sure that you think of the things you went to think about. But once you get yourself in hand — get your mind under control — you can really accomplish something. I have studied aloud many parts on these cliffs, declaiming without fear of interruption; a little self-conscious perhaps when some sea gulls whirl round and listen to me, or when a sheep gives me a contemptuous stare, but secure from the possibility of human criticism.

There are people of means who devote their leisure to traveling round the world — to visiting far distant countries, to gratifying a desire to see everything before they die. This I am sure is a most intelligent ambition. There are other people who pack up and go to one beloved spot year after year, beloved perhaps for its natural beauty, but more often because it is associated with periods of their life that have been full of happiness and free from care. Dull people very likely at dinnerparties — never even been to Tokio; seldom been faced with sudden death. . . . I belong by nature to this class. I do not brag about it. I do not recommend it. I merely state that the "inveterate traveler" can never know the full happiness of saying "Hullo, Brittle" to a village postman, or "Well, William" to a gardener — words of greeting spoken after an absence of seven or eight months spent facing the stern realities of life in metropolitan surroundings. The postman and the gardener may not be good men; they may be perfectly wicked inside, but as postman and gardener they stand as symbols of peace and contentment to the unadventurous individual who has just been released from the clutches of progress.

At the first glimpse of the postman as I arrive in the village of St. Margaret's-at-Cliffe I feel that the dove of peace is descending upon me. And when I say "Hullo, Brittle" and Brittle says "Back again, sir?" I know that life for me has begun. I never see Brittle except on the road. Of course he delivers my letters but I don't even know how he does it. We have a letter box in the front door, but I am sure my letters never come to me that way; it savors too much of city manners. I think he passes them through the kitchen window but I cannot swear to this.

We have no telephone. More than thirty years ago Flo and I joined hands and swore a solemn oath that whatever happened, even if we made a lot of money, we would never have a telephone at St. Margaret's Bay. And we never have. This annoys our friends but brings happiness to the home. It is the only place in the world where we can go for shelter without having a telephone — that disturbing element that breaks in upon one's most sacred privacy without invitation or apology. At one time my bunk on an Atlantic liner was sanctuary — no telephone. Now the garrulous little beast, in imitation ivory, dances round our heads hand in hand with the pillowcases.

But at St. Margaret's — peace. I have seen Niagara Falls, and have at first been disappointed because they are not bigger, and then been amazed because they are so big. I have seen the Grand Canyon and its awful grandeur has moved me more than anything my eyes have ever gazed upon; but its tremendous silence has suggested turmoil as great as Niagara's. I have never seen the Pyramids but at some time in the future, when I stand before them, guidebook in hand, I feel sure that my special dove of peace, which descends so rarely, will decide in favor of the postman at St. Margaret's Bay. It is evident to me that, although I have traveled an average of fifteen or twenty thousand miles a year for the past

106

thirty years or so, I was not intended for a traveler. I think I was intended to live in one room with a pipe and a lot of tobacco and somebody to talk to about the theatre. I should no doubt be doing that now if Flo hadn't had other ideas. I have visited many places that have given me pleasure, but I have found no peace like the peace of St. Margaret's. Of course it is impossible to go anywhere in the world and be absolutely sure that you are secure from interruption. We had great excitement, for instance, when Bleriot flew the Channel in 1909 and left his 'plane on our very cliffs (this being the nearest point to France).

And there was 1914 and those following years, which I try to blot out; for then St. Margaret's ceased to be herself — everything was horrible and unreal. Tin hats and bayonets breaking into our peaceful roads — startling voices bursting out of my special private walks and demanding to know who went there; bombs ploughing up Mr. Eliffe's land, and blowing our windows from the inside out instead of the way we might in our blissful ignorance have expected; great arms of light at night, groping for the zeppelin that could be heard, but not seen. . . . Myriads of airplanes that sped up and down from Dover and spat fire at the zeppelin as it was at last held helpless in those powerful arms of light. . . . The sea gulls, screaming and shouting, always spoiling for a fight — I suspect those sea gulls of having gobbled up the dove of peace. . . . There was no St. Margaret's for me until after 1918. But the postman had been too old for active service, and so had the gardener, and so had I. So when I came back from my Red Cross Tour and I said "Hullo, Brittle," and he said "Back again, sir?" and when I said "Well, William" to the gardener, I realized that I must have been dreaming, because here was St. Margaret's just as it was; and so it has remained until now.

During my London Season of "The Green Goddess" William Archer came to St. Margaret's for a week end. By this time we were close friends; we had passed through the stage of author and actor; the differences of opinion as to what was good literature for the stage and what was merely good literature; we had fought some hard battles but the prolonged success of the play had driven all differences of opinion into oblivion. Archer was acknowledged, in his day, to be England's most distinguished dramatic critic; he was also a literary man of great ability. It was his knowledge of Scandinavian literature that enabled him to appreciate the works of Ibsen and to give us the best English translation that exists today. In so far as he was the first to translate the Scandinavian author into the English language, the great influence of Ibsen on English dramatic literature was due to William Archer. Whatever you might think of Archer as a man, he was bound to command your respect. Less often, I think, he inspired affection, such as I felt for him. I was very proud of his friendship and very glad to have him "all to myself" at St. Margaret's. Archer was a very reserved, very tall, very broad, very erect, very bony Scotchman of about sixty-eight. When you spoke to him he looked at you with a full and clear eye that obviously reflected an orderly brain which was not only taking in everything you said, but was analyzing it so that he could not by any possibility misunderstand you. His answers were therefore direct and capable of analysis by you. But with all that he was not in the least pedantic. At your first meeting with him you would adopt a sympathetic attitude towards him, because you realized that he had come straight from the funeral of some friend. You formed this mistaken impression not from any display of depression on his part for he had, on the contrary, a rather high-pitched sprightly delivery; but entirely from the fact that he was dressed from head to foot in black; nothing by any means strange or out of date — not a long black coat, but a short business jacket closely buttoned; so closely buttoned that you began at length to wonder what was underneath it. A well-dressed man in black, with a black bowler hat and an umbrella. As your acquaintanceship ripened you realized that this solemn black was his customary suit. My confirmed opinion is that if Commander Byrd had wanted him to go on a Polar Expedition, Archer would have accepted and would have made a noble figure amongst the barking dogs in his closely buttoned black coat, his bowler and his umbrella, with a midweight overcoat thrown over one arm and a suitcase containing his evening suit for dinner.

My own wardrobe at St. Margaret's is of a rather mixed and strange character. This is not due to any design on my part to impress the villagers by attempting to look like an artist who has flung off his city responsibilities or is it to affect a carelessness of garb that shall suggest the intellectual abandon of one who descends for a brief while to the level of God's less favored creatures. It is merely due to the fact that when my clothes get so old and worn that they can no longer hold their own, so to speak, in metropolitan surroundings, and Flo insists that they shall be thrown away, I say to myself "These will do for St. Margaret's," and bear them secretly to a drawer containing other treasures to be transported to St. Margaret's when the time comes for our annual holiday. By employing this underhand method I am able to keep about me many old and valued friends — not always in their entirety; sometimes just the upper part; less often I cling to the legs, but even of these I have some excellent specimens. I am repaid for my loyalty when the Dover tailor, called in as a specialist in an effort to put new life into a pair of trousers, says, "Nice bit of stuff this, sir — might I ask . . . ?" "Yes," I answer quickly, "pre-war." "Ah, I thought so. Can't get this stuff today, sir. It isn't made. A little narrow in the leg, or they'd be as good as — No. Not enough turn-in to let 'em out, I'm afraid. But there, fashions change; they'll be wearing them tight again before you can turn round." *

In my invitation to Archer I had impressed upon him the primitiveness of our surroundings; so I met him at the station with some hope — faint, I admit — that he would loosen up a little respecting clothes for the country. But here came Archer himself — in black — closely buttoned; the bowler, the umbrella and the suitcase. It was impossible to suppose that he hoped for any mental relaxation in those clothes. He could never be taken for a week-end guest. He could be none other than the family solicitor come to witness the signing of the will and hurrying back by the evening train. And yet I am convinced that deep in the breast of

* He is a nice, old-fashioned tailor to whom the term "pre-war" has only one meaning — nothing so modern as the war of 1939.

William Archer there was at this moment a holiday feeling, the warmth of which was struggling to make itself felt through the armor plating of the closely buttoned coat. He was a most charming guest. At dinner I was able to see that the insistent buttoning of the coat in the daytime had no special significance. It was not done to make him look thinner or fatter; it was just that Archer, having decided to button his coat in the daytime, would continue that habit forever, against all eventualities. His dinner jacket, although not entirely unlike his other jacket, stood startlingly wide open and revealed a broad and clear-cut expanse of chest that anyone might be proud to exhibit; it seemed a pity that after tonight it should be shut up again until we dined tomorrow.

Of course I led him on to speak of the theatre. He could talk on many subjects but he was a mine of information in theatrical history and I had him to myself. I wish I could recall some part of that conversation which he made so interesting. I have friends who seem to have known from childhood that they would one day be called upon to write their reminiscences; so sure are they that, after a visit from a person of distinction, almost before the front door closes, they have recorded in a diary priceless epigrams and witty sayings which otherwise would be lost to posterity.

I recommend this procedure to all who anticipate publishing their recollections, because although the *bons mots* of the departed visitor had to be spontaneous, the writer of the reminiscences has ample time to think up some little thing of his own which will prove that he himself is not without moments of spontaneous wit and humor. I am unable to recall any scintillating dialogue, but there is one incident in connection with Archer's visit that I like to remember. Although I love St. Margaret's, I have to confess there is nothing much to see there. If the cliffs and the downs don't thrill you, you must be prepared for a dull time. But you always have to be taken down to see the Bay. From our cottage, you can drive down by a long winding road or you can walk down two hundred and seventy steps (count 'em) to the seashore; most of my guests find walking down "great fun" — but while walking up they are not amused. Archer was a good deal older than I, but he said he liked walking so I took him down to the Bay. It was a cold blustering Easter Monday morning. The beach was deserted except for two couples who had obviously come from London for the day. When an English tripper goes to the seaside on a Bank Holiday he has to bathe or he feels he has been cheated. No sane individual would have ventured out on such a day as this. The wind was bitter and the waves were high and heavy. Archer and I had found a stray scrap of sun, just big enough for us to rest in before we walked back. We were talking about a National Theatre and how it might be founded. He and Granville Barker had been working hard for years in an effort to stir up the public in favor of the idea. I had never believed it would be a success launched in the way it had been outlined to me. I was strongly of opinion that if you built a theatre and called it the National Theatre — no matter how many Nationalists subscribed towards it, and even if the Government itself took a hand — that didn't make it a National Theatre.

I have great faith in the actor, but no faith in bricks and mortar. Bernard Shaw doesn't agree with me. He recently told me that he believed if you put up a sufficiently noble building and christened it National Theatre it will in time become one. I told Archer that I believed the only way you could establish a National Theatre in England was through the art of the actor and not through the skill of the architect or even of the producer. I told him I had seen millions of money wasted in New York in building a National Theatre with no other foundation than money. I said my belief was that if you are in a position to get money — public or private — you should use it to establish first of all a company. Engage half a dozen of the best actors and actresses in the country and put them under contract for three years. They will form the nucleus of your company. Hold them together in the heart of theatrical London and give them something worth doing, and at the end of three years you will be likely to have a firm foundation for your National Theatre. The time will then have arrived for you to think about putting up your permanent building.

Archer was listening attentively to my remarks and placing them in their proper compartments in his analytical brain, ready to be brought forth as required, when all of a sudden we were interrupted by a scream; I will go so far as to say a piercing scream. As during a full quarter of a century of experience I had never before heard a piercing scream at St. Margaret's, I felt that however interested I was in the National Theatre, it was my duty to look up. Archer seized his umbrella and sprang to his feet. And there, far out in that horrible sea, was one of those idiotic London trippers, absolutely done for and making signs for help. The other man had reached the shore, but was exhausted and practically lifeless. The two women were screaming lustily towards us. Knowing what the tide was like, and seeing that the waves were getting more and more angry, I felt there was little chance for the bather.

However, I knew there was a hut along the beach where Joe, the boatman and bathing attendant, kept things; so I dashed along hoping to find a rope; fortunately the hut was open and the rope was there. But Joe didn't want people interfering with his rope, so he had wired it up in such a way that it could not be undone except by Joe. You see it was Joe's dinnertime, and although there was no law against people bathing between twelve-thirty and one-thirty, it was their affair if they got drowned. It was obvious that by the time I had released the rope, even if I could, it would be too late, so I looked about for something — anything — that might be of some use. I saw at the back of the hut a long bamboo pole which was used in some way in the operation of catching prawns. It was about twelve feet long and there suddenly jumped into my mind an old play that I had seen years ago in the provinces in which there was the thrilling situation of a human bridge — a number of men held hands and formed themselves into a chain which resulted in somebody being saved. I remembered it very indistinctly but it occurred to me that if all four of us held hands, the front one taking the pole, this suggestion of help might at any rate stimulate the man to make an effort to swim near enough to seize the other end of the pole. I'm afraid I didn't feel very heroic as I dashed out of the hut with my twelve-foot bamboo. I realized in my heart that it was really a futile idea. Fortunately it was never put to the test. Fate had intervened. As I started to run in the direction of the weeping women, I noticed that half a dozen people had collected since I left for the hut. Then I stopped in surprise, for I saw a man was swimming out. He was hardly visible in the heavy sea. But as I stood I had the thrill of seeing him reach the drowning man, and I watched him as he battled back with him. It was a hard fight, and as he got near the shore, the crowd pushed forward and dragged them both in.

As soon as I saw the man was saved, I again felt nothing but disgust and irritation for the idiotic London tripper whose stupidity had caused all the trouble. I hated this happening when Archer was here and I hated keeping Archer waiting about for me in the cold. I didn't join the life-saving group but I turned up towards the road where we had been sitting, to look for Archer. He wasn't there, so I hurried up to a little teashop farther on where I thought he might have gone to get out of the wind.

He wasn't there but as I came back to where we had been sitting, he wandered up — his coat closely buttoned, his bowler firmly fixed.

I said, "Sorry to have left you."

There was something a little strange-looking about him, but I didn't know what.

He said, in that funny, high-pitched tone of his, "I say, Arliss, have you seen my umbrella?"

That was what it was then that made him seen strange: he hadn't got his umbrella.

I said, "No, what did you do with it?"

"Well, I had it here, you know," he said, looking rather wildly round.

I said, "Yes, I know, I saw it in your hand. Don't you remember where you put it?"

"Well, I threw it down, you know, when I went after that chap."

It seems absurd that, although he had been standing before me all that time just as he came out of the sea, I hadn't even noticed he was wet. You have probably never seen a man come up out of the sea in a well-fitting, closely buttoned black "business suit"; but if you ever do, you will be surprised to notice how little different he looks from when you saw him dry. If the hat had been wet I suppose I should have noticed it, but he had evidently picked up his hat as he came out of the water. Of course I realized at once that that heroic figure that I had just seen fighting for the life of a perfect stranger was no other than the quiet gentleman from town who was at this moment looking for his umbrella. That it should be Archer who had done this thing was so entirely unexpected that I just stared at him. He was very serious, breathing a little heavily, quite unself-conscious, and really worried about his umbrella.

"Why are you carrying that?" he said. I realized then that I was still clutching my twelve-foot bamboo.

"Oh, this," I said. "Well, I — er — " I felt a sudden sense of shame — as though some very discreditable act of mine was brought to light, and I had no defense. Here was I, more than ten years younger than Archer, careering about with a long pole, like a circus clown, while he had done the only possible thing that could have saved the man's life. I was grateful that the umbrella became visible at this moment; it rescued me from a momentary embarrassment, and gave him a sense of permanent security. He said, "I'm so glad I've found my umbrella." He was now perfectly self-possessed, while I was feeling more and more stupid. Since I had been surprised with my long pole, I had, so to speak, lost my balance and was overanxious to do something that would regain for me my self-respect. I said, "You stay here while I telephone for a car." But Archer, having brains, said, "No, it's much better for me to walk," so I gave up being helpful.

As we turned to go I glanced at the crowd on the beach. The bather was evidently recovering and there were signs of the whole thing being regarded by his party as a good joke to take back with them to London. Not one of them turned to look for the man who had undoubtedly saved a life. They never knew who it was and never made any effort to find out. As Flo often says to me, "Aren't people strange?" Archer didn't look back; he had apparently forgotten the whole affair. He hadn't really, but he was shy and couldn't bear to be told he had done anything out of the ordinary. "There's something in what you said about the running of the National Theatre . . ." As we hurried home he took up the conversation just where we had left off.

I have told the story at some length because it shows a side to Archer's character that is likely to be unexpected even to those who knew him well, and also I have dwelt on it because he would never let me refer to it without pooh-poohing the whole incident. There is a sequel which I am sure no dramatist would miss.

When we got home of course Archer's clothes had to be dried, a necessarily slow process, because they were of that heavy black material which we associate with Queen Victoria. I couldn't lend him anything because my clothes by the side of his looked as though they belonged to a pygmy. Everyone was ready for lunch, so the obvious and sensible thing was for him to slip on his dressing-gown. This suggestion was conveyed to him as he was taking a hot bath. Meanwhile a young American couple blew in on their way to Dover to take the boat for the Continent. We didn't know them but that didn't matter; we were always glad to see Americans and these honeymooners had brought their introduction from old friends in Boston. They were having a grand time. They loved England, and our funny English manners and customs, and all that. We wished they could stay to meet Archer and they wished they could, but they had to dash off to catch the boat. They were in such a hurry that there had been no time to refer to the adventure on the beach, but just as they were getting into their car, Archer appeared in immaculate evening clothes. He was hurriedly introduced and they drove away in a state of mental confusion, I am sure, as to what particular section of English Society dresses for lunch at 1:30 P.M. Of course, when we came to think of it, to have seen Archer in a dressing-gown would have been impossible. In relating this adventure I have gone back several years — to 1924, when I was playing "The Green Goddess" at the St. James's Theatre. I must remind you, however, that I have now arrived at 1930, having finished the filming of "Old English" and come to St. Margaret's to think.

Chapter 8

THE WEATHER happened to be England at its best, and when the weather is like that in England we talk about it so much that a good deal of time is consumed which under normal conditions might be used to greater advantage. After enjoying this weather for several weeks I was just about to start thinking when I had a cable which enabled me to avoid the effort. Darryl Zanuck had been thinking in Hollywood. Of course Darryl Zanuck doesn't have to think with that same depth and emotion that is necessary for you and me; an unseen agency gives him a sudden shot in some spot above the level of the neck, which makes him jump up, press a button and call a conference. That means that he has the nucleus of an idea that is capable of development. His cable suggested that I should make "The Millionaire." The selection appealed to me and I agreed. The story was by Earl Derr Biggers; it was published (I think) in the *Saturday Evening Post*. I had done it as a silent picture under the title of "The Ruling Passion." Its original title was "Idle Hands" and it was now proposed to call it "The Millionaire." Producers about this time had a craze for changing titles. When I first did "Disraeli" there was some question about changing the name to something more attractive. I remember suggesting that they should call it "Wild Nights with Queen Victoria" but I withdrew the suggestion when I found to my alarm that there was some danger of its being adopted. "The Millionaire" has the "plus" value that I always look for when I am trying to find a subject for a picture. Mr. Biggers not only wrote an amusing story but in addition there is an interesting basic idea — the psychological effect on one who retires from active business too early in life. When you are seeking a subject for a picture or play, if you can find some character or condition that an audience can apply to its own knowledge or experience of life, you have an advantage over the merely amusing or interesting story. If possible give the audience something to discuss when they get home. The plus value in "Old English," for instance, was the vital character of Old Heythorp. In "The Green Goddess" it was the English University influence clashing with the Indian outlook and mentality; it was that which raised Archer's play above the level of mere melodrama. But it is not easy to find stories with this plus value.

The three pictures I had already made were from plays that I had performed on the stage. "The Millionaire" was a new departure, inasmuch as it was adapted only for the screen. I was — and am — fundamentally a stage actor, so I approached the experiment with a feeling of uncertainty. In my previous pictures I knew from experience just how the lines could be given with the greatest effect. I knew also, from having played the parts on the stage, the value of certain glances or gestures, and also the moments when the dialogue was in danger of being broken with a laugh from the front.

The audience had become with me a habit, and I felt that it was impossible for me to give a satisfactory performance for the screen unless I could know their reaction. There is a deep-rooted belief in the theatre that few actors give their best performance of a part until they have played it several times before an audience. Winthrop Ames used to say that I was never at my best until I had played a part for a fortnight. In my opinion the hardest condition that the stage actor has to contend with when he acts for the movies is the absence of an audience.

The screen can create many illusions that cannot be attempted in the theatre, but as a record of the art of the actor it will always have the supreme disadvantage of being nothing more than a dress rehearsal. I felt so strongly about this that I proposed to the Warner Brothers that they should have "The Millionaire" made into a play and let me tour it in some unimportant towns for two or three weeks in order to discover all possible values, before we attempted to put it on the screen. They were nice enough to make a pretense of thinking this over seriously; they didn't even smile. They were always very patient with me. It must have been at once obvious to them as it afterwards was to me that the idea was quite impracticable. The story would first of all have to be made into a full-length play, long enough to run about two-and-a-half hours; stage scenery would have to be built which would be of no use in the picture production; and having consumed two or three weeks on the road, the play would then have to be cut down to movie length with all the changes necessarily involved in turning a play into a picture.

I abandoned the idea, much to my regret, and to the great relief of the Warners.

My earnest desire for an audience, however, led me to evolve a plan that I have adopted in the production of every picture I have made since, a method that I have found most valuable. It starts with a series of intensive rehearsals. I never begin to rehearse until the script has reached its final state — that is, until it is finished. I fancy I hear some of my poor ignorant readers say, "Well, I should think no sane man would!" — but you'd be surprised!

Then I collect the entire cast and read the script to them. Then I rehearse the whole story with the whole company for two weeks. (This is precisely the same method as that used in the regular theatre before production, except that in the theatre we generally rehearse for a longer period.) The last rehearsal but one is known as my "dress rehearsal." It is not really a dress rehearsal, because we do not dress and we have no scenery. But we collect as many people as we can from about the studios — people from other units who know nothing about our picture. They are drawn in as an audience. We also invite all the executives who are likely to have any connection with the making of our picture — including the director, the cameraman, the cutter, and the higher and lower officials. Having got our audience, we go straight through the picture with as nearly as possible the same speed as the film will run when it is shown. There is no reading of parts; all the actors are letter-perfect. Maude Howell is there with a stop-watch and has men ready to put on quickly any necessary props and furniture; she rapidly explains where we are as the scenes change, and the actors act their parts just as they will appear (except for costume and make-up) when the film is actually being shown. We go through without pause from beginning to end, as though it were a play in the theatre.

This is the method I use as a means of finding out, to some extent, the effect of the story on the audience. It also has great value in discovering "holes" in the script. It is surprising how easy it is, even for the most careful and critical reader, to miss discrepancies when reading through a scenario. But when you see the whole story unfolded before you in the space of eighty minutes by the actors who have studied their parts, any inconsistency becomes clear and unmistakable. Of course a single audience made up of stray people in a studio cannot teach you all that you would learn by playing two weeks in regular theatres, but it is a great deal better than nothing.

This mode of preparation can only be accomplished with the co-operation of the management. It is very expensive, particularly in Hollywood where the system of engaging actors is on a different footing from that of England. In England the custom is to engage the actor by the day and pay him on that basis for each day that he is called for work. The leading actors insist on a guarantee of a minimum of so many days' work. This is reasonable, because during the shooting of the picture they have to be on call at overnight notice and so cannot engage themselves elsewhere until the part is finished. This means that they may be tied up with one picture for four or six or eight weeks. The "bit" actors, being easy to replace, are not able to get these guarantees, but their anxiety to stand well with the casting director gives sufficient security to the management that they will be there when called upon. I have found, however, that the directors are very reasonable, and will generally try to fit in the scenes for a small-part actor who has the chance of picking up a few days' work in another studio. So you see in England the actors have to be paid only for the days they rehearse and for the days they work before the camera. A standard contract is now under consideration which may change some of the conditions I have outlined.

In America the terms are far less easy for the producer. The actor there has to be paid from the first day he is called to the studio until his work on the picture is finished. That is why my system was a rather shocking innovation. The producer could nerve himself to withstand the shock of paying for rehearsals, but when the icy cold fact emerged that an actor, after rehearsals, might not be needed in the studio for three weeks, the effect on the budget was alarming. Supposing his salary to be a thousand dollars a week (the leading actors in America are generally engaged on a weekly basis) that makes (three times one is three) three thousand dollars for nothing! I think a certain amount of bargaining was resorted to, but only in the case of the large salaries.

So you see this preparedness plan of mine costs money. I am all the more grateful for the co-operation of my managers because I am not quite sure that they do not regard it as an unnecessary expense which they are willing to bear as a sort of compliment to my steadfast convictions. After nearly ten years in the studios, I am still of opinion that this system of rehearsals saves money in the end. Without rehearsals everyone concerned in the picture is handicapped. An actor is given a bit — perhaps overnight, perhaps on the day of the shooting — and he goes on and does it, having a very hazy idea of what it is all about, and what connection it has with the rest of the story. If there is a miraculously good director, the actor is told what it is about and gives an intelligent performance. If it is a worried director — one of those who claps his hands and says, "Come on, let's get on" — you have a combination of a worried director and a worried actor. The director thinks he tells the actor what it is about but in reality he doesn't. The director makes the actor feel stupid and eventually, inside the head of the actor, a condition of evaporation sets in and the newly acquired words which were just now under control begin to fight for air, and struggle to get out — not by way of natural delivery, through the mouth, but through the roots of the hair; so that when the director says "Shoot," the interior of the head of the actor has become a vacuum, and of course he dries up. Then follows the heartbreaking scene of an actor losing his nerve — I can imagine nothing more tragic — and becoming really stupid. I have known a scene to be taken fourteen times without satisfactory results.

I once took the trouble to reckon up the approximate cost to the management of a case like this — the wasted film, the lights, everybody's time, the overhead generally, and I know it made out a very good case for my system of rehearsals. Nearly all the actors on the screen today have been stage actors. They have been in the habit of rehearsing the play. Once they have rehearsed, they not only know what the play is about and the precise share their part has in the story, but they approach their work in the studio with a feeling of security; the actor is then able to use such ability for characterization as he may possess, and to place himself inside the part, a mental condition which he cannot arrive at if he is struggling to remember words.

The only argument worth discussing that I have heard in favor of discarding rehearsals came from an actor who believed that continual repetition robbed the scene of a spontaneity that it was likely to have through the overnight system of study, followed by the immediate performance. Although on the face of it there is merit in this suggestion, I do not think it is a sound argument against preparation. If there is any art at all in acting, it surely must be the result of experience and work and judgment. Most actors will admit that if they can be unhurried, the time taken in studying a character is well spent. Their final understanding of a part is generally much deeper and better than when they first approach it. I am thinking mainly of the well-written play or story; but I am not sure that it is not equally true of an entertainment that is made up of little more than a string of gags. The only kind of spontaneity that I have found reliable is that which is inspired by the audience — that sudden flash that comes across the footlights from the people whose imagination has been stimulated by the art of the actor. But that, as a rule, is nothing more than an unexpected illumination of what the actor has already placed there. It is study and judgment and discrimination that tell in the long run; spontaneity is not to be depended upon.

Well, having decided that I would go back to Hollywood and make "The Millionaire," I was immediately urged to make other pictures. An English firm wanted me to do "The Devil." I had done it in the silent days but I was afraid of it in the talkies. The Devil's particular hobby was leading nice respectable ladies from the path of virtue. This is an attractive occupation that might tempt imaginative directors beyond limits advisable to be pursued before a family audience, and as that is the class of audience I care most about, I continually have to exercise caution. The play itself is merely a domestic story with simple interior settings, and if done in that way on the screen, with Molnar's amusing lines, it might perhaps be made acceptable even for "my audience." But I am sure no producer would want to do it that way. Its very title conjures up visions of Rabelaisian orgies.

And then of course there is always "production value." You may not know what production value is. I didn't know for a long time. Well, production value can only be attained by spending a lot of money unnecessarily, just as a man who wishes to make a great impression might put on three diamond studs; he is a very ordinary man, but he doesn't want you to know that. He believes the studs will give him an importance which he does not in reality possess; he would really look much better without them, but they dazzle you. You can't talk pennies to a man who is wearing such expensive studs; so he makes a better bargain with the diamonds than without them. And so with the picture: if the producer spends a great deal of money on its production, he is able to get a higher rental from the exhibitors, and the total additional revenue from the rentals is apparently greater than the amount spent in production value. That is why a simple restaurant has to become the Ritz, and why a house becomes a castle; and it explains the reason why the heroine gives such extraordinarily large parties. I am hoping the time is not far distant when production value will cease to be considered necessary. I am in favor of beautiful settings when they belong to the story; and I fully realize that although change of scene is of no special importance in the regular theatre, it is vitally necessary in the cinema. My objection to production value is that it has the habit of crashing in without being invited; that it holds up the interest; that it breaks the continuity of the story by the sheer weight of its magnificence.

There is perhaps another reason for restraint in the introduction of these super-gorgeous settings. The audience is becoming a spoilt child; it is being given too much. It not only doesn't gasp when shown a scene that costs thousands, it ceases to notice. Or, at any rate, it doesn't remember it when it leaves the cinema. But it will talk about the way an actor spoke a certain line and will recall some effective piece of "business." From the time the picture begins — as soon as the characters are introduced — the audience is waiting to see what is going to happen to those characters; it is anxious to join them in their joys and sorrows, their trials and tribulations. Its interest is centered on the actors — or should be; it is eager to follow them from one incident to another and it becomes impatient if the story is halted or cluttered up with extraneous matter. If the hero is to be shipwrecked, by all means let us have a thrilling shipwreck, with real water. But if the heroine is to be kidnaped, don't introduce a number of elephants unless elephants are really needed.

The introduction of animals is, more often than not, resorted to merely as production value; it is seldom that animals are necessary to the story; more often they are an interruption. In my films I have many times struck out scenes in which animals have been introduced, and generally the cut has proved to be good for the story.

The shooting of all scenes in which animals appear should be carefully watched by some trustworthy official of a humane society. No director or other person connected with the making of a film intends to be cruel; in the ordinary way he is far more likely to be gentle and considerate of animals. But to get what is intended to be a tremendous effect a director would not spare cat, dog or horse; man, woman or child. But men can shout, women can scream, children can cry for protection — and get it. Animals are mostly patient creatures — they suffer in silence; or if they cry, their cry is not heeded. Anything for the good of the picture! The average director does not understand that the thrill which involves obvious cruelty to an animal defeats its own ends. When an animal is seen to be suffering, the interest of the audience is violently ruptured, and the people who are intended to be thrilled feel nothing but horror and repulsion.

In my opinion the art of constructing a story either for the screen or the stage is fundamentally the same. It is perhaps more simple to write for the screen, because you can show in detail what can only be subtly

129

suggested in a play; moreover, the writer for the screen is spared the necessity of those more or less mechanical climaxes obviously designed for the ends of the acts. But the "build" should be the same; the interest should be built in the same ratio to the advancement of the story as that which is marked by Acts I, II, III in the theatre. Inasmuch as all people who go to the theatre for entertainment must go with an open and receptive mind, it may be said that the mental attitude of all people is more or less the same as soon as they become part of an audience in the theatre. I do not mean that all are on the same level of intelligence, but for the time being they are just primitive human beings; they are in the same school with the children who listen to the bed-time stories. The theatre usher tucks them up and they wait for the curtain to rise on "Let's suppose . . ." The art of the actor is appreciated more by one person than another, but the story is the chief consideration with practically everyone. This must always have been and must always be, if we admit, as I think we must, that the primitive in human beings remains unchanged through the ages. I am arguing that production value is not a true value; it seldom advances the story — more often impedes it. It leads to dangerous competition in lavish spending and not infrequently ends in bank-ruptcy. The fact that it has become a virtual necessity for producers to spend large sums on every feature pic-ture is liable to result in the shelving of many good stories which do not look like a sure thing and on which therefore they dare not take a risk.

In my opinion, expenses in nearly all branches of the picture business are too high. Picture houses are too

costly, advertising can be ruinous; the army of middle-
men in all departments must be a perpetual drain. Although there is today nothing like the waste there was
in the "old days," there is something wrong when every
feature picture has to be rated either a "knock-out" or
"a flop."

I am aware that I am laying myself open to criticism
in discussing the managerial side of pictures — a part
of the business in which I have had no real experience —
but I venture to do so because of my practical knowledge
of audiences and their taste. I have had a long experience
of the public and I believe them to have simple tastes;
by simple I mean ingenuous and unsophisticated, and
that they are neither entertained nor amused by production value.

In considering the cutting down of expenses of production, the question is bound to arise: "What about
the large salaries of the actors?" Well, I may be prejudiced but I am afraid that however much we may object to these salaries, however much we may regard
them as being out of proportion to the deserts of the
individual, there is nothing to be done about it. We
must just grin and bear it. In the entertainment world,
where people pay money for admission, the value of
one who entertains cannot be gauged by his deserts,
by his brain-power, or even by his ability; it is bound
to depend on how much money he draws to the box
office. Whatever the cause, — it may be a woman's
charm, or a man's unusual personality, or five babies
all born together, — whatever it is, if it draws money
to the box office, competition arises between managers
and the salary is bound to go up. But my opinion is

(and I offer it as consolation to the managers) that there is only one sure asset in the world of the theatre, and that is the actor. The play is a gamble, the settings may mean little, but the one known quantity is the ability or the popularity of the actor. No actor or combination of actors can save a really bad play from failure, but actors of distinction can frequently save a mediocre play from being a dead loss at the box office.

Some of the proposals made to me at this time might have had interesting results if I could have accepted them. Leon M. Lion was anxious for me to do "Old English" under his management; he had identified himself with Galsworthy's revivals and "Old English" would probably have been a sure thing for a limited run. But I did not wish to do odd jobs in England. After my season with "The Green Goddess" I should have been willing to continue at the St. James's Theatre indefinitely, forming a partnership with Gilbert Miller, much as my old friend Gerald du Maurier did with Frank Curzon and afterwards with Miller. Or I should have been willing to make a similar arrangement with Frederick Harrison at the Haymarket, but such contracts, although mooted, could not be made at that time. Another proposal came from Maurice Browne, to produce "Disraeli" at his theatre. "Disraeli" was produced in London in 1916 with Denis Eadie in the part, but it had a disappointing reception. The success of the picture has tempted several managers to approach me about doing it again in London. It would give me a certain satisfaction to do it in England (I played it for five consecutive years in the United States); but I am always dubious about reviving a play that has been tried and failed, especially when it has had the advantage of an actor as good as Denis Eadie.

Shortly before I sailed for America, and while I was still at St. Margaret's, two mysterious gentlemen leapt into a Rolls-Royce in London, and leapt out again about midnight in front of our cottage, after we had gone to bed. If a similar visit had been paid me in America, I should at once have suspected a hold-up or a kidnap. As it was, the interview commenced coldly through a window, but by degrees I gained sufficient confidence to permit of the front door being opened, and of the visitors being let in without being frisked. They proposed that I should begin a season in London immediately. It transpired that one of them was buying, or already owned, or had leased, the Duke of York's Theatre. I think they must have read in a book somewhere that the way to do business was to dash at it, take the other man by surprise, and carry the day, before he could recover. Or perhaps, knowing my association with American managers, they thought that was how theatrical business was carried on over there. Of course they couldn't know that the one thing nobody has ever succeeded in doing is to hurry me, either mentally or physically. (Flo has often threatened to have WAIT A MINUTE carved on my tombstone.) But it was a nice summer night and I daresay they had a very pleasant drive home.

James B. Fagan, who had recently written "And So to Bed," had just bought one of those delightful old farm-houses in which you knock your head. Mrs. Fagan is quite six feet high, but she loved it. I wanted Fagan to write me a Voltaire play. I had tried Shaw and

133

Maurois, but I still persevered. So Flo and I went over to the farm and sat with the Fagans in front of one of those tremendously picturesque fireplaces that take up all one side of the room and have all sorts of iron hooks and things lying about — those fireplaces that sell farmhouses and look so wonderful on Christmas Day when there's a fire lighted in them, or on some important anniversary, when there's a fire lighted again. We had a charming visit and talked Voltaire and many other characters. I think something might have come of this, but poor Fagan died within the next year.

Shortly before we sailed we dined with the John Drinkwaters. He was very full of Charles II — I think he was writing a "Life" at the time, and he was anxious to make it into a play for me. I was not enthusiastic, but I suggested that he should write me a Richelieu play. The Lytton version was good, but decidedly old-fashioned, and it seemed to me that Drinkwater should be able to write something better or at any rate more suitable for the theatre of today. If I remember rightly he promised to start on it when he had less work in hand, but I think he was a busy man to the end, and it was never begun. It will be seen that up to this time I still had no thought of "deserting" the stage; the pictures, for me, were still only an interlude; I was always looking for a play.

However, there was "The Millionaire" to be done, so we started back for Hollywood. When we arrived in New York Harbor there was no tender to meet us, it is true, but there was Richard Beamish, which answered just as well. Richard could always take care of everything. When Richard came puffing towards you, you discovered that the world was yours. Richard could make me believe that New York had slumped into a state of depression during and in consequence of my absence; that my appearance was waited for with breathless excitement; that there had been a three minutes' silence throughout the United States when the populace heard of my safe arrival; that every theatrical, picture, and radio manager was waiting in a condition of painful anxiety to hear whether he, Richard, could persuade me to accept the largest salary ever paid to any . . . etc.

CAST

The Millionaire

James Alden	. .	GEORGE ARLISS
Mrs. Alden .	. .	FLORENCE ARLISS
Babs . . .	.	EVALYN KNAPP
Bill Merrick .	. .	DAVID MANNERS
Schofield .	. .	JAMES CAGNEY
Carter Andrews .	.	BRAMWELL FLETCHER
Peterson .	. .	NOAH BEERY
Davis . .	. .	IVAN SIMPSON
McCoy .	. .	SAM HARDY
Dan Lewis .	. .	J. FARRELL MACDONALD
Briggs . .	. .	TULLY MARSHALL

ℯℓ

Director .	. .	JOHN ADOLPHI
Story, "Idle Hands"	.	EARL DERR BIGGERS
Camera .	. .	JAMES VAN TREES
Dialogue .	. .	BOOTH TARKINGTON

Chapter 9

"THE MILLIONAIRE" was finished in less than seven weeks, including two weeks' rehearsal. This of course does not take into account the time needed for picking the cast. Perhaps I should tell you how a cast is picked.

It is the custom for the casting director to read the final script and then discuss the cast with me. By this time I know the manuscript thoroughly and have a definite idea of how I think each character should be played. The casting director is a miraculous individual; if anybody has ever done anything, he can remember it; he can recall exactly how the actor did it and in what picture, and can form a fairly accurate idea of his capability of playing any given part. There are so many actors in Hollywood now that have played with me in the theatre, besides those I have met on the screen, that as a rule it doesn't take long to agree upon the majority of the cast. But there are always one or two difficult spots, generally, strange to say, in the choice of a young woman or a young man. There are as you know clusters of young women of all shades, but it so often happens that there is not one amongst them that has the particular quality you need. You can't tell a girl this because she would immediately ask you what quality you did need, being convinced in her own mind that she had it in stock. But you can't explain, and if you could, the best she could offer would be a poor imitation. It is there or it isn't. Those who have it are either starring or holding out for a part that gives them greater opportunity. If you are lucky enough to make a "discovery," so much the better for you and for her; she will shortly be amongst those who are holding out for greater opportunity — and getting it. The right kind of young man is worth his weight in gold. I cannot tell you what particular ingredients or what special attributes are required to create this valuable specimen; he may be handsome, he may be plain, short or tall, dark or fair. I will however go so far as to say that he must be interesting to look upon, he must have imagination and he must be alive; beyond that I will not commit myself except to say that he needs about fifty other manifestations that I can't describe.

So when we strike any difficulty in casting, we are generally in for a long and laborious search. You cannot tell what an actor can do by looking at a studio photograph, or by meeting him once in the casting office. But you can get some idea by seeing him on the screen in other parts. A casting director may remember everything, but he wants me to see for myself. So a certain number of films in which the actor or actress has appeared have to be collected from other studios, that I may see them run off. In company with Maude Howell we sit through half a dozen, sometimes more, according to the number of people under consideration — before we finally decide.

Just now and then I can feel sure of my man by one brief interview, in the casting office. There was a small but important part in "The Millionaire" — the part of an insurance agent. The scene was entirely with me, and was the turning point in the story. I knew it depended largely on the actor of this small part whether my change of mental attitude would appear convincing. I saw several promising young men without being much impressed one way or the other; but there was one more waiting to be seen; he was a lithe, smallish man. I knew at once he was right; as I talked to him I was sure he could give me everything I wanted. He wasn't acting to me now; he wasn't trying to impress me; he was just being natural, and, I thought, a trifle independent for a bit actor; there was a suggestion of "Here I am; take me or leave me; and hurry up." As I came to my decision I remember saying, "Let him come just as he is — those clothes — and no make-up stuff. Just as he is!" The man was James Cagney. I was lucky!

I am always relieved when the casting business is over. It is painful to have to turn actors away. If I had never been through the mill myself I suppose I shouldn't mind so much, but I know just what is going on behind those anxious eyes. I have no special gift for character reading, in fact I often fail to recognize what afterwards seems so obvious; but when it comes to dealing with people in my own profession I suppose my long experience endows me with a sort of instinct. In Hollywood there are a certain number of small-part actors who are always in demand and who make quite a large income. These are the lucky ones; but there are the others, the great crowd that just manage to live — always waiting from year to year for their "chance." There is a large and important publication known as a casting directory. It contains the portraits of innumerable actors and actresses, and tells their line of business, their addresses or the address of their agent. If the miraculous mind of the casting director does not of its own volition immediately hit upon a likely actor for a part, this book is used as an aid to memory. Supposing there to be three parts of which we are uncertain, it is usual to send a call for about half a dozen people for each part, so that there may be as little delay as possible in making a selection. The men and women who are interviewed in this way, in their effort to make a good impression, are generally seen at their worst; they are strained and unnatural. To be one's own natural self one must be at ease, and I defy anyone to be at ease who is undergoing a critical examination — and knows it. A girl generally has a definite plan of campaign. She knows the interview will last about five minutes — at most, ten — and she decides in advance the kind of girl she is going to be for those five or ten minutes. If she knows the type of part she is needed for, she will endeavor to suggest that type. But if, as more often happens, she knows nothing, she has to make up her mind what is the best mood to assume — the aloof, nonchalant, opulent; or the terribly artistic I-live-only-for-my-art; or the trusting, adoring, anything-just-so-that-I-can-act-with-you! This is all very tricky, very artificial, the little humbug! I wish I could be amused — but I can't. I find it so pathetic, because I can feel behind it all — she needs the money. I know she has very likely spent her last dollar on some little bit of finery that she thought would just make her look "it." I know that she has probably been on her knees this morning and prayed to God that she may get this job, because she knows that once she gets her chance, her luck will turn.

I am not exactly bidding for sympathy for those in hard luck in my business; I know that many of them have no right to be in the theatre at all. But how are they to know this until they have tried? And, once in it, it is very difficult to get out. Who can blame them for never realizing that they have no ability? I think it is as well that theatregoers, particularly those who get their information from movie magazines, should be told that there is this hard-working, sober, earnest class — courageous men and women, young and old, who, year after year, wait and hope for their chance; who experience the worst kind of deprivation, that genteel poverty that must never be confessed. Sometimes one of these will have pluck enough to get out before it is too late, and take a steady job in some business. But more often they go on waiting, — through middle age, — still hoping, and never realizing that from the very beginning they have been fighting a hopeless battle. And that is why I am glad when the casting is over. It is hard to have to say "Off with his head" as one after another is brought before you. I know a girl — the dark, exotic, Anglo-Indian kind — who applied for a part and was told she was entirely unlike the type required. She dashed back to her lodgings, put on a fair wig and a great deal of make-up, hurried back to the office, sent up a different name, pranced in unrecognized, and got the job. But that is the sort of thing that happens only once in a lifetime.

I like acting with people I know and who have worked

141

with me before. I suppose if I had no one to control me, I should have almost the same cast in every picture I make. As it is, the casting director always says "I suppose you want Simmy" (that is Ivan Simpson). Of course I want Simmy. I know that he will give a fine performance; and the better the actor I work with, the better I shall appear to be. And "Of course you want Charlie Evans." They think I want Charlie Evans merely because for years he ran a play that I wrote. Well, that is one reason, but I also want him because he's good. He lights up any part he plays. Although he has been his own manager all his life and his own star, he plays those bits in my pictures with all the zest of the moneyed amateur starting his career.

I had a very good cast in "The Millionaire" including Flo, who played one of those wives that the people like to see her play; they like to see her taking care of me; and she can do these parts without having to draw very deeply on her imagination.

During the shooting of "The Millionaire" I am quite sure that a great many screamingly funny things happened but I can't remember any of them. I really have great sympathy with the movie interviewers — I mean those in search of snappy paragraphs; they are always in despair about me.

They say, "Now, Mr. Arliss, what happened during the filming of this picture that stands out clearly in your mind?"

I look at them with glazed eyes.

"Well, I mean — Mr. Arliss, something must have happened — how long have you been making the picture?"

"Six weeks."

"Well, there must be something — some anecdote, that's what we want, a story — something funny."

"An anecdote? Well, Mr. Beery told me a good story one day when we were on location — I'll get him to tell — "

"No, we want something that happened to you, yourself. Didn't you hurt yourself one day? Fall over a dog or something? Ben Silvey was telling us something about . . ."

"Oh, yes, I did hurt myself one day."

"Well, that'll do; tell us about that."

It's all very discouraging to the interviewers. That's one reason why I so seldom figure in the fan magazines. Nothing ever happens to me. I was confiding in my friend Godfrey Davies last spring at the Huntington Library. Godfrey Davies knows everything that happened two hundred years ago. When I am studying an historical character I sometimes go to him for advice. This time I called on him because I wanted to broadcast "Richelieu" and I wanted to make Richelieu say to his cat, "A cat may look at a king; but I don't advise it, Mistigris." But I wasn't sure whether it would be an anachronism. Godfrey told me immediately who said it first, and assured me that Richelieu might have quoted it. Then I suppose he noticed that I was looking pale and wan and interesting, and being of a sympathetic nature he asked me what was the matter with me. I told him that the reason he found me in this interesting condition was that I was about to become an author — that is to say, I had promised two publishers, one in England and one in America, that I would write for them my Life

143

and Adventures on the Screen, and having taken up my pen to write had discovered that I hadn't had any adventures, and that the worry of this discovery was so troubling me that even my life was ebbing away.

Godfrey in an effort to encourage me told me he liked my first book of reminiscences. I said: "Yes, that was written about my earlier days. That was pie compared with this." And then I remembered that he had just published a book called *The Early Stuarts* and that his knowledge of modern English had perhaps got rather rusty, so I quickly translated the word "pie" for him, so that he should not feel embarrassed. "I mean, Godfrey, that was easy compared with this." Godfrey Davies, who has always been a seeker after truth, said "Why?" And so I explained that if, when you are young and rehearsing, the stage manager swears at you, and if you swear at him back, and he then smacks your face, that is adventure; and if a little later in your career you lock your manager in his room and threaten to keep him there until he pays you your salary, and then when you relent and go to let him out you find that he has escaped through the window and taken the money with him, that is adventure. But all that belongs to Volume One. When you reach the period of your career that seems to call for Volume Two — what happens then? You are a star in pictures. A successful star as soon as he arrives on the set is monarch of all he surveys. Everybody is sweet to him; they may not want to be sweet, but they are sweet. Even the director is nice to him; he may have a glint in his eye, but he has to be nice to the star.

Everybody knows that much depends on the star; the best that is in him must be encouraged and nurtured;

he must be made to believe that everyone there thinks him wonderful. They don't know that although you are the star you may think yourself awful in this part; they all believe you think you are wonderful. You enter the studio in the morning. The director comes towards you, shakes you warmly by the hand and says "You look wonderful"; says loudly, "Where's Mr. Arliss's chair? Bring Mr. Arliss's chair! No, not there — not in the draught — put it here." If a mad bull now dashed into the studio, and you hit the bull and saved the life of the leading lady, or even of the director, that would be adventure. But it doesn't happen. Nothing happens. . . . "You see, Godfrey, there is nothing to write about. From now on, everything is just routine."

Godfrey showed an entirely unexpected reaction to this final remark of mine. I will not say that his frame shook with emotion, but he did in reality show great excitement. He rose and said: "Wonderful! Write it — it will be wonderful!" I said "Write what?" "Routine!" he answered and his voice would have rung out if he had one of those voices. "If I could only find *that* in my research work! Everybody writes of the great happenings — the high lights — you can find them in a hundred books; but it is the routine that we need to have recorded in order to describe life as it is in any period. Routine! Write it! And in two hundred years' time your book will be a classic."

This has encouraged me tremendously. It has given me a feeling of security and authority. If what I write seems dull to the reader that merely shows his stupidity; he hasn't intelligence enough to realize that I am writing for posterity. So when you feel, reader, that I am being dull almost beyond endurance, I want you to understand that that is when I am being most literary and most classical and most inspiring to our great-great-grandchildren. I admit that I do wish Godfrey could have made it a little less than two hundred years, but he knows, and so I have made no effort to get him to modify the term required for development.

I have pointed out how difficult it is to find plays and stories for me, so although the executives of the Warner Brothers were by no means idle, nothing had been decided upon to follow "The Millionaire." We happened to be going through one of those periods that I have mentioned, when some unseen agency is revealing to producers the fact that costume plays will be poison at the box office. I was therefore very much surprised when Jacob Wilk, who was the head of the story department, suggested "Alexander Hamilton." I had always liked Hamilton (I played it for two seasons on the stage) but I was diffident about proposing it because I was part author (Mary Hamlin was the other part) and I know that an actor who has written a play is regarded by managers as a dangerous person to encourage; and if the actor, being a star, should suggest his own story — well, that's going a bit too far.

However, the suggestion came from the executive; Darryl Zanuck agreed with some enthusiasm — which of course meant that it would be done. I decided to go away while the working script was being made. If I took a hand in the making of the scenario, there was an obvious danger of too much George Arliss. So I suggested that Mary Hamlin, that model collaborator, should be brought from the bosom of her family in Canandaigua to act as adviser, and that she and Maude Howell and Julian Josephson should all work together. (Julian Josephson had worked with Maude Howell on the script of "Disraeli" and had proved himself not only an excellent writer but one who was peculiarly sympathetic to my limitations, with an unusual talent moreover for keeping within the atmosphere of the story.) I therefore had an unexpected opportunity for a holiday trip between pictures.

Flo decided that the first thing to do was to dash up Mount Wilson and see Edwin Hubble in his observatory. It's always a holiday to see the Hubbles. So we telephoned Grace to find out whether Edwin was up the mountain today. It is necessary to do this, because the stars are very touchy about weather; they are so close to Edwin up there that if, for instance, the weather doesn't exactly suit Venus, she will say, "Nothing doing tomorrow night, Edwin; not coming out, old dear," or words to that effect, and then Edwin stops at home with Grace. But word comes that he is up the mountain today, so we pick up Grace at Pasadena and up we go. The drive to the Observatory, up, up, for six thousand feet, used to be a hair-raising experience; you were threatened with destruction at every bend in the road. It is now widened and graded and made suitable for those people to whom sudden death is not attractive. But it is still a little trying for Flo, because at four thousand feet I always "pass out" — the car begins to jump about and have its own private earthquake; that is how it seems to me. So I have to be helped out and spread flat on the ground. After about ten or fifteen minutes I am sufficiently recovered to go on, and when I get to the top I am quite well. And we always have a good time. You are liable to meet anybody up there — Will Hays, Doris Kenyon, Sir Trevor and Lady Bigham (Sir Trevor was at one time Chief Constable of the Metropolitan Police). They all go up to see Edwin and his telescope. There is a little hotel there where Grace Hubble always orders a special meal for us. Sometimes, when Margaret Gore-Browne comes with us, we can make up a four for bridge while we are waiting for the stars to arrive. I wish I could be a little more intelligent about the heavens. When we get up there, I mean inside the observatory, and stand beside Edwin on that little platform, and Edwin is all beaming because by good luck some star is behaving particularly well tonight, I wish I could be more interested in Sirius than in Bill down below, who with one touch of his finger makes the whole roof revolve. Edwin can't make the stars move to order, but with a few unintelligible words to Bill below, the structure moves round to the star, or the moon or whatever Edwin has ordered for you. And then, if it happens to be me, I look through the telescope and say "Wonderful!" And Edwin tells me how many "light years" away the thing is that I'm looking at, and I say "Not really? Isn't it wonderful!" And I'm wishing that Bill would push some more buttons, so that I could see the wheels go round. Before Edwin gets his two-hundred-inch next year I really must rub up my astronomy.

We now had three weeks in which to do as we liked. Flo wanted to see the Carlsbad Caverns in New Mexico and to take in some other places on the way. This would mean about a three-thousand-mile drive by the time we got back. But that was what attracted Flo. She loves adventure; it was just a bitter practical joke Fate played upon her when he tripped her up and made her stumble into my arms and so condemned her to a life of dull, monotonous security.

We spent the first night at Palm Springs and then made for Yuma. Now this was the time that we should have had an adventure. Close to Yuma there was a cloudburst; it was dreadful: terrible rain; bridges washed away; railways torn up; cars and people missing; rescue parties sent out. Here would have been something to tell the interviewers. But unfortunately it all happened while we were asleep in Yuma. I knew nothing about it until the next morning when all the danger and drama were over.

We were marooned in Yuma until the third day, when the waters subsided sufficiently for us to get away. So, as usual, I missed the adventure, and merely came in for the inconvenience. There was nothing exciting in Yuma. It is one of those little settlements that you meet so often when you motor in the West. You wonder who put it there, and why. It has an hotel, a cinema, an amazing ironmongery shop where you can buy every kind of tool and shovel, and other shops where you can buy a dress-shirt or a nifty overcoat — in fact anything that might be needed in the desert. We were told that there was only a limited stock of provisions and that if the waters did not settle within a certain period, we should be starved, because there was no way of getting food. That would have been exciting. But the waters did settle. When at last we were leaving, I got the chauffeur to take a photograph of our car up to the hubs in water, with me seen through the window, distressed; but after I got it developed and printed, it didn't look at all thrilling; it was just a car in some water; so it never reached the press agent. I wish for Flo's sake that Yuma could have been an adventure.

Then we went on to Phoenix, Arizona, where there is a settlement of the Navajo Indians; they told me that in their religion anger is considered the greatest of all evils. This struck me as a very sound conclusion. Then a beautiful drive on to Globe. In a quiet spot we were hailed by two motorists who turned out to be Mr. and Mrs. Kellogg. We had crossed with them in 1928, when Mr. Kellogg was coming back after signing the "Peace Pact." Then to the Roosevelt Dam, and then through a long stretch of desert, which some people find so attractive, and then to Carlsbad.

I am not going to attempt to describe the Carlsbad Caverns; it is interesting, however, to know how they were discovered. A man was watching a swarm of bats, which suddenly disappeared. He followed their course and found that they had flown into this hitherto unknown cavern. I may be wrong. Perhaps he saw them fly out; but in any case it was the sudden flight of bats that excited his curiosity. The next day he went again armed with a rope and a candle and discovered what I believe is the largest cave in the world. We entered along a steep, sloping ground and then walked on and on, deeper and deeper, for some six miles. I believe thirty miles have since been explored, but at this time only six miles were open to the public. Some electric lights were placed so that one got the beauty of color conjured up by the fascinating stalagmites and stalactites. As everybody knows, the stalactites are the ones that come down from the ceiling and the stalagmites are those that come up from the floor; I didn't know it till then, but I am given to understand that everyone else did. The effect is amazing. You may get some idea of it if you imagine vistas of royal apartments, of the most beautiful proportions and the most beautiful colors, — more magnificent even than anything you have seen in the movies, — all carved in delicate sparkling traceries such as icicles would make, but all remaining solid and firm and unchangeable. Flo was entranced. Superintendent Boles, who was kindly devoting his time to us, was proud and happy that she should be so appreciative. She said, "Isn't it wonderful? All this solid structure, and yet so delicate it looks as if you could push it aside with your hand." And she put up her hand to push it; and she pushed it, and it moved! She didn't faint nor did I, but we might have been forgiven if we had. Even Captain Boles was unprepared for this phenomenon, because he had not noticed the particular spot on which we were standing; but he was considerably amused for it appears that this is the only piece in the whole of the caves that moves; it is so balanced that it has a slight play and sways at the least touch.

Anyone who has seen the Carlsbad Caverns will think that I am unappreciative in dismissing them with so scant a description. But this is not a book of travel. In fact my main reason for telling about this holiday trip is that it may be some sort of answer to my friends of the theatre who are continually asking why I don't return to the stage. If instead of making "The Millionaire" I had produced a play in London or New York, I should possibly have been tied up for six or eight months, and could never have had these hairbreadth adventures. The life of a successful actor in the theatre is a very narrow one geographically, and by no means broad socially. If ever a man is tied to apron strings, it is the actor. He dare not move a distance covering more than an hour or so from the theatre at any time; even his meals are regulated by the rise and fall of the curtain; having led this life for a great many years, I welcome a little more freedom. It is not so much laziness as a desire to escape the prolonged exaction of the theatre.

Well, we left the Carlsbad Caverns and pushed on — properly impressed by the Painted Desert and the Petrified Forest, and so to the Grand Canyon. Perhaps I am not very susceptible to the beauties of nature; while others swoon I am likely to murmur a few impressive words of approval. Until I looked upon the Grand Canyon I have never been taken by the throat and rendered insensible of my own world — never been shown anything so grand, so tremendous, so alone. For the first time I was lifted out of myself and became just a tiny speck in an unknown universe. It seemed peculiarly fitting that Professor Einstein should be there — on his way, I think, to Pasadena.

While still at the Grand Canyon I was brought back to earth by a telegram from Warners' telling me that the play "Alexander Hamilton," the picture rights of which Mrs. Hamlin and I had sold to them, was not ours to sell. I realize now why it is that producers have to be so meticulously careful to establish their rights to everything they use, so fearful of infringing other people's copyrights. If in a picture I want to hum a few bars of

"Comin' thro' the Rye" or "Way Down upon the Swanee River," the whole machinery of the legal department is brought into play in order to make sure that there is no living creature who has rights in either of those classics.

When I played "Hamilton" on the stage I was under the management of Klaw and Erlanger. The season ended and the play reverted to Mrs. Hamlin and myself without any question. In the meantime, Klaw and Erlanger had dissolved partnership. Erlanger had died, and now, ten years later, the trustees of the Erlanger Estate claimed that "Hamilton" was part of the Erlanger property. After a great deal of trouble and expense our right was established. There would probably have been a much more serious delay but for the good offices of my old friend George Tyler, who had been a party to the original contract.

It made it clear to me why every movie concern has its own legal department. One of the most frequent causes of dispute is the claim made by unknown authors of plays that their stories or scenes from their stories have been stolen. Most budding dramatists believe that whatever else may be said against their play, nobody can deny that it is an original idea. Whereas I should think I am well within the mark when I say that if a professional reader of plays finds an original idea once in five years he may consider himself lucky.

I have no experience of the unpublished novelist; perhaps he can write a novel and still remain a more or less normal person. But let a man write a play and he loses all sense of perspective about his own work. It is possible that the novel may take a passive place in the mind of its author, as literature for the library, and that he is content to let it go down to posterity side by side with Thackeray and Dickens and Galsworthy and the others.

Not so the playwright; he has written a play! His play is forever rising up and making spectacular pictures in his brain. He sees the theatre, or the cinema; he sees his characters being portrayed by his favorite actors and actresses who are speaking his lines, playing his big scenes and drawing tears and laughter and applause from the audience. His mental condition is such that he cannot realize that these great moments exist only in his imagination and are not in the manuscript at all. He loses all sense of proportion. He is a dramatist! All the old stuff that he has written down takes on the guise of originality because he has written it. So when he sees the same situation dished up in a movie that is innocently produced by one of the companies to which he happens to have sent his manuscript he immediately brings suit against them for plagiarism. I believe most big firms now return all packages that look like manuscripts unopened, unless they are known to be sent from some reliable source. I do not wish to discourage prospective playwrights, but merely to impress upon them that the writing of plays is perhaps the most difficult branch of literature and that if they wish to become dramatists, the only safe way is to begin by learning the rules of the game.

I felt a certain satisfaction that "Hamilton" should be filmed, not only because of my share in the writing of the play, but because I had always had a great admiration for the man. I think he did more for his country than many of the others of his period whose names are better remembered, including Thomas Jefferson and James Monroe, both of whom we introduced in our play. When I was doing some research work in Washington during the writing of "Hamilton" Mr. McAdoo, who was then Secretary of the Treasury, was exceedingly kind in opening up all the Hamilton records for me — although when he saw the play I think he was rather shocked that any Secretary of the Treasury could behave in such a way! Before we made the picture I was curious to know what the name of Alexander Hamilton meant to the average man, so I asked a group of American citizens in the studio and found that it meant nothing; only one of them seemed to know anything about him and he said he wasn't sure what Hamilton did, but he knew he had something to do with Nelson. This puzzled me until I suddenly thought of Lady Hamilton. I have come to the conclusion that today the man-in-the-street, as he is called, doesn't know anything about the history of his own country, and doesn't want to know. Whether this is due to the cinema or the radio or the motor car, or the determination of everybody that youth shall be served with large helpings of physical culture and very little else, I have no idea. Perhaps it is that there are so many autobiographies that the reading public have very little time for the really dead ones. Or perhaps it has always been so. I had a further instance of the incomplete knowledge regarding historical characters displayed by the rising generation when I received a most charming letter from a lady who expressed her keen enjoyment of "Hamilton" and said that she was particularly interested in the character of Jefferson because her grandfather had once seen him play "Rip Van Winkle."

About this time there were a number of gold medals and awards flying about in Hollywood. "Disraeli" came in for a share of the swag. I got a gold medal that was not awarded to me. And I think it pleased me more than if it had come to me first-hand. A really important movie paper called *Photoplay* presented a gold medal to H. M. Warner as the head of the firm (that's the Harry Warner I mentioned before — the one who whistles the money off the trees) in recognition of the "Disraeli" picture. "H. M." knew this was to be given to him (producers know everything), so he got hold of the medal in advance and surreptitiously had another one made just like it. After the ceremony of the presentation had been duly applauded by a large audience, "H. M." proved to the audience that he was a good producer by producing the duplicate and handing it to me with a very charming little speech. And I wish to impress upon my readers the fact that this was not one of those base-metal medals that are given for valor, but a real solid eighteen-carat gold — just as solid as the key I got in London — and it was made by Tiffany. I like to record that these movie magnates are not all as hard-boiled as they are sometimes believed to be.

Another gold medal came to me from a source about three thousand miles from Hollywood and unconnected with the movies. It was from the American Academy of Arts and Letters in New York, a very distinguished institution. The medal was awarded to me for Diction. As I was in Hollywood and the presentation had to be made in New York, I got my old friend Frank Gillmore to represent me and to read for me an address conveying my thanks and appreciation. I quote from that address because it expresses certain views on diction which may not be out of place here. All those who know Frank Gillmore will realize how fortunate I was to have him as my proxy: —

. . . If in the past anyone had told me I was likely to be awarded a gold medal for diction, I should probably have retired to my study to find out what was the matter with my method of speaking. This, I suppose, is because I always imagined that people who got medals for diction were those who spoke beautifully. It used to be so in my early days. When I was a very obscure member of an elocution class the students who got medals for diction spoke wonderfully. Their diction was so unmistakable that you could almost see the medal moving towards them of its own volition; and before they were halfway through "The Dream of Eugene Aram" the medal was firmly between their teeth.

It is hard to eradicate these early impressions. But I am bound to conclude, and I do so with great satisfaction, that those Directors of the American Academy of Arts and Letters, this world-famed institution, who are responsible for this award, have a far different appreciation of the art of the actor than had the judges of my student days. . . . If an actor speaks particularly well and knows it, he should at any rate conceal from his audience the fact that he does know it. There are actors of whom we say: "He has a beautiful voice but he is always listening to it." That means that he is not only conscious of this superior quality, but that he wishes the audience to be aware of it also. It is, in my opinion, a great mistake for an actor ever to appear to rise superior to his audience. Such an attitude annoys them and distracts their attention from the subject matter. When I am rehearsing a part and meet a word about which there may be some difference of opinion as to its pronunciation, I do not consult a dictionary in order to find out which is right; I endeavor to discover which is the most general way of pronouncing it, and I adopt that way. I always try to avoid teaching an audience anything, or at any rate, I make a great effort not to be found out. For it is well-known in my business that the public will run a mile from the theatre if they think there is going to be any attempt to teach them. That is why plays written as propaganda are generally failures. An audience resents being corrected or coerced or in any way "done good to."

If, for instance, the American Academy of Arts and Letters said, "We are interested in a campaign for better spoken English and regardless of expense we will form a company of actors which shall comprise all our Gold-Medalists for Diction" — suppose they did it, and sent the company round the country with such advertisements as "Come and hear how English should be spoken" or "Listen to the silver-tongued Gold-Medalists" — do you think the people would come near the theatre? I assure you I should be very sorry to be on sharing terms.

There is no doubt that good diction is far too rare. By "diction" I mean the speaking of words correctly and easily. That is what we are concerned with at the moment, although I suppose the word "diction" means a good deal more than that.

Of course, we are handicapped because English is the language of a diversity of people scattered in many parts of the globe. But there are only three kinds of English that I am familiar with — the English of England, the English of America, and the English of the telephone operator. This last I do not propose to consider, because it is almost a language of its own and is, moreover, spoken more or less in confidence. But the difference between the English of England and the

English of America is mainly one of diction. It is futile to assert that the English of the two countries is not one language. There are some differences in pronunciation of certain words and occasionally a given word will have a different meaning. But, as a rule, it is only the difference between the English of England of today and that of a hundred and fifty years ago. America has frequently maintained the purity of the language which in course of years has become vitiated in England. We all know that many Old English words and phrases are now regarded in England as Americanisms.

The chief fault in speech in America I should describe as sloppiness, and the outstanding defect in England as snippiness. The English of England has been distorted by people who really ought to know better, the upper classes. Unfortunately the less educated class, particularly in the suburbs of London, in an attempt to ape their betters become so refined that at times they are hardly understandable. The American is never guilty of this straining after superiority, but in my opinion he errs on the other side. He is so afraid of being meticulous in his speech that he allows himself to become careless.

I have noticed amongst the youth of today that there is frequently a decided objection to speaking well, a feeling that there is something unhealthy in good articulation. I know nice parents — well-spoken parents — with children who speak vilely. Frequently when a boy speaks very badly the mother looks at him with pride and says "Isn't he a little man?" I can see no good in this. There is nothing clever in speaking badly — anybody could do it with a little practice. One can speak well and still be a little man — or a big man. I say nothing against slang. I rather admire it; it enriches the language. But I can see no excuse for a lazy and careless delivery of words. Laziness in diction leads to laziness in phraseology — to the perpetual use of the words "Fine" and "Grand" and "Sure" —

monosyllables which can hardly be said to be a healthy stimulus to conversation. . . .

I have said that actors must never appear to be making an effort to teach anything; but what we should do is to set a worthy example which the youth of today may be inspired to follow. And with the advent of the talking pictures our responsibility becomes far greater than ever it was before; not that the masses go to the movies to learn how to speak; but young people are inclined to be very imitative, particularly of those actors and actresses whom they specially admire.

Looking back, it seems to me that gold must have been much easier to obtain just at this time than it is at the present moment. Dame Madge Kendal gave me a gold ring made out of Lord Fisher's trousers; and gave Flo one too; also made out of Lord Fisher's trousers. The title First Sea Lord, which was Lord Fisher's, carried with it a great deal of gold braid. This gold braid does not seem to descend from trousers to trousers. The new trousers do not inherit the braid of their predecessors. When a First Sea Lord has worn out his trousers, he apparently casts them off like an old glove — braid and all. Dame Madge was a very observant and original woman. Having discovered that gold braid of this period contained a great deal of pure gold, she followed the matter up until she got Lord Fisher's discarded glory, took the braid to an old-established gold refiners', which still carries on business opposite the Garrick Club, and had the gold extracted and made into gold rings as souvenirs of her old friend Lord Fisher. Madge Kendal was an amazing old lady. She was more than eighty-six when Flo and I last lunched with her. She talked for two hours without stopping and held our interest every moment. Like most people of pronounced and autocratic character, she was greatly loved and greatly hated. I think the people who knew her best and were well acquainted with her family history were the ones that loved her.

CAST

Alexander Hamilton

Alexander Hamilton	.	GEORGE ARLISS
Betsy Hamilton	.	DORIS KENYON
William B. Giles	.	DUDLEY DIGGES
Thomas Jefferson	.	MONTAGU LOVE
George Washington	.	ALAN MOWBRAY
General Schuyler	.	LIONEL BELMORE
James Monroe	.	MORGAN WALLACE
Mrs. Reynolds	.	JUNE COLLYER
James Reynolds	.	ROLF HAROLDE

&

Director	. .	JOHN ADOLPHI
Story	. . .	GEORGE ARLISS AND MARY HAMLIN
Adaptation	. .	JULIAN JOSEPHSON AND MAUDE T. HOWELL
Camera	. . .	JAMES VAN TREES

Chapter 10

DURING the shooting of "Hamilton" I once more began to think seriously of returning to the stage. I had not yet admitted to myself that the pictures had "got me." I missed the glamour and excitement of the theatre, although as compensation I was spared a great deal of nervous strain. But Darryl Zanuck and the Warner Brothers were meanwhile settling my future for the next two years or thereabouts. They offered me a contract by which I was to make four pictures. Of course I didn't have to sign it, but Flo and I liked Hollywood; I liked the people with whom I worked; I was relieved of long periods of touring — with railway journeys that made me sick. It is true I had the long trip from England and back, but that was comparatively easy. I could arrange my working months in Hollywood, a land of sunshine, to conform to that period of very uncertain English weather November to April. Moreover I was playing to an audience to be counted in millions instead of thousands. So I signed.

"Hamilton" being finished in May, we at once sailed for home, anxious to be in time for the English spring, which when it is good can be so very very good that I am always willing to take a chance on it. This was in 1931, when American producing companies were beginning to make a serious move towards establishing their own studios in England. Jack Warner came over and opened Warner Brothers Studios at Teddington. When we lunched together at the Carlton I promised to make a picture in that studio the following year, providing the equipment was as good there as in Hollywood.

"The Man Who Played God" was definitely decided upon as my next picture. But as that was only one of four needed to fulfill my contract I was busy reading a great many plays and stories. The manuscript of "Rothschild," a play in four or five acts, came to me during this summer, although I did not make it for the screen until two years later.

Our annual summer holidays in England (which as years go on seem to follow each other with confusing rapidity) vary very slightly one from another. Some outstanding event, such as a coronation or a war or my painting the coal-cellar door at St. Margaret's, is the only aid I have to memory. Each year before returning to America we go through a routine which, for the benefit of posterity and Mr. Godfrey Davies, I will here set down.

All those who have experienced the business of leaving their house for six or seven months will know the amount of thought and trouble it entails. We have two doses. First there is the cottage at St. Margaret's to close up. You know the thousand and one things to be seen to — how tiring it all is. On these occasions I am bound to admit that I am always very thoughtful about Flo. If the weather is fine I will take a long walk so as not to be in her way. You know how terribly in the way a man can be. And then after she has got the curtains down,

"The Millionaire"

"The Working Man"

Scenes from "The Working Man"

The author as Richelieu

Scenes from " Richelieu "

Scenes from "Alexander Hamilton"

The author in "The House of Rothschild"

"The House of Rothschild"

George Arliss as Voltaire

Scene from "Voltaire"

Scene from "Dr. Syn"

The author in "Dr. Syn"

George Arliss as Disraeli

Scene from "Disraeli," with Florence Arliss

Scene from "His Lordship"

"The Green Goddess"

Scenes from "The Green Goddess"

"East Meets West"

The author in "The Last Gentleman"

George Arliss as Shylock

The author in "Old English"

LEFT TO RIGHT: Darryl Zanuck, Joseph M. Schenck,
George Arliss, Samuel Goldwyn

The author being received by Queen Mary at the première
of one of his pictures

Scenes from " The Iron Duke "

Filming "The Iron Duke"

Scene from "The Guv'nor"

The author in "The Guv'nor"

George Arliss in " A Successful Calamity "

and things like that, I will come back and greet her with a few cheery words. If the weather is bad, I am there in the house; always ready to be called upon for advice, but never interfering — just quiet, with a book, moving from room to room so as not to be in the way. If there is any very heavy job to be done for which Flo needs more assistance, I am always ready to dash off to the village to find somebody.

Then there is the garden to be seen to. You know what gardeners are if left to themselves; you'd come back and find nothing but cabbages. So explicit directions have to be given to the gardener as to what he has to do at certain periods of our absence. This I leave entirely to Flo. She loves her garden and I always find that the best way to help her in matters of gardening is to leave her absolutely alone. I have sometimes made suggestions, but they seemed painful to Flo and the gardener, so, although it is an effort, I refrain from offering advice, even though I know it to be good. When we have finished our work at the cottage, we go back to see about the house in London. But first of all there is the dog to be disposed of.

At the time of which I am writing it was Buster, but he has now passed away and has been succeeded by Sadie Thompson. When Buster died after a long reign, Flo was heartbroken and declared that she would never have another dog. (She always does this.) But our old friend Louise Boulton said secretly to me, "I cannot bear to see Flo without a dog," so she conceived the idea of asking Flo to take care of her newly acquired Yorkshire while she went away on a prolonged visit; this being planned with the full intention of never claiming it again. Flo fell into the trap and Sadie Thompson has been our dog ever since.

When I say *our* dog, I am merely speaking as the head of the family. I am always very fond of Flo's dogs, but they are her dogs and no one else's. They are never happy unless she is in sight. If I tell Sadie to do anything, she gives me a slow look, turning her eyes until the whites become very expressive and clearly indicate, "While *she* is here I don't have to do anything but what she tells me."

Sometimes at St. Margaret's when Flo is busy she will beg me to take the dog for a nice long walk. I prepare to go obediently; Sadie demurs; Flo says encouragingly, "Now go with the Master," — the Master! — and Sadie comes, obediently. After we have walked about seven minutes towards the downs and I am enjoying life, Sadie shows signs of great fatigue. I say, "Come on now, you can't be tired yet." She revives slightly and comes on, but in a very few minutes she is so worn out that she can hardly drag one leg after another. I say sternly, "Now none of this" and she comes on, using the whites of her eyes to create a look of heart-rending appeal, but I will have none of it, and push on. She now continues, little by little, to slow down; and when she is about ten lengths behind, she turns tail and makes, hell-for-leather, for home. I tear after her calling "Sadie!" appealingly, commandingly, thunderously, without avail. At last my anger becomes so terrific that even Sadie is appalled and stops and crawls towards me. I say, "Now my girl, you've asked for it! Now you're going to be put on the lead." I produce the lead and my prisoner is now securely handcuffed, so to speak, and I resume my walk, firmly, lead in hand. It is the work of an instant for Sadie to institute a sit-down strike; this she does with complete success. No man can pull by the neck a sitting dog for any prolonged period. The work is not only hard but degrading. So we turn back for home. Sadie is released, and with an occasional victorious backward glance at me, gambols merrily to her mistress.

Flo has always had a dog from the days when she was quite a small child; during our married life one dog has succeeded another. But of course we have never been able to take any one of them abroad with us. Every English dog-owner knows that if he goes out of England he cannot take his dog. Not that other countries will not accept it, but because he may not bring it home again, except under specific conditions which he knows will, at least, mean agony for his dog, and possibly result in its death. Six months' quarantine for a dog that has all its life been petted and cared for by one person! I have been through all the business of rebellion against this wicked law. The answer is: "That is the law." You proceed to explain that the dog is never allowed out alone, that it has been with you for so many years and has a spotless record! They say: "That is the law about dogs; it would be impossible to make exceptions." You say "Why?" They answer: "If you do it for one, you must do it for all."

Why? Why not make exceptions? A passport is insisted upon for humans, so every Tom, Dick and Harry can get one. Why shouldn't my dog have a passport? Not every dog, not any stray dog, but my dog and your dog; the dogs that can be vouched for by responsible British citizens who have passports of their own. Our dogs are likely to be far less dangerous to the community than Tom, Dick and Harry, and our dogs' passports far more truthful. I maintain that this is not a stupid suggestion put forward by a dog crank; it is reasonable and it is common sense. We English believe that we show greater humanity to animals than any other country in the world and yet this ridiculous law still survives. And what is it all about? It is a law instituted to stamp out rabies.

Without going into the question of what percentage of danger there would be from rabies if all the stray dogs that could find their way into England were allowed to stray in, let us consider your dog and Flo's. If either Flo or you were allowed to take your dog out of the country and bring the same dog back to your home, surely that dog would be of far less danger to the rising or declining generation of British subjects than if you left it behind, or than if you placed it in quarantine for six months after you landed. I know of no greater mental suffering for a dog than to be parted from its master or mistress. If a dog develops madness, it seems reasonable to conclude that it is a mental condition — a condition that might be brought about by mental anguish. This will be disputed; perhaps someone will even go so far as to attempt to explain rabies. If he does, his explanation cannot in the least weaken my argument, that the present law is cruel and stupid. When will the humane societies of England make a concerted effort to have this law repealed?

So as our dog cannot go with us, he is taken each year to our old friend Edith Wilkins at Chipping Norton. Edith is of the "county family" type and is one of those characters whose word and loyalty can be relied upon under all conditions. She would sacrifice her own comfort any time for any dog — and once she has taken on the responsibility of Buster or Sadie Thompson, we know that that is a sacred trust and that she would much prefer death to dishonor. Chipping Norton is one of those pleasant little places that has never grown up. It has had a few growing pains, I believe, to which it seems to have succumbed. At one time it made some blankets; during the World War it turned out some khaki. I am not sure whether or not the present war has brought it once more to life — I doubt it. Chipping Norton is known as a hunting center, which probably accounts for its stunted growth and its lack of progress. I cannot maintain that hunting is the sport of the ignorant; there might be some excuse for it if it were; but it is a brainless and barbarous occupation. Chipping Norton has a faded town hall and market place surrounded (as in most English villages) by pubs. Once a year in this market place a fair is held which is still called "the Mop" because in the old days the maidservant who wanted a job went to the fair with a mop over her shoulder, which was a sign that she was there to be hired.

This leaving the dog behind is always a wretched business and we never get hardened to it. Flo, unfortunately, not only knows what a dog is talking about, but also knows what it is thinking about, which makes it more difficult for her. So we always stay a few days at Chippy to give Sadie time to become familiar with her temporary home before we sail. During this time we never fail to pay a visit to dear Mary Anderson (Madame de Navarro) whose home is less than half-an-hour's drive from

169

Chippy. Broadway, which has long been known as one of the prettiest of English villages, is now famous for being the home of Mary Anderson.

When I look at "Mamie" now, she is so little changed that I cannot believe it is fifty odd years since I first saw her at the Lyceum Theatre — when I used to sit in front night after night, because she was the greatest actress and the most magnificent creature I had ever seen. Just how great an actress she was I cannot say; but I do know that she took London by storm and was able to hold her own with all the English actresses then playing. The fact that she left the stage when she was thirty and yet is still vividly remembered by all old theatregoers seems to me to prove that she was an actress of great charm and ability.

She and Dame Madge Kendal were close friends, and although Mamie is very unlike Madge, she has certain characteristics common to both. They both loved the stage and loved to talk about it. Dame Madge's recollections of the theatre were much richer in detail because she had had long years of experience as a manageress both in London and in the English provinces; she was a great social favorite, but she never lost her admiration of the theatre and her respect for the art of the actor. Mary Anderson loves the stage no less, but there is a part of her that is devoted to music; she has met all the great musical artistes of her day, and I have sometimes suspected that she would rather have been a great operatic star than a great actress. In another respect she resembles Dame Madge Kendal: she likes giving things. We never leave her without taking with us some concrete evidence of her affection. In her latest book she mentions giving me a brilliant emblem of St. George which was originally owned and worn by Edmund Kean. Each Christmas she sends me a pocket diary with a flattering inscription which I do not hesitate to flash in front of my less fortunate friends. Madge Kendal passed away in 1935, but Mary Anderson still enjoys every moment of her life in Broadway.

So there are many reasons why we always regret saying good-by to Chippy.

When we close up the house in London I take charge of all the important details that need attention before we sail, such as leaving our change of address at the bank, buying such clothes as I am likely to need, calling at my club, and such things as only a man can do. I show the same discretion about the arrangements in the house as I did about the cottage. Flo, who has a well-balanced mind about other things, has strange ideas about cleanliness. Carpets, for instance, must be taken up bodily before we go, and sent to the cleaners. Perfectly ridiculous, of course; what are those infernal machines for that howl and moan through the house every morning if not to keep the carpets clean? For what other reason does that noise continue for hours? A servant using one of those instruments of torture can hear nothing else that is going on in the world. A fire engine might arrive and remain puffing away without a word of welcome from within. Servants love to use these vacuum cleaners for long periods, because the noise they make constitutes a perfect alibi for disregarding bells of all descriptions.

All this cleaning-up in a house is in my opinion like cutting down a venerable tree in a garden. Why is it that men of taste feel so warm and comfortable in a study or snuggery of a bachelor friend? Because there is that welcome warmth that only years of undisturbed dust can bring. Where could we find our fine old black oak and rich mahogany if our ancestors had ever thought of cleaning things? So to avoid any sort of discussion I leave all this entirely to Flo. The arrangements in London are less difficult than at St. Margaret's, because there are John and Mrs. Jackson left behind, both of long and trusty service. And there is Miss Crumpton, my secretary, who looks after my letters during our absence, including my fan mail — which is delivered by the postman in the regular delivery, and not sent in sacks direct from the General Post Office as I learn from the fan magazines is the method adopted by the Government for other film stars.

Celia Crumpton is known in my study as "the terrible Mr. Crumpton" because of the number of complaints I get from begging-letter writers, who tell me in a personal letter that they have received a reply from Mr. Crumpton, but they are sure he never showed me their appeal. They can't put anything over on her, because she never forgets a name or a handwriting. I have always been unable to dictate anything longer than an ordinary letter, and even then I get confused and halting and mixed; it is Celia Crumpton who tells me where I repeat myself and it is she who gives me the word I am searching for when I suddenly stop dead.

So all these things being done, there is nothing to be considered now, before we leave, but Dinky Bits; his full name is Dinky Bits Hail Columbia God Save the King, but for short . . . I hope I'm not boring you with these domestic details; after all these are my reminiscences and I must tell you about Dinky, who traveled with us for more than thirty years. If you say to me, "We like you, Mr. Arliss, but we don't want to hear about your furniture and livestock to the uttermost detail," I answer, "You have brought it on yourself. When you bought or borrowed this book you must have known the risk you ran. You know what autobiographies are. You must take the consequences. If my dear gray-headed lady acquaintances edge me into a corner and start telling me about their wonderful grandchildren, I consider that I have a perfect right, after ten minutes, to draw myself up to my full height, walk out of the room and slam the door after me. But if I have said to them 'Oh, do tell me about your wonderful grandchildren' then I should be patient and affable. Are you answered?"

Dinky, then, was our parrot, who, I repeat, had traveled with us for more than thirty years. His traveling cage was made to go inside a case that looked like a hat-box. This was intended to deceive officials of all kinds and prevent the possibility of his being consigned to the baggage-wagon or the guards van. Although again he was our bird, he of course belonged really to Flo. All animals belong to Flo. She called him "a dear little bird" and "What a pretty creature!" and "a nice 'ickle bird," all of which he repeated to himself when alone, with great dramatic feeling. But he was not in reality quite such a darling as he thought he was, or as Flo believed him to be. He was beautiful to look at — gray, with a perfect crimson tail — and he excited great admiration from passers-by — if they passed. He was an autocratic bird. He was allowed out of his cage and given entire

173

freedom at home and took unwarrantable advantage of it. He objected to me on principle, unless it happened that Flo had to go away for any length of time, in which event he would fawn upon me mawkishly. But when she was within call, and he was therefore free from all danger of my retaliation, he became most insolent to me. If he saw me reading or writing, in obvious enjoyment of a certain quiet and seclusion, he would think for a few moments and then decide that I was assuming airs of proprietorship which by right belonged to him and that I must be put in my place. He would then proceed to approach me from behind with great stealth. When he walked he could make the most devilish row with his feet if he wished to attract your attention, but if he had any subtle and secret design which might be foiled were he observed, he could walk with absolutely noiseless footsteps. By this secret manner of approach he would reach a point so near my ear that with his piercing eye he believed he could see the drum. He would then give out a most startling *Click!* — a sound so full of meaning and determination that it could hardly be duplicated by any man-made instrument. Coming unexpectedly it is more terrifying than a pistol shot, and causes the subject to jump and to break out in a cold perspiration. It means, in fact, "Stick 'em up." This is no practical joke on Dinky's part. It is done with stern determination and set purpose. "Get out of that chair; you've sat there long enough. I don't care where you go, but I'm tired of the sight of you."

He was not a really accomplished parrot. He could not say all this, but he implied it. Sometimes I have presence of mind enough not to jump up, but to slide myself just far enough from the back of the chair where he is poised for attack to defy him. I say, "Go back to your cage! Go home! You wicked little bird!" If his mistress had said this he would have gone immediately. But in me he recognizes a weak-minded individual without power or authority. He gives another threatening *Click* and takes a short flight on to the table. At great personal danger I rescue my fountain pen; his beak misses me by a hair's-breadth. Then he grinds his teeth. How he learned to do this I have no idea. We read of people grinding their teeth, but I have never known anyone who has actually heard it done. But Dinky gave an unmistakable imitation of a person grinding his teeth. He now gives a hasty glance round and suddenly becomes, quite unexpectedly, gay; performing a most ridiculous and abandoned dance, with his toes turned in even more than usual. It suggests, "Oh, let us be friends. All is forgotten and forgiven." This, however, is merely to put me off the scent; having danced near enough to a little bottle of ink which I keep on my desk, he makes a sudden vicious jab at it, well knowing that one crunch and it would be all over. At this moment Flo, having heard my screams, enters and says, sternly, "Dinky! What are you doing?" and Dinky at once becomes the most docile, the most loving and lovable of birds. He gets on Flo's outstretched hand, nestles under her chin, coos, calls himself a "nice 'ickle bird" and almost swoons with virtuousness. Flo takes him away with much stroking and sympathy and says a little resentfully to me as she goes, "You evidently startled him."

In thirty years, Dinky was the only one of the family that showed no sign of age. He crossed the Atlantic more than sixty times; he traveled thousands of miles up and down the United States; submitted himself to the caresses of many attractive leading ladies, and bit many un-suspecting colored porters. When we were in our draw-ing room on the train, we always took the cage out of its case, but when anyone knocked at the door we threw something carelessly over the cage, so that it might not be seen. If a garrulous colored porter rested his hand negligently on the covering for what the writers of detective stories call "a split second," Dinky had his finger. Dinky always listened intently when covered up and no matter what kind of cover was over him he had an uncanny instinct of the moment when a finger was within reach. In some of the old trains the top-light in the drawing room had to be put out by the porter. You got into bed and rang the bell and the porter came in, stood on a stool and put out the light. Our colored porter was of course entirely ignorant of the existence of Dinky; he stood on the stool, put his hand down for a moment to steady himself, and as the light went out a mighty howl went up into the night — it emanated not from Dinky, but from the innocent colored man; not so much a cry of pain, as a wail occasioned by the religious conviction that the Devil had got him at last.

Unfortunately for us, great scientists discovered a disease and great scholars discovered a name for it. It is called psittacosis, and is supposed to be contracted through parrots. So the great guardians of the public health of England and the sage and mighty ones of the United States decided, with their usual intelligence, that no parrots should be allowed to "enter" either country under any conditions whatever. So Dinky was left behind, caught a cold and died. Flo mourned his loss, and with all his faults I loved him very much.

Chapter 11

"THE MAN WHO PLAYED GOD" was adapted from a drama called "The Silent Voice" which was originally played in the theatre I believe by Otis Skinner. It was an artificial but exceedingly effective story. A musician loses his hearing and after a period of despair learns lip-reading, which brings about his salvation. There was a short scene between the deaf musician and a professor of lip-reading; and although I had read up about this system of teaching, I thought it would be more satisfactory if I had a chat with an actual teacher. So I applied to a school of lip-reading.

As I am an actor of long and varied experience, I had thought of the professor as a nice, elderly gentleman with rather long hair — I have always played them that way. At the Elephant & Castle Theatre, on the Surrey side of London, where all my early experience was gained, no one would have dared to come on as a professor without a profusion of gray or white hair and a bandana handkerchief, partly out of the pocket — and possibly a snuffbox.

When the real professor arrived I was really surprised to find myself shaking hands with a dapper little man of about thirty-five who might have been the assistant manager of any big business house. He had never been in a studio and had never before met an actor. The way he described his method of teaching was so direct and clear-cut, so much more convincing than the way we should have done it at the Elephant & Castle, that I asked him if he would play the part — which he did, with ease and authority, not quite realizing I think that he was actually being "taken." The result was an attractive little scene which bore a stamp of truth.

I hasten to confess that from a professional, that is, a theatrical, point of view, this is a very bad precedent. It is often dangerous to run counter to the generally accepted notions of character; if you were to set a thief to play a thief, he would probably appear to be the most virtuous person on the stage. Men who are born in the purple if they venture on the stage will often convey the impression that they were born in the attic; while one who was raised in the attic (if that is possible) can convince an audience that he is absolutely riddled with veins of blue blood. It was only because ours was a very little bit that we were able to get away with it.

The deaf person is taught to watch and study not only the action of the lips, but the movement of the muscles of the face and neck. Our teacher told me that the best results are not as a rule obtained from the most intellectual people. He said that his most promising pupil at the moment was an iceman.

It was in "The Man Who Played God" that I first met Bette Davis. We were having difficulty in finding a girl with some ability who looked a little different from the average ingénue. It was Murray Kinnell who suggested Bette Davis; that same Murray Kinnell who had done such valuable work in "Old English" both on the stage and screen. He had played with Bette Davis in a picture called "The Menace"; he thought she had possibilities and urged me to let her rehearse. In the theatre and on the screen, by the time I come to rehearse a play I know every character thoroughly; I don't mean that I know all their lines, but I know the characters and the opportunities they afford the actors who are to play them. I know just what I want to do with my own part, and I am acutely conscious of just how far I fall short; one may have a vivid imagination without the power of achievement. And so I never expect to get from the other people all that my imagination has conjured up.

I think that only two or three times in my experience have I ever got from an actor at rehearsal something beyond what I realized was in the part. Bette Davis proved to be one of these exceptions. I knew she had a "nice little part" important to me — so I hoped for the best. I did not expect anything but a nice little performance. But when we rehearsed she startled me; the nice little part became a deep and vivid creation, and I felt rather humbled that this young girl had been able to discover and portray something that my imagination had failed to conceive. She startled me because quite unexpectedly I got from her a flash that illuminated mere words and inspired them with passion and emotion. That is the kind of light that cannot be hidden under a bushel, and I am not in the least surprised that Bette Davis is now the most important star on the screen. I was fortunate, too, in having Simmy again, particularly as nearly all his scenes were with me. Flo felt that she was too old for the part that

I should have liked her to play, so she slipped out of it and Violet Heming slipped in. Miss Heming and I had not played together since 1913, when she followed Elsie Leslie as Clarissa, the ingénue in "Disraeli." The stage version of "The Man Who Played God" lent itself easily to screen adaptation. Maude Howell made a working script and it was passed by Darryl Zanuck with very little time lost in conference.

During the entire period of my connection with Warner Brothers I was fortunate in my business connections in the studio, inasmuch as the only member of the executive with whom I had to confer was Darryl Zanuck. Jack Warner I met occasionally when contracts had to be discussed, and Harry Warner now and then at "social gatherings"; but Darryl Zanuck had entire control of the actual production of the pictures. There was no red tape. I could go to him and get a final decision on any point in a moment. Luckily for me he had some regard for my opinion.

This is more surprising than some of my "fans" may realize, because most of the young men who have grown up in the pictures are slightly contemptuous of the theatre — well, perhaps not contemptuous, but they regard stage plays as old-fashioned in construction and stage actors as fellows to be carefully watched and controlled. They have practically no knowledge of the drama, past or present; they think of the cinema as having superseded the theatre for the reason that it is better. If you speak of Henry Irving or Forbes-Robertson they search their memory and say "What picture was he in?" I am not holding this against them; this blind devotion to a cause by its followers is what gives more power to the elbow of the leaders. Zanuck is a born leader, not a blind follower. But he knew that, however different the pictures may be from the spoken drama in the theatre, they are nevertheless both built on the same foundation. And it was because he realized this, and believed that my working knowledge of the theatre must in a great measure apply to the screen, that he and I were able to save a good deal of time in the production of my pictures.

We could not entirely eliminate the conference: the specialists had to be called in for their opinion on the story; that is one of the laws of the studio; the operation on the manuscript is not performed by one specialist; there are several. Each specialist is allowed to take a jab at the patient where he thinks it will do him the most good. The specialists all do this until they are exhausted. The patient is then taken away, a bleeding mass, and when the wounds are healed up, he is brought back and they do it again. Sometimes mortification sets in and a leg has to be cut off and replaced by a wooden one. But this is so skillfully done that when it is seen on the screen nobody knows it is a wooden leg except the audience. The reason I got on so well with Zanuck was because he had faith in his own judgment and in mine. After one conference, which probably produced some good suggestions, he and I would get together and decide on a final script which he would O.K. without further trouble or delay.

I first met Darryl Zanuck in 1928, when I was playing Shylock in Los Angeles, and when the talkies were still being called the "movie-tones." He was then in his twenties. I had finished my New York season with "The

Merchant of Venice" and was touring the country. Jack Warner brought a party to the theatre and afterwards they all came to our rooms at the Biltmore Hotel. We talked of the possibility of my playing "Disraeli" on the screen. Zanuck was tremendously enthusiastic about it — walked up and down, outlining, with much gesticulation, an entirely new opening to the screen version which struck me as being exceedingly clever in construction. Jack Warner chuckled and said: "He does all the work at the studio now. I just add up the figures."

As Zanuck ran on and on with his ideas about "Disraeli" I remember thinking: "You talk too much, young man. I should have more faith in you if you didn't have quite so much to say." Although I find it difficult to form an opinion of the silent man, I cannot help at once mistrusting the capacity of the man who talks at great length about the things he is going to do. I suppose I judge others by myself. If I have an idea and talk about it, my enthusiasm evaporates in the process of talking and I seldom get as far as putting the idea on paper. But I had no means of knowing, in this brief meeting, just how artful Zanuck was. I couldn't know then, what I have since discovered, that he talks a blue streak with the full intention of exposing his own weakness. He will pour out his ideas one after another, tumbling them on each other's heels, lashing himself into such a state of excitement that the words can't come out fast enough. It took me some time to get on to the fact that all the time he was apparently lost in his subject, he was watching everybody at the conference, particularly the two or three people whose opinion he respected, and getting a fairly shrewd idea of what effect he was making. When he is holding forth in this manner he is really having what to an actor would be a dress rehearsal. He is not only watching others, but he is listening to himself and registering his own weakness as he goes along. He is trying to stimulate the others into going one better, but most of all he is trying to expose to himself the vulnerable points in his own arguments. It is an ingenious method, but in using it you must be careful not to be surrounded by too many "yes-men."

Zanuck never hesitates to throw over his own ideas as soon as he gets a suspicion that they are no good. He has the most amazing memory for detail that I have ever come in contact with. He will have half a dozen great pictures under his control at one time and yet the story, and construction, and sequence of scenes of each one will be clear in his mind at a moment's notice. I have gone to him during the shooting of one of my pictures with a suggestion of some slight change in dialogue, and although it may be two or three weeks since we last discussed the story, he will remember every detail of the scene. If you get a decision from Zanuck it is not given because he is worried and wants to get rid of you, but because he understands exactly what you want and why.

When you go into his office in the morning you never know what you are going to find there. Sometimes it is a quiet, rather insignificant, simple little man in a dark suit — a man that you feel you should advise to take some sort of tonic. That is Zanuck. The next morning you see a broad, swarthy individual in a magnificent green shirt, open at the throat, a pronounced Lord Byron effect, exposing a full, strong neck and a great breadth of chest; amazing trousers, or breeches or top-boots — according to how he felt when he got up. That is Zanuck. The morning after, you will find him sitting at his desk enveloped in an enormous camel-hair overcoat. He now has the appearance of a man who has been told by his physician that if he leaves his bed that morning he will surely die, but who has come to his office in defiance of his doctor's orders.

If it is a conference, he will sit and listen with eyes glazed, obviously at the point of death. The writers who have been summoned, finding they are not interrupted, gain confidence, and heated discussions go on about the story for which the conference is called. Zanuck sits immovable. He has a small, well-shaped head which, rising above his huge coat, suggests to one watching him a snail which in a moment of surprise has let its head come out of its shell. The conference becomes more heated — how to get the girl on to the desert island and having got her there, how to get her off again; or whether she ought to be there anyway. Zanuck is obviously not interested; looking at him one might guess that he was thinking vaguely that he ought to have made his will before he left home. His body seems to be getting smaller and his coat larger. A specialist gets an idea: "Suppose she's put on the lifeboat with the boy, see, and just as they've got well away, a damn big wave comes along . . ." Zanuck is now evidently fast asleep; a close observer would have noticed that his head has been gradually disappearing since the early part of the conference, and now there is nothing visible but the top, which in snails forms a sort of lid to the shell. The specialists out of respect for their sleeping chief are now speaking in hushed tones, but they are all talking at once and arriving nowhere. Suddenly the body of the snail leaps so far out of its shell that it nearly sheds it, and with eyes blazing it says, "I've got it!" And he has. He's been listening to what everyone has said; he has heard and examined every argument, and suddenly he has hit on the solution. That is Zanuck.

He's not always right; but he generally is, and at any rate his suggestions are in the right direction; and he always has some good men about him (in my time there were Lucien Hubbard and Ray Griffith) who can be trusted to develop his ideas. Being now resurrected, he makes up for the period of his disappearance by doing nearly all the talking for the remainder of the conference, which may last from two to six hours — during which time he recites the entire scenario, without a note, in much more minute detail than the writers could do, and probably speaks all the dialogue impromptu two or three times over, not exactly as it is to be written, but expressing the substance of what all the characters say to one another from beginning to end. This is a conference.

It would serve a very useful purpose if it stopped at this; if the original author of the story or some one reliable writer now set to work, with occasional prompting from Darryl Zanuck, and finished it. But it isn't done that way. After the conference, the writers responsible go back to their office and work on the lines now agreed upon. It seems fairly obvious that when there are two or three men of some literary and inventive ability working together on a story they cannot be tied down hand and foot. The consequence is they now get new and brilliant ideas which they incorporate in Script No. 2.

At the next conference it is discovered that the new ideas throw the whole story out of gear, or that they don't seem as brilliant as they looked in the writers' office. Zanuck is annoyed, takes the floor again; brings out new and brilliant ideas of his own; the conference comes to an end, the writers go back to their office and prepare Script No. 3. Then there is another conference.

This procedure goes on for an indefinite period, depending as a rule on whether the story under discussion was good or bad to begin with. It often happens that a great deal of time is devoted to a scenario before it is discovered that the idea was no good from the start. This is likely to take longer to find out if there are many specialists at the conferences. In that case, they are all so anxious to contribute something good and original that their embellishments for the time being disguise the initial weakness of the story.

Speaking from my own experience I believe I am right in saying that those pictures of mine which proved to be most to the taste of the public were the ones that were produced without too many cooks. In justice to my friend Darryl Zanuck and as a side light on his character, I think I cannot do better than insert here an open letter written by him to all writers under Warner Brothers management. It is on a quarto sheet, pink, and typewritten: —

Warner Bros. Pictures Inc.
and
First National Productions Corporation
Burbank, California.

INTER-OFFICE COMMUNICATION

To all Writers.   Date: *Nov. 30, 1931*

From Mr. Zanuck.   Subject _____

The reason we hold story conferences is to exchange and discuss ideas and decide on a definite procedure for the respective stories on which we are working. The ultimate result of a conference should be a decision to proceed upon certain lines, and it is expected that the writers will then go ahead and follow out the instructions as agreed upon at the conference.

Of late in several instances we have definitely decided upon certain things at the conference and discovered that the things we agreed upon have been ignored, changed, or so twisted around that the situations cannot be recognized as the same situations decided upon at the story conference.

I know that it is often very necessary to change a number of minor details — dialogue, little pieces of business and such must be smoothed out, and incidents slightly altered.

However, from now on when we decide in conference on a definite line of procedure from sequence to sequence I want it followed out. When the script is finished you can voice your ideas at the next conference, but we can at least have the opportunity of reading the script written the way we decided it should be written.

Changes made contrary to discussion in conference often cause a great loss of time and money, and a great loss of sleep on my part. I assure you I get no kick out of sitting

187

to them. It brought me many letters from people who by reason of some physical infirmity had given up all hope but who, having seen the picture, were inspired with determination to face their trouble and to find consolation in trying to help others. One of the most satisfactory letters that reached me was from a group of deaf people who told me that they had never thought of attempting lip-reading until they saw this picture, and that now they were all learning rapidly, and that a new life had opened up to them. Unfortunately for me, the man who played God was a very rich and very generous person; he gave away large sums of money; so of course begging letters came to me in great numbers; some of them very pathetic but most of them obviously from professional beggars; all of them praying that I would play God to them. In requests for money my American followers were more courageous than my own compatriots. The requests from England were for various sums, but seldom for more than five pounds. In America they ranged from a modest five dollars to a bold five thousand.

The writers generally said that if I would send the money at once, I could trust to their honor not to tell a soul about it — not even the members of their own family. Some wanted new furniture for the entire house. One bright youth wanted a new motor car; he had a car but he wanted a new one; to save me any trouble in selection, he mentioned the make and the price. Mothers wanted me to undertake the education of from one to three children (all lovely). A student in Palestine was much more modest; after assuring me of his admiration for my work he said: "I beg not to think me one of the flatterers who merely want money, no sir, but if you want to encourage me by sending a present, I beg it to be a thing that is suitable to a student as a set of Eversharp fountains pens or a drawing set or anything you want. Lastly I ask God to remain an everlasting star, faithfully yours."

A young man in South Carolina suggests a method of raising money which will be satisfactory to him, and at the same time will not be a burden on my personal resources: —

Dear Sir,

I am a young man 21 years of age. It has been my lifelong ambition to get into the movies. I had enough saved to pay my way to Hollywood, due to a misfortune I had to spend it.

I have saw you play in several pictures which I enjoyed very much. I travelled with a road show once and had some experience there. I have a good voice for immitating annimals especially the laughing hyena.

If you will get several of your friends to donate and buy me a ticket to Hollywood it will be highly apriciated and I will pay for it as soon as I get straight.

Very truly yours . . .

to devote to those friends and acquaintances that, as I have said, are liable to blow through Hollywood in a most unexpected way.

John Hays Hammond had just arrived in Pasadena; he was a friend of many years' standing (he was special ambassador and representative of the United States at the coronation of King George V) and we were glad to be free from the studio and able to have some little "visits" with him. Hays Hammond had more charm than any man I have known, except perhaps his son Jack. It is unfortunate that his many activities as the greatest mining expert of his day did not allow him more time to devote to the diplomatic service of his country. He was really a born diplomatist; he had a way of displaying the keenest interest in what *you* were doing — of making you the central figure, the really important person. As is the case with most men who have led adventurous lives, it was difficult to get him to talk about himself; but sometimes one could lead him on to speak about his life in South Africa during his close association with Cecil Rhodes and Dr. Jameson. Now and then I was able to get him to tell of the time when he was sentenced to death, and imprisoned within such easy distance of his place of execution that he could hear the workmen cheerfully erecting the gallows.

During his visit to Pasadena, he was writing his reminiscences, and from time to time he would come to me for advice; he didn't need it, but he made me think he did — it was one of his pleasant ways of making the other fellow feel important. His sister, who had been his constant companion, was collaborating with him, and later, when the two volumes were published, it was obvious that he needed no other advice, either as to style or substance.

Other unexpected visitors who came at this time were Commander Byrd, Helen Wills (I believe I succeeded in making her smile once), and Aldous Huxley, then of King's College, London. I put these three celebrities in a group because they all looked so very young to have accomplished so much. Although I must confess that Professor Einstein, whom we met at the invitation of Dr. Millikan, the President of the Executive Council of the Institute of Technology, did not look much older.

I could not talk fluently about the North Pole to Commander Byrd, but he knew of my interest in the anti-vivisection movement, so he talked animals to me. I was impressed by his great affection for his dogs; he told me that if one died on his expedition, he felt it as keenly as if he had lost one of his family.

I continue to be surprised at the different types and classes of representative people who travel thousands of miles to visit Hollywood without any apparent reason. I like to spend two or three winter months there even if I am not going to do any work. In my case, however, there is a reason. I have many friends and many pleasant associations connected with my seasons at the studio. But who would expect to meet Lord and Lady Byng in Hollywood — six thousand miles from Scotland Yard! (It is evidently of no use for Englishmen to go to California to escape the Metropolitan Police.) Lord Byng and I had one thing in common: we both smoked the same little pipe, which we bought at the same shop in the Haymarket. He always smoked it during the Great War, and it was christened (and is still sold under the same name) "the little Bingo." When the Tommies saw him smoking his pipe they would say, "Here comes the little Bingo" — a familiarity which Lord Byng by no means resented. He had a sense of humor that would have pleased my Uncle Charlie (although my Uncle Charlie would have been rather surprised at its being possessed by anyone outside his immediate family). He told me a story which I found amusing, although I am afraid it has no point unless you happen to have watched the "Black Maria" arrive at the police station and back up to the entrance so that the prisoners, as they step out of the police van, practically step into the station.

"Well," Lord Byng said, "we were invited to a swanky dinner party — a duchess or somebody — and we wanted to be quite at our best. It happened that my chauffeur was suddenly taken ill, so, as I was head of the police, I borrowed for the night one of the police drivers. When we arrived at the duchess's mansion, the driver, to our horror, deliberately backed through the gates and up to the front door."

The "writers" had now succeeded in making an acceptable script of "A Successful Calamity." The original play was written by Clare Kummer, with her usual delicacy of touch. It seemed to be quite an up-to-date little comedy, and it was only when you analyzed it that you found it was composed of all the old stuff: the rich father who pretends to be ruined; the young wife (played by Mary Astor, looking so beautiful that Mr. Pepys, could he have seen her, would surely have put her in his Diary and oh, Mary, how you could

196

have put him in yours!) who was supposed to have
run away with a handsomer man, but hasn't; the spend-
thrift son and daughter, who immediately reform and
rally round the ruined father; even the old butler (you
can imagine how perfectly Grant Mitchell played him)
who offers his master the savings of a lifetime — it was
all there and I gloried in it, because I like the old stuff
and believe in it.

I don't know how far the picture was financially successful, but I think it was worth doing, and it was
wholesome entertainment. Wait — I believe I can remember an adventure during the filming of this picture:
not an exciting adventure, but terribly instructive to
students of moving-picture mechanics. You realize that
during the shooting of a scene — that is, during the
time that the camera is actually grinding — there must
not be a sound in the studio; not a breath must be heard,
except that of the actors, and even they must breathe
in the politest way. One device after another has been
tried to prevent any sound escaping from the machinery of the camera itself.

One method was to place each camera and its operator
in a large glass case, which was wheeled about to its
required positions. The next device was a heavy, padded
cover which was placed about the camera, making it
look as though it were dressed for an Arctic Expedition.
The present appliance is a fairly compact metal covering in which the camera is placed. It is called a "blimp"
but I don't know why. The glass-case invention was, I
believe, effective as to sound, but the fact that the
picture was necessarily taken through glass robbed it of a
certain clarity. Moreover, the operator was almost en-

tirely deprived of air. This fact was regarded as relatively unimportant — just so long as it didn't kill him, nothing mattered. The slogan of the studio is "Anything for the good of the picture." The individual is expected to suffer any kind of inconvenience in order that the camera and microphone may show good results. And, strangely enough, everyone is willing to make this sacrifice and to make it without a murmur, from the meanest of the staff to the inevitable star. An extraordinary spirit of ambition seems to enter into everyone concerned in the making of a picture, — the mechanics, the actors and the staff, — a determination to make the finest picture that has ever been turned out of the studio; it is a sort of religion that belongs to the pictures and which I do not believe exists in any other business or profession. It is, of course, quite understandable in the case of the stars, but to me it is entirely unaccountable amongst the rank and file of workers, because they get no more money or credit out of a good picture than they do out of a bad one.

Well, now for the adventure. It is interesting to note that certain sounds which are almost inaudible on the set register with startling significance through the microphone. The placing of a cup back into the saucer may come out with a bang which suggests that the heroine has been shot in the next room. The crackling of paper, such as may be caused by the ordinary opening of a letter, registers rather like the arrival of a regiment of artillery. In "A Successful Calamity" I had a scene in which I was discovered sitting in an armchair and lighting my pipe. There was to be a rather long pause as I smoked and gazed into the fire. The camera started; I gazed into the fire, lighted my pipe, and continued gazing into the fire with much feeling. I was about to go on when the sound man gave that irritating buzzing signal which means that there is something wrong, and the scene was stopped. He came out of his box and explained that there was some creaking and crackling going on all through the scene. I knew there was perfect quiet around me, and I knew that where Adolphi, the director, stood there must be a deathly silence. But Adolphi was a martinet — the type of director who would stand no nonsense. So, although everyone about him had almost refrained from breathing, he gave them an angry reprimand and told them to keep still. And we did it again, with the same result. It was decided that it must be the chair creaking — so we got another chair. Again the same trouble. It must be the boards. So then the carpet was taken up and the floor hammered down. Once more I gazed into the fire, lit my pipe and continued to gaze into the fire; and again came the maddening buzzer from the sound man. I'm afraid it might be boring to describe the various attempts we made to discover the root of the trouble, so I will no longer keep you in suspense. I think I have already admitted that I am really and truly a stage actor. The lighting of a pipe on the stage is not as simple as it looks. If it takes a shade too long, it slows up the scene. So I had, with great foresight, prepared some tobacco — made it very dry, so that it would catch light easily. The noise that registered was the burning of the dry tobacco in the bowl of my pipe, which to me was entirely inaudible until after the ingenious sound man had at last suggested it.

"A Successful Calamity" being finished, Flo and I left for England via Paris. We sometimes dropped off at Cherbourg and spent a few weeks in Paris during the spring or summer. Before leaving Hollywood, I again approached Zanuck about making "Rothschild," but the story was once more shelved.

During the summer, after we had left Paris, I had the satisfaction of introducing Ernest Pascal and his wife to St. Margaret's Bay. I think they liked it, but you cannot expect an author who is writing a play or a movie to be enthusiastic about anything but his play or his movie. Pascal had brought a complete scenario of "The King's Vacation," the story that was to be my next picture. It was his original story, written so far without interference.

I walked him on the downs to Dover (four miles); but we did not talk about the sea gulls or the view, or the way the coast is sinking inch by inch; we talked only of "The King's Vacation." I ventured some suggestions. Ernest behaved like a gentleman and listened to me with great restraint. He didn't lay a finger on me. Next day I walked him on the downs to Deal (seven miles) and again I made suggestions. It is lonely up there, as I have said — high up, on the edge of those white cliffs. Anybody might fall over. And, of course, the slightest push . . . But Ernest is a kindly man. And, after all, authors do not kill stars, intentionally. I think perhaps Ernest must have agreed with some of the things I said, because he and I remain the best of friends today, a condition which I cannot claim to have maintained with all the writers assigned to me. I like to think that some of the charm of St. Margaret's went into "The King's Vacation."

It was now decided by cables from Zanuck that my next three pictures should be (1) "The King's Vacation," (2) "The Adopted Father," (3) "Voltaire." Maude Howell, who was now associate director in all my pictures, "sat in" with Ernest Pascal on the final working script of "The King's Vacation." Maude has a keen, analytical mind which discovers the barren spots in a scenario with surprising accuracy. The first instinct of the writer is to resent her, but he always ends by freely admitting the value of her advice. She can cut and prune and revamp better than anyone I know, and she has an uncanny instinct of what will go with an audience and what is likely to fall flat; she has the happy faculty of being able to gain the confidence of the people with whom she works, and after a time, even the most dictatorial of directors will confer with her without any apparent fear of losing his dignity. No star has ever had a more faithful and valuable lieutenant than I have in Maude Howell.

We were particularly fortunate in the cast of "The King's Vacation." Marjorie Gateson had a most difficult part and played it with great skill. Flo had a part that suited her to perfection, and, of course, she stole all my scenes.

"The Adopted Father," my next film, was an adaptation of one I did under that title in the silent days. We now decided at the last moment to call it "The Working Man." It was an amusing story. A rather nervous and pedantic young man, a bachelor, lives with his sister; they have no other ties. One day the sister brings home a child that she proposes to adopt. It is a boisterous little boy about five or six years old, and the brother objects; there is a furious quarrel, and the brother slams out of the house. In order to teach his sister a lesson, he now proceeds to adopt a father. He chooses an impecunious old gentleman who is feeding in a cheap coffeehouse, and takes him home to his sister: he does it in a spirit of retaliation, expecting that the entire episode will be closed by the next morning, and the old gentleman and the boy returned from whence they came. But the funny old gentleman has insisted upon a signed document setting forth his rights as a father, and the young man now finds that the document is legal and that he is at the mercy of the funny old gentleman — who, of course, turns out to be a rich old gentleman and not at all the self-effacing person he was believed to be. That is the basis of the story; it was not high-brow, but I thoroughly enjoyed making the picture.

For many years, long before I ever thought of making pictures, I had a desire to play Voltaire in the theatre. Although, even then, I had a great many historical plays sent to me, nobody apparently had thought of Voltaire. I approached various authors without any satisfactory result. During one of my periodical visits to Philadelphia, an old acquaintance of mine, Lawrence Dudley, whom I had known only as a lawyer, happened to hear me mention that I wanted a Voltaire play, and promptly said, "Well, I will write you one." This did not strike me as being an answer straight from heaven to my prayer. My heart always sinks when one of my friends suggests writing a play for me. It is difficult enough to tell any author — even somebody you have never met or heard of — that he has written a bad play; in fact, it isn't done. Even managers become quite unaccountably tender-hearted when they return plays.

Instead of saying, "Your play is awful, why waste my time with it?" they write on beautifully engraved paper: "We have read your play with the greatest interest, but . . ." and something quite nice to finish up with. There is, I believe, an instance on record of a very angry manager sending back a manuscript with a note, "My dear Sir: I have read your play — oh, my dear Sir!" but that is an exception. I would always rather nobody ever wrote a play for me. When they write with me in mind they always pander to my vices — put in all the things "I do so well." If they would only write it for some other actor and then give it to me, there might be discovered in me depths and versatility undreamed-of.

It is possible that the gentle reader has never had a play written for him by one of his friends, in which case he cannot possibly know the amount of finesse that is required to evade the play and keep the friend. But you must not think because your friend writes a stupid play that he, the author, is a stupid man, and that you have been deceived in him all these years; he is still the same intelligent friend. But just as there are people who are perfectly sane in other respects, and yet believe that they are a teapot, or a divinity, or Napoleon, so there are men and women who, having written a play, believe forever after that they are dramatists.

I did not encourage my friend Lawrence Dudley to carry out his threat, and as time went on I believed I had escaped. But he had secretly taken unto himself a collaborator — George Gibbs, a fellow townsman — and sure enough, "Voltaire" arrived.

And wonder of wonders, it was very nearly a good play: it had drama, character, and was written with considerable skill. This took me so by surprise that I at once set to work to see if it could not be produced. Dudley was not a practised playwright and Gibbs was a writer of novels, so they gave me a free hand to make what changes I thought advisable. Voltaire is such a complex character that I do not see how it is possible to do him justice within the limitations of the theatre. Cinema, and even theatre, audiences have a very superficial idea of most historical characters — when they have any idea at all. As an average audience, we think of Voltaire as a tremendous figure in history — a great philosopher, a friend of the people, a master of propaganda; one whose influence is believed to have brought about the fall of the Bastille, and finally the Revolution. This is possibly a correct estimate. But these great results were achieved by a little man sitting in his study or his bedroom, writing, writing, far into the night; bathing his eyes with cold water, drinking strong coffee, and writing, writing. A keen little man with an amazing genius for directing his pamphlets and propaganda into the right channels.

All this makes good reading and good drama for the library; but it is infernally difficult to make it interesting on the stage. All Voltaire's great achievements were the result of his writing, writing, writing. It is the other side of the man, his domestic side we may call it, that lends itself to the stage: his childish cunning, his unexpected pettiness, his loves and hates, his lack of all sense of humor in situations where he himself was the central figure. There are half a dozen comedies to be written if one could sacrifice Voltaire entirely to comic episodes. But who would dare to do this? One might take the chance with Mr. Pepys, but not with Voltaire.

However, after we had all spent a good deal of time in rewriting and polishing, it looked to me like a reasonably good play. I was then under the management of Klaw and Erlanger. I submitted the play to them through George Tyler, their representative, and it was accepted for my next production. Before the contract was signed, however, the manuscript was read by Mr. Klaw's son; he didn't like it, the firm withdrew their offer, and the play was shelved. I don't blame young Mr. Klaw. I was never quite satisfied with the play, either.

It was long after this that I had the interview with Bernard Shaw when I suggested that he should write me a Voltaire play. So I never played the character on the stage. I had very little hope that it would be accepted for the screen, but as we were considering many possible characters, I mentioned it on the off-chance. It was a bold suggestion, and its reception was at first anything but enthusiastic; but gradually Zanuck became interested. He had to admit, however, that it was a gamble — and undoubtedly high-brow. Voltaire! The very name might scare away the movie public. So it had to be submitted to the Brothers. Strange to say, it went through. Jack accepted it, and even Harry, who was very pessimistic about historical plays — even he agreed. I was very happy because I knew that they would give it a beautiful production, far more lavish than would be possible on the stage. It was set in a picturesque period and I was aware that a great deal depended on the way it was presented. Much preliminary work was necessary, in which I was involved even more than usual, because "Voltaire" was regarded in the studio as *my* play and I had a certain amount of useful knowledge of the period which I had stored up when I worked on the original manuscript.

I always feel relieved when the camera begins to grind on the first shot of any one of my pictures, because then the hardest part of my work is over. It is all the preliminaries, the preparation, that I find irksome and laborious — all the details that cannot be arranged in an orderly way. Of course, I have nothing to do with the building of the scenes, but the designs are brought to me that we may be sure all doors and windows and fireplaces are just where they should be for the business of the scene. Apart from these details, and a general idea of the suitability of the scene submitted, I have no responsibility as to the scenery, and no fear. The heads and the staff of the construction department are amazingly efficient; in an industry which in many ways leaves much to be desired in general management, the scene designers and builders, the property department, and the working staff generally, are surprisingly reliable.

Historical pictures, as a rule, require a great deal of research work. In "Voltaire" we had a scene on the terrace of the Petit Trianon which was so faithfully reproduced — in measurement, in sculptural and architectural decoration, in every particular — that when I visited the actual spot the next summer, I could hardly believe that I was not standing on the stage at Hollywood — in fact,

I almost spoke my lines. I wish that audiences could realize more fully the credit that is due to the designers and the builders of scenes in the studio.

It is while conducting the more personal preliminary details that a star most needs his patience and endurance. I have spoken of the choosing of the cast and of the rehearsals; but there is also the selection of furniture, — which is important, — the "tests" and the trying-on of costumes, the "studio" photographs, and many other preliminaries, nearly all of which come during my rehearsal period when I wish to devote my time entirely to the play.

I have said the choosing of the furniture is important; this could be left with perfect safety to the head of that department, if the star didn't have to sit in any of it. A settee, for instance, is generally placed upon the set so that the star may use it when he wishes to be particularly nice to a lady. But if it is too high or too low, or if the seat dips down at the back so that the star feels he is gradually shutting up and disappearing from sight, or if during the scene, when he wishes to appear most charming, he is trying to save himself from either falling off, or falling into the lady's lap, he is not likely to be seen at his best.

Then there is the armchair. If you play young and dashing parts this is an item which need give you no concern. But if you are to be a statesman or a business magnate, or even a mere father, you will find that the armchair enters largely into your life. If you are a king, you need not have the same anxiety about your throne, because no king can look really comfortable on a throne. Just as there is no disguising the uneasiness of the head that wears a crown, so it is difficult to conceal, in another direction, the physical discomfort of a throne. But a statesman has to be subtle, and to be subtle you must be at your ease; if your armchair has been chosen without duly consulting the dimensions of the desk which is, as it were, to be its partner, the results can be very disconcerting to a star. (It will be noticed that my anxiety appears to be only for the star. This must not be regarded as just selfishness on my part. I am merely taking on the atmosphere of the studio, where everything revolves around the star.)

Any such difficulties as these must be discovered before the day of shooting, because when once the camera and the microphone make their appearance, that means that the entire staff is at work, and that the overhead is enormous. If the expense works out at five thousand dollars an hour, and it takes twenty minutes to get a different chair from the property department, it will be seen how disastrous it may be to leave anything to chance. In the English studios, some of which are sadly restricted for space, it may take an hour to get a chair from some distant furniture store.

Then there is the unhappy day that has to be devoted to "tests" — that is, the photographing of make-up and costumes. All the characters have to go through this examination and registration, a procedure which depresses me in about the same degree as if I were at the police station for the purpose of recording my fingerprints. But if an actor is to play Voltaire, it is obvious that his make-up must be tested in advance in order to see whether he looks anything like the character.

The make-up man loves his work and is never more

happy than when he is producing a definite character. He approaches his subject joyfully, as a master. He has no thought of time; he knows that in this preliminary test nobody dares to hurry him; and so the actor remains as quiescent as if he had been given an anæsthetic. I am rather troublesome because I have made myself up for so many years that I cannot refrain from making occasional suggestions. And the make-up man is further handicapped because I will not allow him to "build up" my face — that is, I don't have anything plastered on which makes that part of my face static.

If I had my chin built up and a piece put on my nose, I could probably be made to look exactly like Voltaire. But I am strongly of opinion that no actor who is playing a long and important part should have his features monkeyed with. Make-up specialists now admit that the thinner the layer of grease paint, the better for the actor; every feature, every part of the face should have freedom of movement. Every pore of the skin is a window of the soul — that not only sounds like an overstatement, but it is. It expresses, however, exactly what I mean. The slightest twitch of the nose or mouth may, at a given moment, express something which cannot be as well conveyed in any other way.

As the make-up man works on and on, I watch with admiration his efforts to make me look like Voltaire, and I realize with great concern that the more he tries to change me, the more like George Arliss I look. That is how it seems to me; but after two or three hours' work, the make-up man is happy and I go to Stage 6 to be photographed.

Nothing is more depressing than a stage that is prepared for the taking of tests. Just a corner is lighted — enough for the purpose. Substitute furniture is placed before the camera; nobody is keyed-up; there is a feeling that the whole thing is a great nuisance, but it has to be done. It is likely that the cameraman who is to be *your* cameraman when the picture is made is working on another picture and has had to be borrowed for an hour or so. This helps to accentuate the feeling that you don't belong there and that everyone will be glad when you've gone. The supporting actors have little to do beyond being photographed back and front for the inspection of wigs and costumes. I, on the other hand, have to go through elaborate contortions — to make an entrance, to walk about, to sit down, to read and write, to suggest the character in as many ways as possible in order to give the cameraman ideas for his light effects.

I make my appearance in this cold, depressing atmosphere, and the camera starts grinding. I am really very anxious; I not only want to see how I look and how my clothes look, but I want to take this opportunity of giving myself some idea of what I am going to be like in the part. And I know the camera is grinding and is taking down everything in evidence against me; so I try — oh, how hard I try! And the more I try to feel like Voltaire, the more I feel like Disraeli or Hamilton, or any other character I happen to have played; or else I feel only like myself doing ridiculous antics. Well, it seldom comes out quite as bad as it feels, but it is always unsatisfactory and has to be all done again another day.

And there are other nerve-destroying preliminaries; the trying-on of costumes is perhaps the most wearisome. We always had to be fitted when I was acting in the theatre, but there we had more time. In the movies, everything is crowded together; it has to be. The factory has its schedule of pictures to be made during the season. Each one in its turn has to be got out of the way to make room for the next.

The costume people in the studios always arrive when I have had a long and tiring day; I think I have finished, when lo! they appear like ghostly messengers bringing me my shroud — shrouds — armfuls of them. They are gentle with me; tailors are very gentle people; they say they did not wish to disturb my rehearsal, so they waited outside the door for hours, until I should come out to my dressing room. If I ask them why they did not give me notice that they were coming, they smile gently and ask me which I will try on first. So I go into my dressing room and the tailors follow me.

And presently Ben enters. I don't think I've mentioned Ben — Ben Silvey I mean. I ought to have done so because through all this nightmare of preparation his figure can be seen moving slowly and inevitably like the mills of God. Ben is a large man. When I was very young and used to be taken to the Zoo in Regent's Park, there was a very large elephant that the children used to love. It was called "Jumbo." Well, Ben Silvey always reminds me of Jumbo. He lopes a little and treads softly; as he comes towards you, you know he is not going to hurt you, but you are aware that he is approaching you with intention, and you know that you can't escape him. He has under his arm a manuscript of considerable bulk encased in a strong and solid cover. This is always under his arm; no living creature within the walls of the studio has ever seen him without it. And there is a good reason.

The sheets of writing within that cover are the result of days and weeks of Ben's labor. They tell just how long it will take to make the picture from beginning to end; what scenes are to be shot on each day and the names of the actors required in each specific scene. This prophetic document is called a "breakdown," and can be drawn up only by someone of judgment and experience.

I think I have mentioned that it is impossible for all the scenes that have to be used in the making of a picture to be kept standing and that scenes cannot therefore be shot in their proper sequence. So the man who draws out the breakdown has to be able to gauge the length of time each scene will take to shoot; it is important that this should be definite in order that the date he gives for each succeeding scene may find the scenery ready and the actors prepared. But Ben does much more than this. As the preparations for the picture develop, the portfolio he carries becomes more and more bulky. He makes notes of everything. Captain Cuttle would have gazed at him with admiration. I have never seen Ben eating or drinking or smoking or sitting down. I do not think that the ability to do any one of these things is denied to him by Nature: I believe it is merely that during the making of a picture he regards them as relatively unimportant.

When the tailors have taken possession of me Ben enters softly, and unobtrusively joins the group. By a clever movement of the body he contrives that the portfolio falls open and, while still holding it in his arm, he makes copious notes. If I am to wear a modern costume, and I see him looking with the eye of an artist at the region of my neck, I may in an evil moment say,

"I'm not going to wear this tie, Ben." Ben is surprised, disappointed, hurt, and loses faith in human nature. He says in a low voice, as one who is possessed of a guilty secret: —

"You're not going to wear that tie!"

"No, Ben, I'm just fitting on these clothes; I haven't changed my shirt or anything like that."

He says, "What tie are you going to wear?"

"Oh, I don't know, Ben, exactly; just — something sort of suitable — "

"Dark?"

"Oh, I should think so — something of that kind."

"A stri-ped tie?" I have never known why Ben always says "stri-ped," instead of "striped," like other people. I imagine his mother used to say it. I am very tired and I do not answer. But you can't do that sort of thing with Ben — useless to try. "A stri-ped tie?" he repeats.

"Yes," I say unconvincingly.

Ben says: "Or spots?"

I say: "Yes, something of that sort."

Ben says, "Stri-ped or spots?"

"I really don't know, Ben. I've got a lot of ties."

Ben now makes a long marginal note. Then he fixes me with an appraising eye, and suddenly, with surprising agility, becomes a performing elephant — he goes down on his haunches and supports himself by elevating his heels just as the elephants do at the circus. This reduces him to about two-thirds of his normal height and enables him to examine, in great detail, my trousers. This garment seems to take a place of honor in Ben's portfolio, for it is the subject of an exhaustive note. I like Ben very much, but now I wish he would go away; he's so

213

exacting; and just now when I am being pinned up by the tailors I don't want to be pinned down by Ben. Having finished with my trousers, he resumes his human form and, in the process, conjures the portfolio back under his arm; I think he is leaving; but he says, "What hat are you going to wear?"

"Well, Ben, I think I'll wear a bowler."

"A bowler? Is that a topper?"

"No — no. You know, a darby."

"A darby."

"I mean a derby."

"Oh, a derby. You're a Prime Minister in the picture. Would a Prime Minister wear a derby?"

"Oh, I think so, Ben. Mr. Chamberlain wears one."

"Oh, yes. Are you going to carry an umbrella?"

Ben has his little bit of fun when business is disposed of, and generally makes his exit chuckling. You will no doubt realize the reason for Ben's meticulous care of every little detail. If, for instance, I were seen in the picture to be wearing a spotted tie, and, as I walked into the next room, the tie suddenly became a stri-ped one, the audience might not notice it, but the whole of Hollywood would be in convulsions, and Ben would never hold up his head again, although the responsibility of a slip of this kind really belongs to the script girl.

Attached to every picture there is a script girl, who never leaves the set during the shooting of a scene. It is her duty to note every item of dress that is worn on the set. If for instance a woman's sash or bow or ornament of any kind is slightly out of place, and by an oversight has been photographed like that at the beginning of the scene, the script girl must see that it is so displaced throughout the entire scene — which may last three days. When I go out, holding my gloves in my right hand, it is for her to watch that when I am taken later — perhaps the next day, appearing on the other side of the door, I am not holding my gloves in my left hand. And my hat must be at exactly the same angle as when I put it on. The position of the arm, the movement of a finger during a speech, are all noted in the script girl's script. We are apt to think that young girls should not be trusted to fill positions of great responsibility, but in all my experience I cannot recall an instance of any one of these girls being caught napping. But Ben cannot trust anyone but himself; the picture is his religion; his portfolio is his Bible, in which he must be able to point to chapter and verse for everything.

CAST

The Working Man

John Reeves . . .	GEORGE ARLISS
Jenny Hartland . .	BETTE DAVIS
Benjamin "Napoleon" .	HARDIE ALBRIGHT
Tommy Hartland . .	THEODORE NEWTON
Hank Davis . . .	J. FARRELL MacDONALD
Freddie Pettison . .	GORDON WESTCOTT
Haslett	CHARLES EVANS
Butler	EDWARD COOPER
Mrs. Price . . .	RUTHELMA STEVENS

∾

Director . . .	JOHN ADOLPHI
Author	EDGAR FRANKLIN
Adaptation . . .	CHARLES KENYON AND MAUDE T. HOWELL
Camera	SAM POLITO

CAST

Voltaire

Voltaire	GEORGE ARLISS
Pompadour . . .	DORIS KENYON
Nannette Calas . .	MARGARET LINDSAY
François . . .	THEODORE NEWTON
Louis XV . . .	REGINALD OWEN
De Sarnac . . .	ALAN MOWBRAY
Captain in Play . .	GORDON WESTCOTT
Dr. Tronchin . . .	DAVID TORRENCE
Emile, Valet to Voltaire	MURRAY KINNELL
Mistress in Play . .	DORIS LLOYD
Old Merchant in Play .	IVAN SIMPSON
King in Play . . .	DOUGLAS DUMBRILLE
Madame Denis . .	HELENA PHILLIPS

ᐁᐁ

Director . . .	JOHN ADOLPHI
Authors . . .	GEORGE GIBBS AND E. LAWRENCE DUDLEY
Adaptation . . .	PAUL GREEN AND MAUDE T. HOWELL
Camera	TONY GAUDIO

CAST

A Successful Calamity

Wilton	GEORGE ARLISS
Peggy Wilton . .	EVALYN KNAPP
Eddie Wilton . . .	WILLIAM JANNEY
Emmie Wilton . .	MARY ASTOR
Connors . . .	GRANT MITCHELL
Mr. Belden . . .	HALE HAMILTON
Butler	CHARLES COLEMAN
George Struthers .	HARDIE ALBRIGHT
Larry Rivers . . .	RANDOLPH SCOTT
Partington . . .	DAVID TORRENCE
Curtis, the Broker . .	MURRAY KINNELL
Barney	TOM BROWN
Lizzie, the Cook . .	HELENA PHILLIPS
Furniture Mover . .	CHARLES EVANS
Maid	NOLA LUXFORD

෧

Director . . .	JOHN ADOLPHI
Play	CLARE KUMMER
Adaptation . . .	JULIAN JOSEPHSON, AUSTIN PARKER AND MAUDE T. HOWELL
Camera	JAMES VAN TREES

CAST

The King's Vacation

Phillip	GEORGE ARLISS
Lord Chamberlain . .	DUDLEY DIGGES
John	DICK POWELL
Millicent	PATRICIA ELLIS
Thorpe	O. P. HEGGIE
Wilhelmina . . .	FLORENCE ARLISS
Helen	MARJORIE GATESON
Anderson . . .	JAMES BELL
Mrs. Seymour . . .	HELENA PHILLIPS
Amalia	MAUDE LESLIE
James	CHARLES EVANS
Men-in-Waiting . .	ALAN BIRMINGHAM
	HAROLD MINJER
	DESMOND ROBERTS
Barstowe	VERNON STEELE

༄

Director	JOHN ADOLPHI
Author	ERNEST PASCAL
Adaptation . . .	ERNEST PASCAL AND
	MAUDE T. HOWELL
Camera	JAMES VAN TREES

Chapter 13

WHILE we were making "Voltaire" there were things going on in the outside world that forced themselves on our attention. Banks began to break in Hollywood and several of my friends lost all their savings. These bank failures spread so alarmingly that for a time the Government closed all banks throughout the United States. This drastic action affected the picture industry in more ways than one.

A great deal of money has to be credited to Hollywood banks from local banks in cities all over the United States where the great producing companies own large picture houses. It is obviously necessary to have large sums of ready money in Hollywood in order to meet the heavy expenses of production. This long-established method of transferring capital becomes impossible with the banks closed. The only way to get the money was to ship the actual cash. This of course was a temporary condition, but actual losses were being sustained through the stagnation of business all over the country. The producers appealed to the actors to shoulder a share of the burden, and as usual, the actors responded with a good deal of generosity.

It seemed rather a hard fate that at this particular

moment there should be an earthquake. It was my first definite earthquake. I had experienced an occasional jump, but nothing alarming. This evening I had just arrived home from the studio — about six o'clock. I was sitting with Flo in her room when without warning, the floor seemed to come up, the carpet waved, and the walls appeared to be going wild. It was very like a rough day on the ocean, without the rhythm of the sea; it was so like it that it made me feel very seasick. It did not require any special intuition on my part to realize that this was an earthquake. Quick as a flash it came to me that years ago my brother Fred, who had spent many years in India, told me just what to do if ever I was in an earthquake. But I couldn't remember what it was. I said to Flo that I thought the thing to do was to go down on our hands and knees and crawl out. And I went down on my hands and knees and commenced to crawl. Flo is active in a crisis. She gave a quick look at me, and didn't laugh — not then; but she has since given, to a picked circle of her friends, imitations of me escaping from an earthquake: a most undignified performance to which I will make no further reference. But this was a tense moment and all she said was "Come on, let's get outside" and made for the door and the staircase and the garden. As soon as we got outside I remembered what Fred had told me to do. It was to stand in the nearest doorway, this being the safest place to protect you from falling bricks or timbers. It would have been a manly thing to do, with Flo held protectingly in my arms, if I had thought of it in time.

As an offset to the earthquake, I have much pleasure in recording that while we were having these unfortunate experiences, the sale of beer was legalized. I am not particularly dependent on beer, but I had been in America long enough to realize the evils brought about by prohibition and everyone knew that the legalizing of beer was just a forerunner of the repeal of that unfortunate act.

Just as we were finishing "Voltaire" we had what I may call a domestic upheaval in the film colony, and that was the break between Darryl Zanuck and Warner Brothers. As I remember it Zanuck withdrew from the Warners on Saturday, and I am told that by Monday he had received an offer from every producing firm in Hollywood. He decided, however, that he would in future have a free hand, so he accepted Joe Schenck's suggestion to form a new company and together they established Twentieth Century Pictures, which has since absorbed the Fox Corporation and is now one of the most important and prosperous companies in the business.

Although I had been very happy with Warner Brothers, I made my next contract with Zanuck; this was an obvious step for me to take since my association had been entirely with him ever since I started in talking pictures. I think mine was the first contract to be signed by the Twentieth Century Company.

It was decided that "The House of Rothschild" should be my next picture and that the story should be founded on the play that I have already referred to. Although it was obvious that the story of the Rothschilds is not private property, the author of this play had conceived and carried out a definite line of construction, and whether or not we adhered to that, it was a great advantage to have a ready-made plot that should keep the picture writers within bounds.

During my years in the theatre, — I mean my pre-picture days, — when I accepted a ready-made play about an historical character, I took it because the story, as the author had written it, was dramatic and interesting, and because I believed it would stand on its merits as a play even if the audience had never before heard of the character. I then made it my business to read everything I could find about the central figure with the object of enriching the character without interfering with the drama. I have found that the most frequent fault in many otherwise well-written historical plays is that the author, having a mass of knowledge about his hero, is anxious to put it all into the play; the consequence is that without being a frankly episodic play there are so many side issues that an audience has no sustained interest in any one of them.

Having so far decided then on "Rothschild" for my next picture, I was anxious to get home. I had made certain definite engagements in England, and it happened that the only boat that would get us home in time was the *Bremen*. So we booked our passage and sailed. This was in 1933, before Germany's treatment of the Jews had become a world scandal. I was therefore genuinely surprised to get within the next few weeks letters from my Jewish fans in all parts of the world expressing their disappointment and surprise that Flo and I should patronize a German boat. I confess I felt rather guilty about this because the Jews have always been good and faithful adherents of mine both in the theatre and in the cinema. No one has a keener appreciation of what the world of science and art and literature owes to the Jews than I, and no one has greater sympathy with them in their unequal fight against savagery and ignorance.

As soon as possible after our arrival in England I made for St. Margaret's where I knew I could work on Rothschild without interruption. An historical character has certain advantages over a character of fiction inasmuch as the actor never reaches the end of its possibilities. Side lights are continually being thrown from unexpected quarters. I could hardly have expected to learn anything new about Rothschild at St. Margaret's Bay. But I did; I struck an unexpected mine of information. Flo and I paid a little visit to Flora Lion at Sandwich; there we met Lord and Lady Jessel, who happened to ask if they might call and see our cottage. When they came I think they were a party of five. I had been working on the script of Rothschild in my little study — I say "little" study because it is little. It is about eight feet square. I can sit at my desk and reach anything in any part of the room without getting up. So if one looks in at the door of this sanctum one can read, with ordinary eyesight, anything that is open on the desk. It was therefore next to impossible for my guests not to observe a number of books concerning Rothschild. As nothing had appeared in the press about the possibility of my doing a Rothschild picture, my friends expressed surprise; and the reason why they were surprised was that every one of them was by birth a connection of the Rothschild family. The result was that I obtained a certain amount of information that I could not otherwise have got. I have had similar strokes of luck in connection with other historical plays, but never anything quite so surprising and unexpected.

We began the filming of Rothschild in December 1933 and finished it by the end of January. It was one of those very pleasant experiences in which everything goes smoothly. Flo played my wife and was particularly convincing in the lines in which she told me to take my hands out of my pockets — a command which she gives me several times a day in real life. Darryl Zanuck gave me a magnificent cast — in fact I don't remember any of my pictures that can boast of so many well-known names. Most of the actors I knew well; I had either met them on the screen or played with them on the stage. The only one I had never met or seen in private life was the terrible Boris Karloff — the professional bogey-man. I was therefore considerably surprised to find him one of the most retiring and gentle gentlemen it has ever been my lot to meet — which only goes to confirm my previous remarks about stage villains.

When Rothschild was finished there came the usual hectic search for a subject for my next picture. I cannot say how many plays and stories are submitted to me at these times, but an unbelievable number. Sometimes there comes something outstanding that relieves us from any indecision. But more often the selection is a matter of much discussion.

Finally Maude Howell discovered a play by Katherine Clugston called "The Head of the Family" (afterwards christened "The Last Gentleman"). I was very uncertain about this story because there was a moving picture scene in the last act, which although probably effective on the stage was likely to be confusing on the screen — a picture within a picture. Darryl Zanuck, however, saw no danger in this, and he was proved to be right. The screen version was made by Leonard Traskins and Maude Howell who succeeded in delivering a script that was at once satisfactory to me — this I believe is regarded by all other writers who have worked for me as a miraculous feat.

It was my good fortune to have associated with me in this picture Janet Beecher, whom I had long admired in the theatre; Miss Edna May Oliver, who can make me laugh longer and more spontaneously than any other actress on the stage; and that matchless comedian Joseph Cawthorn. Cawthorn played only a small part, but his great ability made the scene one of the high lights of the picture. When I recall Cawthorn as a star in musical comedy only a few years ago I cannot help holding a grudge against the movies for luring him away from stardom and from the theatre. He and other fine artistes who were the backbone of the American stage are now more or less lost in the long list of supporting actors on the screen.

What is the reason for this? It isn't that they are old or infirm or that they have "had their day" in the theatre. Joe Cawthorn is capable of doing all the things he used to do on the stage and of doing them just as well. The fact is that actors get tired of wandering over the earth; of having no settled home; or of having a settled home and not being able to settle in it. A popular star in America may play for a year in New York, and then inevitably he has to travel with his successful play for at least two years through the great United States — living comfortably enough, but always moving on.

On the other hand, a talking picture can be made in six or eight weeks; for the actor that is the end — it is done with; he has no further responsibility. And because a successful picture can return fabulous sums, the producers can afford to pay large salaries for small parts. The directors of these big concerns are wise enough to know that a fine actor in an important "bit" is worth every cent they pay him. The star of the theatre who has for years been enduring an unrestful life may reflect that although he makes great successes in the theatre, he also makes costly failures. He decides to side-step into the movies and finds that in the end he is likely to make almost as much money playing small parts on the screen as he can make by remaining in the glamour of stardom on the stage. He can make his pictures in Hollywood where the climate is beautiful and he is able to have a settled and extremely comfortable home. That is the reason why so many fine actors are "lost to the stage." Now, don't say, "But has he no love for his Art?" Of course he has. He was loving his art for years; from the time he got up in the morning and dashed off to rehearse, till after eleven o'clock at night. It's all very well for you. You can telephone to the office and say you've caught a chill and tell your secretary to telephone if there is anything important. And then about dinnertime you can conclude that you were mistaken about the chill and you can decide to go to a "show." You can say, "Let's go and see Cawthorn — he's always worth seeing." Yes; well, *he* can't afford to have a chill; *he* can't telephone to the audience and say, "I shan't be

227

down till ten tonight." He loves his art. And if he loves his art very much, he's also got to love bazaars, and love returning thanks for the guests at testimonial dinners. Supporting actors are as a rule long-lived; but has an actor-manager ever lived to three-score years and ten? I can't think of one who has, unless he gave up his responsibilities in time. He's worn out; the life is too exacting.

For a businessman — something in the City — I should highly recommend dying in harness. But an actor should give up before his audience is beginning to say "I remember him in his prime" or "Isn't he wonderful for his age?" Madge Kendal knew this. I don't think anyone thought of her as getting old, on the stage. She knew when to stop. And if ever a woman loved her art, she did.

In these remarks about retiring I am speaking of course of the stars, who in their long years as popular favorites should have saved enough to keep them in their old age. The small-part, the supporting actor, generally has to go on till he drops, or is dropped. And I think that is good for him. I have a theory (which is probably quite unsound scientifically) that the reason this class of actor lives long and has good health is because for a certain period during every day of his acting life, he has to forget himself and become somebody else. It is well-known in my business that an actor can go to the theatre with a headache or a backache, or a chill or some such discomfort, and forget all about it as soon as he walks on the stage. This, of course, is equally true of the star, but the average small-part actor has no exhausting social responsibilities outside the theatre. His is an easy

228

and pleasant life when once he gets a job. No, I can't blame Joe Cawthorn for hiding in the movies; I think I blame the producers for allowing him to hide.

It was about the time that I was making "The Last Gentleman" that the English movie concerns were arriving at the conclusion that the only way for them to compete with Hollywood was to spend a lot of money. That, at any rate, was the impression I received; and there is no doubt they were thinking in the right direction. If, in reality, they decided that they ought to be in a position to spend a lot of money if necessary, then I think they were entirely right. I have given my opinion on production value — the futility of spending a fortune on a scene that is dragged in by the hair — but there is a time when the great palace is a necessary effect, and that is the time when money should be available. Picture audiences know so much about pictures that they are not easily fooled. That is why I never allow the illustrated weeklies to take photographs of the inside of my house — a diversion in which they sometimes show a desire to indulge. They would surely photograph "a corner of Mr. Arliss's study" the setting for which would have to be prepared by massing together all the books I possess, a bust of Shakespeare, a signed photograph of one of the Royal Family, and a picture of Flo at the age of eighteen to suggest domestic felicity.

But the public of today gets on to this. They don't believe it unless they see the other corners. So many of the English pictures, through lack of capital, have had to resort to this subterfuge of the single corner, to the detriment of the production. When the interior of a palace is necessary to the story, you cannot create the illusion of space and grandeur by cutting from one corner to another. The decision of the English companies, then, to create a large reserve of capital, was a wise one. Whether or not the money is wisely spent must depend upon the judgment of the producers.

If one believes that our English companies are sometimes open to criticism in the way capital has been used, it must be remembered that the making of pictures in England on a large scale is a comparatively new industry. In Hollywood it is an old-established business, run by men who have grown up in the work; its wild oats have been sown — lavishly; in my opinion, there is little waste in the American studio today.

The problem of making commercially successful pictures in England is a very difficult one. It is obviously dangerous to enter into competition with America. From New York to San Francisco is three thousand miles with a cinema in every street. This gives a tremendous domestic market for the Hollywood producers. Even without the English and foreign markets open to them this would obviously allow them to spend a great deal more money on the production of any one film than an English firm could spend, unless the American market were freely open to them. America can afford to spend a million dollars on a picture and still make a handsome profit. England cannot spend half that sum without courting disaster.

I believe we should take advantage of all the amazing technical knowledge which has developed in America during long years of training and research, but that we should disregard production value, and make no effort, for the present, to make pretentious pictures. What the audience is hoping for is a good story and good acting. I have had a great deal of experience of American audiences, and it is my opinion that if England could forget all about the American market and make films with only British audiences in mind, we should be more likely to produce something that would appeal to America than if we tried to follow the lead of Hollywood. From my experience, I should say that there are no audiences in the world who can adapt themselves to a foreign atmosphere as easily as the Americans. When I say "foreign" I refer to countries other than their own. In particular they are quick to adjust their minds to an English environment and to appreciate the best English plays. The greatest successes made by British playwrights in America have been with plays that were written with no thought of American audiences. My opinion is that the future success of English studios lies in making films, within reasonable limits of expense, for the English market — films that depend mainly on the story and the acting. I believe in time we could excel in such films, just as Hollywood excels in the spectacular productions. By this means the American market would be automatically opened to us. The companies of the United States that control the cinemas have shown that they are not slow in making a bid for any British films out of which they believe they can make money.

By the time I had finished "The Last Gentleman" the Gaumont-British Company was becoming very active. They seemed to have arrived at a determination to break into the American market. They apparently came to the conclusion that if they could produce pictures with a star who was well-known to the American public, they could more easily make a deal with American distributors. I had always wished to make a picture in England, but I was not encouraged by the quality of work turned out by the British producers. A good deal of influence had been brought to bear upon me from time to time, including that very powerful argument patriotism. But although I love my country, I could not bring myself to jeopardize such reputation as I had made by taking a somewhat obvious risk. So I held off. But now, when Gaumont-British were showing some anxiety to make a contract with me, I felt the time had come when I might safely accept their offer. They had been turning out some very good pictures recently and there seemed to be no reason, with the large capital that they now had at their command, why they should not improve by leaps and bounds. But I was very loath to break with Zanuck. Joe Schenck was against my going; not that he would say a word against the English companies, but he contended that Darryl Zanuck and I made an ideal combination for my pictures, and, arguing from his own experience, he maintained that a perfect business relationship such as this can seldom be duplicated.

Richard Beamish was no longer making himself responsible for my career; not that he had lost interest in me, but he had become quite a figure in the political world, and had less and less time to devote to the unrealities of life such as the movies; and knowing Richard as I did, I was bound to face the fact that within a few years he would probably be President of the United States and would be likely to insist on my becoming a senator, in which capacity I could scarcely do him justice. So I placed myself in the hands of Rufus Le-Maire.

LeMaire is the type of active American businessman who lives up to the slogan "Do it now." He is the man you read about in books who gets an idea at twelve, boards a plane at one, catches the boat as the gangplank is being hauled into the air, and arrives in time to do some noble deed. The average Englishman becomes exhausted by merely watching Rufus. While I was still in a state of uncertainty in Hollywood, turning over in my mind what Joe Schenck had said about the danger of breaking a successful business alliance, LeMaire had flown from Hollywood, arrived in London, settled terms, and pledged me to make my next picture with Gaumont-British. So, towards the end of April, Flo and I took a fond farewell of Hollywood.

CAST

The House of Rothschild

Mayer Rothschild Nathan Rothschild	.	.	.	GEORGE ARLISS
Ledrantz	.	.	.	BORIS KARLOFF
Julie Rothschild	.	.	.	LORETTA YOUNG
Captain Fitzroy	.	.	.	ROBERT YOUNG
Duke of Wellington	.	.	.	C. AUBREY SMITH
Baring	.	.	.	ARTHUR BYRON
Gudula Rothschild	.	.	.	HELEN WESTLEY
Herries	.	.	.	REGINALD OWEN
Nathan's Wife	.	.	.	FLORENCE ARLISS
Metternich	.	.	.	ALAN MOWBRAY
Rowerth	.	.	.	HOLMES HERBERT
Solomon	.	.	.	PAUL HARVEY
Amschel	.	.	.	IVAN SIMPSON
Carl	.	.	.	NOEL MADISON
James	.	.	.	MURRAY KINNELL
Talleyrand	.	.	.	GEORGES RENAVENT
Prince Regent	.	.	.	LUMSDEN HARE
Amschel's Secretary	.	.	.	LEO McCABE
Prime Minister	.	.	.	GILBERT EMERY
Nesselrode	.	.	.	CHARLES EVANS
Doctor	.	.	. .	LEE KOHLMAR

Stock Traders	. . .	{	REGINALD SHEFFIELD BRANDON HURST HAROLD MINJER HORACE CLAUDE COOPER CRAUFORD KENT
Rothschild Children	. .	{	GERALD PIERCE MILTON KAHN GEORGE OFFERMAN, JR. CULLEN JOHNSON BOBBIE LA MANCHE
Tax Collector	. . .		LEONARD MUDIE

∾

Director	.	.	.	ALFRED WERKER
Associate Producers	.	.	.	WILLIAM GOETZ AND RAYMOND GRIFFITH
Screen Play	.	.	.	NUNNALLY JOHNSON
Based on a play by	.	.	.	GEORGE H. WESTLEY
Associate Director	.	.	.	MAUDE T. HOWELL
Camera	.	.	.	PEVERELL MARLEY
Assistant Director	.	.	.	BEN SILVEY

CAST

The Last Gentleman

Cabot Barr	.	.	GEORGE ARLISS
Dr. Weston	.	.	JOSEPH CAWTHORN
Augusta Prichard	.		EDNA MAY OLIVER
Marjorie Barr	.	.	CHARLOTTE HENRY
Allan Prichard	.		FRANK ALBERTSON
Mrs. Helen Barr	.	.	JANET BEECHER
Judd Barr	.	.	DONALD MEEK
Henry Loring	.		RALPH MORGAN
Claude	.	.	EDWARD ELLIS
Retta Barr	.	.	RAFAELO OTTIANO
Professor Schumaker	.		HARRY BRODLEY
Matilda	.	.	HELENA PHILLIPS

ↄϟ

Director	.	.	SIDNEY LANFIELD
Author	.	.	KATHARINE CLUGSTON
Screen play	.	.	LEONARD TRASKINS AND MAUDE T. HOWELL
Camera	.	.	BARNEY McGILL

Chapter 14

WHEN I arrived in England I found myself being carried off to the Carlton Hotel, where I was placed in a large private room, in which were stored about twenty gentlemen of the press, each of whom expected me to say something snappy, which, of course, I was quite incapable of doing. But it was evident from this large and friendly gathering, to say nothing of the high quality of the refreshments, that Gaumont-British were not going to do things by halves.

After working in the Hollywood studios, set in an expanse of mountains and blue skies, it seemed most strange to me to arrive at a studio in the heart of London surrounded by little shops, and tenements, and small lodging-houses. All the more strange because although I am a Londoner and know my London fairly well, I never had any idea that there was a studio at Shepherd's Bush. For the benefit of those who do not know Shepherd's Bush, let me explain that the name is misleading. There is no bush to be found, and no evidence of a shepherd ever having made even a fleeting excursion there with his flock — except perhaps for an occasional crook picked up by the police.

It was rather a shock to find that my dressing-room accommodation consisted of two little rooms — a violent contrast to my large reception room, large dressing room with cupboards running from one end to the other, dining room, bathroom, fully equipped kitchen; that may seem like overdoing it, but some of the stars work so many hours at the Twentieth Century that they really need a home from home.

I have frequently been asked to give my impressions of the difference between working in the studios of Hollywood and those of London. I have no doubt that if one worked in the newly built, up-to-date studios in the suburbs of London that there would be practically no difference at all. My experience, however, was confined to Shepherd's Bush and even there when one actually got down to work in the studio, it was very much the same as Hollywood. All the same mechanical contrivances were there; but there were less space and less facilities for intensive lighting.

The main trouble with Gaumont-British as far as I could judge was that they had grown too rapidly from a small concern to a big one. They kept growing bigger and bigger and had no time to move. When they needed another studio, they built it on top of the last one and when they wanted more office room, they took the house next door. If they could have foreseen their possibilities I suppose they would have moved out of town long ago. But apart from small dressing rooms and a few minor restrictions, I found little difference in the actual working conditions.

The chief contrast is in the way the work is approached. Nobody hurries, nobody hustles. The fan magazines in Hollywood, when they want to say something funny about me, always fall back on my cup of tea at half-past three: "Everything must be suspended while Mr. Arliss has his cup of tea." That is a great joke in Hollywood because it is the only cup of tea on the set. At the Gaumont-British, at all times of the day, you had to be careful of your elbows in turning, for fear of causing inconvenience to somebody drinking a cup of tea. In the lift, which was strangely small — designed originally I should think "to carry not more than sixteen cups of tea" — you were likely to be crowded out by tea-trays on their way to the various studios. But everything was very pleasant and restful. If I wanted a distinguished actress for a part that was unworthy of her, M. E. Balcon didn't interview her in a discouraging office of the company; he asked her and me and Victor Saville to lunch at an engaging hotel within easy distance of the studio — which was very clever of him because it made all the difference in the engagement. The dining room of this hotel was a sort of clubroom for the executives. And once there, nobody hurried; there was no such thing as a "quick lunch." I don't remember, as a consequence of this, anyone being late for an appointment at the studio, or late on the set for business, but nobody hurried; digestive organs were not impaired by an effort to appear busy.

M. E. Balcon was in the same relative position at Gaumont-British that Darryl Zanuck had been in at Warner Brothers. He was in charge of all productions. So it was his responsibility to submit within a given time some subject that should be acceptable to me. Angus MacPhail was head of the story department; he had a great store of knowledge of books and he left no tome unturned. All kinds of suggestions were made for my picture; and all kinds of stories which at first looked tempting had to be discarded after mature consideration.

"The Forsyte Saga" seemed like a wonderful idea, but after long discussion it was found to be too cumbersome to adapt faithfully. It might have been done, if we could have had a guarantee that every member of the audience was a disciple of Galsworthy.

I was very keen on Nelson — always have been. I thought I might make a good Nelson; it's so easy to get the sympathy of an audience if you have only one eye and one arm. Again I turned to Louis Parker. I felt sure he was the man to write it. He was eighty-two, but just as bright and alert as he was when he wrote "Disraeli" for me — and today at eighty-six or eighty-seven, he is as keen as ever. But Parker, who had written a hundred plays, knew too little about the movies to undertake the job seriously. I have had more Nelson plays sent to me than you "could shake a stick at," as my American friends say. But none of them has been good enough. The best one was written by Tony Pullin. Tony lives in the Temple and is a Doctor of Everything — law, medicine, science — and gives advice gratis to all his friends on each of these learned subjects. When in distress, mental or physical, we ring up Tony. He may be overworked and tired but he never fails to respond to a friend. After looking me over and writing out a prescription, he will go to Whitehall or Woolwich in answer to a call by the British Government and give advice on the testing of metal with X-rays. He will then take the chair at the Pepys Society, and after that he will go home and, if Kitty Pullin has gone to bed, he will finish writing the Life of Newton.

So, hearing I wanted a Nelson scenario, Tony sat down and wrote one; and although he is a friend, and as I have pointed out, I am always fearful when my friends write

239

plays, it turned out to be a better Nelson than any of the others. But Nelson is a very difficult subject. I don't think any Nelson play has ever been a real success. The fact is, no one would dare to write a play about him and not make him a hero. You can't keep him in Trafalgar Bay during an entire play or picture. Battles either on land or sea become tedious and confusing; when I see a long-drawn-out battle in a picture, I lose interest because I never know which side is winning. What an audience likes is domestic details, and that is just what you have to avoid in dealing with Nelson. So perhaps I shall never do Nelson. It got into the newspapers that I was undecided as to the subject of my next picture, with the usual result — an influx of plays and stories of all sorts with parts of all ages from seventeen to seventy, all intended for me. One lady had such faith in my versatility that she paid me the compliment of sending me a play in which I was to appear as Henry VIII in Act I, Duke of Norfolk in Act II, and Queen Elizabeth in Act III.

Several weeks were devoted to the preparation of a Pepys scenario. But after due consideration the idea of playing this character was abandoned. Finally, after a great deal of discussion, we decided on the Duke of Wellington. When Darryl Zanuck heard of this he was a good deal concerned on my account and strongly advised me not to do it. He pointed out to me that Aubrey Smith had made such a pronounced success as the Duke in "The House of Rothschild" that any Duke of Wellington who didn't look like Aubrey Smith would not be accepted in the movies. I explained to him that the old Duke was in reality exactly my height; that, compared with Aubrey Smith, he was actually a small man. Zanuck argued that that made no difference; that, apart from Aubrey Smith, the public only knew Wellington on horseback and if he wasn't big, he looked big. I knew this argument to be sound; I have already mentioned it as one of my own pet theories — the danger, while portraying historical characters, of running counter to the preconceived ideas of the general public. It can be done in books; in fact amongst historians it has been rather fashionable of recent years to attempt to reverse reputations; to drag down the virtuous and elevate the wicked. But it is dangerous to attempt it on the stage.

The reason I fell into the trap was that I knew too much about the man to start with. If my knowledge had been more superficial I should have seen him with the public eye. But when you dig deeply into the life and records of Wellington, you become rather fascinated with his character. It was soon after we announced that the picture was to be called "The Iron Duke" that I had an interesting letter from one of the Duke's descendants begging me not to call it "The Iron Duke." It was then, however, too late to change the title. I regard Mrs. Goodchild's letter as illuminating, so I have asked her permission to copy it: —

> The Alassio Lawn Tennis Club
> Alassio, Italy.
> *Thursday, June 21st, 1934.*

To George Arliss, Esqr.

Dear Sir,

I learn today from the papers that you have selected my great grand-uncle the Duke of Wellington as the subject for your first English film. I cannot tell you why, but for a long time past I have felt that you were going to do so. I am glad for I feel you are the only person I would care to trust with so precious a subject.

I have been engaged in writing his life for the past seven years, and so perhaps I may without undue boasting claim to a little knowledge on the subject.

I am so *very very* anxious that the right Arthur Wellesley should be presented to the world, and not the fictitious one, who is supposed to be hard and stern and to say "By God" or "damn" about every second phrase.

I can show you someone very different to this, I will show you the man who is England's great national inspiration and who has remained so in spite of all the iconoclasts have done to try to pull him from his place.

Please do not call the film "The Iron Duke" — he particularly disliked the appellation, and it strikes the wrong note. The name "the Iron Duke" came from an iron battleship built during his period and called after the duke. But the iron refers to the ship and not the duke. If you portray the real duke you will kill for ever the title "Iron," or at least iron in the sense of inferring hardness.

God send that you may use your great talents in the cause of truth — I know you can make a wonderful thing of this if you will use the material which I have offered to the Gaumont-British Company for just good will and nothing more.

Yours truly
Muriel A. Goodchild

In a further letter to me Mrs. Goodchild said: —

. . . Since the publication of my two books "The Man Wellington" (Constable, 1937) and "Wellington in Civil Life" I am better known in this connection as Muriel Wellesley (my maiden name) under which name I brought out my two books . . . for the critics have acknowledged me as an authority on Wellington and have declared my work to be of permanent historical value.

Unfortunately Mrs. Goodchild was suddenly called to Italy, and so I never had the opportunity of meeting her. I felt some satisfaction, however, that my estimate of the Duke's character was borne out by her more intimate knowledge.

Routine: Preparation for a picture in Shepherd's Bush same as in Hollywood. The casting — costumes — make-up — tests — all much the same . . . There were some moments for me more difficult than in Hollywood; notably, the casting. Old actors associated with my young days, men and women whom I had believed dead long ago, wrote to me or appeared at the studio — ghosts of the past! Sometimes one could be placed but more often they once more had to fade away.

The conferences on the first scenarios were held under conditions that were hardly in accordance with the usual routine. Flo and I had made some appointments in Paris, so H. M. Harwood, who had undertaken the writing of the scenario, would fly over every now and then and conferences would be held in my hotel. It was while we were in Paris that we got news of the death of Dinky Bits. We were at the Jan Hambourgs' listening to Jan's new interpretation of Bach (since published by the Oxford Press) when Edith Wilkins, telephoning from Chipping Norton, broke the news. Dinky had become a habit. Some trick of sound will often make us think we hear him now, calling out as he always did, when his sharp ears detected our coming into the house.

"The Iron Duke" was the first picture I had made without the spontaneous constructive suggestions of Darryl Zanuck and the sound criticism of Maude Howell. I missed them both. But I am deeply indebted to M. E. Balcon for his keen and helpful collaboration and to my old friend the late Campbell Gullan for bravely stepping into the place of Maude Howell. I think it took from three to four months to concoct and write and polish the scenario of Wellington. But at last it was done to everyone's satisfaction including that of Victor Saville, the director.

Directors are proverbially difficult to get on with. It would have made it so much easier for me now if Victor Saville and I had fought all through the picture. I might have recalled biting things that he had said and my clever repartee. But it happened we had no disagreement of any kind, which says a great deal for Victor Saville with his great responsibility and his long hours of intensive work. In spite of my years of experience, I have never been able to understand how it is that certain people in the picture business, directors and cameramen in particular, can go on working indefinitely — often all day and half the night. An actor may be allowed to go to bed without stopping the picture, because the director can switch to another scene; technicians have their unions to protect them. But a director must be at his post every minute, and I have never known a cameraman to delegate his work to an associate except in the case of illness. The actor may have long waits between his scenes, but the director and the cameraman are working always. I suppose you can't compare picture people with any other workers; the director of a picture, for instance, is not a bit like the director of a bank or of a gold mine. And the head cameraman is really an artist. I can only conclude that they are so interested in their work that they forget to get tired.

I found a great deal of pleasure in making pictures in London. Of course I missed the wide sweep of the Hollywood country, but it is surprising how much rural beauty you can find in London. Have you ever walked through Hyde Park between seven-thirty and eight-thirty in the morning? Well, I know you haven't. Nobody has, except a few people, and I know them all. Hyde Park is lovely at any time, both in the fashionable and the unfashionable sections. But never so lovely as in the early morning before other people are up. Then you have the park to yourself except for just a few kindred souls whose love of walking urges them to get up an hour earlier than is really necessary. I say I know them all, because I see them every morning, the same people in the same order of appearance. I don't know what they do for a living, but with one or two exceptions they are obviously all in business. They are mostly comparatively young. There is the young man with a small portfolio under his arm; he I am sure is in quite a good position somewhere. Next comes a young woman who I should say has a scholastic appointment; then there is the man with the dog. Then the elderly lame gentleman whom I should place as being in some Government appointment — except for the early hour — something very superior anyhow, because he sometimes wears a tall hat; after him a girl who is probably something in a

245

teashop; then a young man and a girl walking together, not as lovers, but as though they had some common business interest; then comes the mysterious young lady in a Gainsborough hat and a sort of riding-habit who walks rapidly, her head held high, one arm swinging, and who never looks at anybody; she might be alone in the desert or on the prairie.

I took the same walk every morning from 1934 to 1936 on my way to the studio at Shepherd's Bush — and during all that time the procession, day after day, was almost identical. When I first appeared these pioneers showed a little surprise at a stranger being in their midst, but when they found I was a regular attendant, they accepted me as one of the family and everyone had a smile and a "Good morning" for me in passing — except the mysterious young lady. In the course of my walk there were quite long stretches with no sign of human life; so I was surprised one morning to come upon a tramp sitting snugly under a tree, with a large red handkerchief spread out before him, which judging from its contents served as a dressing-case; the tree supported his back, his knees supported a fragment of looking-glass, and he was happily shaving. England, the land of the free! No doubt about it.

Every morning in the summer months, when I rounded the Serpentine, I was greeted with a few friendly hoots of recognition from long-sighted bathers on the opposite bank, who evidently believed themselves safe from observation, because at that time in the morning I can assure you the nudists had nothing on *them*. From the Serpentine I walked to the Achilles Statue at Hyde Park Corner, where I always saw a girl sitting on a seat

246

reading her morning paper and absent-mindedly throwing crumbs out of a paper bag apparently unconscious of the fact that she was a subject of consuming interest to some hundreds of anxious sparrows that crowded about her. Or sometimes I would turn off towards the Albert Memorial where the flowers are particularly beautiful, and my car would pick me up there. The park gardeners have a pleasant way of attaching a label to the flower so that the visitor may know what to call it if he meets it again. (I wish people would wear labels.) Now and then, if I had time to linger, I would make a note of these Latin names, particularly of some varieties that I knew we had in our London garden; I would study three or four of these, and write them down, with great secrecy, on a piece of paper, so that I should not forget them. You see Flo knows all about gardening and knows flowers by all their mysterious names (I can't conceive who are the godfathers and godmothers who gave them these names) and she is always severely patient with me when I describe a flower as "You know, one of those yellow things" and move my fingers about in a frantic attempt to be more descriptive.

You will begin to realize why I made those notes so furtively. Looking at our garden at home that evening I say carelessly, "I am glad to see that this salpiglossis is getting on so well." Without looking, I am conscious that Flo has received a slight shock. She doesn't compliment me, but I know that she is a trifle flattered that I have remembered the name that she has so often tried to drum into me. After what I consider is a safe length of time, I say, "I think we might have some more cineraria; they seem to do so well here." Flo becomes a trifle suspicious,

247

but she doesn't register suspicion — she may be wrong; perhaps I am beginning to take an intelligent interest in the garden. Eventually of course I get too confident and I overdo it. She finds me out — the piece of paper is discovered, and I am ignominiously exposed.

Perhaps the most trying days for me during the shooting of this picture were those when I looked most like Wellington — I mean when I was on horseback. Some men feel at home on a horse. I never had that kind of home. I was brought up in London, where horse-riding was the exercise of the rich. But, as an actor, I can generally be relied upon to do any business I am told to do. So if I have to ride a horse, the director gets a man who is at home on a horse, and he tells me exactly how I should behave. As Wellington I was in the saddle for three or four hours at a stretch, which I found much more tiring than being in anything else that I have ever tried. I had a very welcome compliment paid me, however, which I think with all due modesty I may repeat.

During my morning walk, of which I have just spoken, on my way from my home to the park I used always to pass a small but military-looking man of sixty or so, who sold newspapers outside a public-house. In the early morning he was allowed to stretch a cord across his pitch, and he made quite a good display, not only of the morning papers, but of the picture magazines. Always as I passed he would give me a military salute, but our acquaintance never got further than that until "The Iron Duke" was produced and pictures of me began to be published in the magazines. Then, as I passed, I would see myself proudly displayed in a star position on the line and the salute became so tremendous as to be quite embarrassing. At last when there appeared a particularly handsome picture of me as the Duke on horseback, my military friend could restrain himself no longer and with the picture in his hand and the admiration of an expert in his eye, he came three paces forward and said:

"Excuse me, sir, but there's one thing I will say, you know 'ow to ride a horse."

I accepted the compliment with all the dignity of a Field-Marshal.

"And there's another thing I'll say sir, if you'll excuse me, you know 'ow to sit a horse, I will say that, sir."

I smiled tolerantly, the smile of one who is so obviously a master that he is beyond flattery.

I said (with dignity of course): "You seem to know something about horses yourself."

"I ought to, sir. Years enough of it."

"Really?" (I unbent and showed interest.) "In the — er — "

"One of the old Forty-Niners." And he drew himself up with pride.

I expressed surprise, and again said "Really?" I was rather confused. It seemed to me I ought to know something about the old Forty-Niners. Was it something to do with the Charge of the Light Brigade, or was it perhaps something American? It flashed across me that I had heard something about the old Forty-Niners over there; but I don't think that was a battle. I believe it was a gold rush. At last I almost had to admit my ignorance. I said "The old Forty-Niners — let me see — that was the — "

"Yes, sir, the good old days. Many's the time I've

249

picked up Madame Modjeska and she's rode beside me — "

I had a confused picture of Modjeska on the battle-field.

"Yes, sir. The good old Forty-Nine 'bus. That was long before the time of all these 'ere motors. Used to run from Brixton to Liverpool Street. We was reckoned the fastest on the road, and my 'orses was always up to scratch. There's nothing nobody can tell me about a horse."

And the ice having been broken, there was nothing, after this, he didn't tell me about the Brixton 'buses.

I suppose no actor is a very good judge of his own pictures but it seems to me that Victor Saville made a good job of "The Iron Duke." It was not the easiest picture in the world to make in the studios at Shepherd's Bush. There were many difficulties which only a very expert director could have overcome. It was my first English picture and I had every reason to feel happy about my surroundings and my associates. I have heard so much about the tantrums of leading ladies — their temperament — that it pleases me to record that Gladys Cooper, whose very important position in London might easily have excused her for being a little troublesome with a strange star, was as pliable and open to suggestions as if she had been a rising student from the Royal Academy of Dramatic Art. I had hoped Flo would play the Duchess, but she decided against it; we were fortunate in getting Lady Hicks for the part (then Mrs. Seymour Hicks) — looking just as beautiful as when I first fell in love with her as Ellaline Terriss. We had great difficulty in finding a good Lady Frances; it was a difficult part, but at last we found Leslie Wareing who played it charmingly.

I was very happy to have in the cast two of my oldest friends. One was Gerald Lawrence, whom I had known ever since he had married my still earlier friend Fay Davis; and the other was Farren Soutar who dates back to the time when we used to produce our own plays in the cellar, and bribe other boys to come in and see us act. After that we graduated together to the Elephant & Castle, and later he acted in a blaze of glory, and a lovely tail coat and striped trousers, as my best man when Flo and I were married.

There is only one disadvantage in having a good "personal representative" — he regards you as a piece of machinery of his own invention that will deteriorate unless kept in constant motion. While I was busy winning the Battle of Waterloo, Rufus LeMaire was arranging with Darryl Zanuck that I should go back at once and play "Richelieu" for the Twentieth Century, and fearing that I might contemplate a prolonged holiday after that, Gaumont-British suggested a contract for two more pictures to follow "Richelieu," a contract which I eventually signed.

During the time I was working on "The Iron Duke" I was thinking seriously of making a picture in which I should impersonate Colonel House — who will be remembered as President Wilson's Ambassador-at-Large both before and during the Great War. Colonel House was a peculiarly interesting character. On first meeting him, you might take him to be a rather insignificant, retiring little man; one who could easily be talked over and brought round to your way of thinking. But when you came to know him you would discover that your estimate based on this gentle exterior was entirely wrong. He had an analytical mind, great determination, and indomitable perseverance. You came to realize that there was a good reason why Woodrow Wilson entrusted him with missions of diplomacy — perhaps the most delicate that had ever been delegated to one man. Although he came into the limelight from comparative obscurity, I don't think he could ever have been fooled by flattery. It was because of his sound common sense and entire absence of self-consciousness that he gained the confidence and the friendship of most of the greatest statesmen of Europe. His tact and judgment were I believe admitted beyond dispute. I am not sure that it is generally known that he did his best to dissuade Wilson from leaving Washington and from going into the midst of astute European diplomats, who might lead him to make decisions without his customary deliberation. House knew that Wilson's power was far greater while he was on a pedestal in the United States of America than it would be after he had stepped down and mingled with the crowd at Versailles.

The story of Colonel House would, I think, make a valuable historical picture; it is a thousand pities that it could not have been made during his lifetime, when we should have had all the advantage of detail that only he could supply. Some day, years hence, it will be made; the David and Goliath contrast has always been good drama. Colonel House, the quiet little unobtrusive man moving noiselessly amongst giants and compelling their attention, is too dramatic to be overlooked. He and I had often discussed the possibility of such a picture, and at last the idea seems to have occurred to one of the big producing companies. Some brief extracts from my correspondence with Colonel House may be interesting (I have withheld the name of the picture corporation.)

Beverly Farms, Mass.
June 15th, 1934.

My dear Friend,

The enclosed letter partly explains itself. The —— Picture Corporation have been urging me to let them do a picture written around the World War in which they wish to make me the central figure. They produced [here is mentioned a well-known war picture] a year or two ago, and it was a great success, not only from a public standpoint but from that of the producer. They plan, so they tell me, to put whatever is needed in this new venture to make it a success.

I have told them repeatedly that I would consider it if they could get you to take the leading part, and I am sending this letter to find your reaction in the matter.

What is done needs be done quickly, for they purpose sending a man or two here to Beverly Farms shortly to discuss details.

Mrs. House joins me in the hope that you and your wife are well and enjoying the summer. We shall be here until the middle of September.

Yours always,
E. M. HOUSE

To this I sent a reply that my agreement with the Twentieth Century to make "Richelieu" and my further contract with Gaumont-British kept me tied for at least a year, and expressing my interest in the idea and the hope that it could be held over until I was free. I give Colonel House's reply: —

It is interesting, my dear friend, to have your letter of June 25th.

It pleases me to have you say that you would "not wish anybody else to portray the character of Colonel House." I have a similar feeling and have told the —— people this.

My thought is that a great historical picture could be made if you were the one to make it. My idea is to have the first scene in the White House, with President Wilson and myself in his study, where I express the belief that a world war is imminent if Germany does not refrain from her determination to build a navy equal, if not superior, to that of Great Britain. I say, at this conference, that in my opinion England will never consent for Germany to have the largest army in the world at her doors, and in addition a navy as large as her own. Wilson agrees and authorizes me to proceed to Europe, and to do what I can in the name of the United States Government to prevent the impending catastrophe.

The next scene should be in Potsdam. Here could be shown the great military display which was put forward to impress me. The Army, the Kaiser and his staff in all the splendour of their trappings, receiving me. The luncheon at the palace with the flower of the German army in their brilliant uniforms in contrast to my inconspicuous dress-suit.

Later my conference with the Kaiser on the terrace and my warning of what would happen to Germany if he did not change his policy. My proposal and his acquiescence that I go to London and try for a meeting at Kiel with himself, Sir Edward Grey, and myself.

My departure for England from France and the mighty display of the British Battle Fleet as I entered the harbor at

Dover. My conference in London, the assassination of the Austrian Archduke, and the precipitation of war upon a thoughtless world.

In London could be shown my luncheon with the King, and the quiet, dignified simplicity of Buckingham Palace and the royal household. I will not tire you by going on, but have in mind conferences and decisions made with Clemenceau, Balfour, the kings and premiers of Belgium, Italy, and elsewhere.

The romance and human interest could be woven in around a German spy and some beautiful woman in Washington, London, or Paris.

With you to do it, I believe a picture could be made that would leave a lasting impression on this generation and the next and would be of value to historians who are trying to gather the facts about the mighty events of this period in order to preserve them for the coming centuries.

My love and good wishes are always with you.

E. M. House

If it could have been written and produced for all it was worth, I think it would have made not only an interesting picture but one, as Colonel House points out, of a good deal of value to historians. But when I came to talk it over with the producers, the difficulties became more and more obvious; we were likely to meet opposition at every turn and our hands would be tied always. The producers, who always have to be so wary of legal complications, and claims for damages, foresaw half a dozen libel suits in no time. We could have made a semi-fictitious story with Colonel House as the hero, or perhaps a different one with Colonel House as the "goat," but we eventually realized that if we were going

255

to tell the truth and make a really vital document we should have to wait until a great many of the *dramatis personæ* were dead.

It is entirely for this same reason that I have never consented to play the part of John D. Rockefeller. For many years — ever since the late John D. commenced to look like me — I have been pursued by people who begged me to do a Rockefeller picture. It is obvious that I should find myself confronted with the same difficulty. I should be continually running up against some living person who would object to the way his character was represented. Moreover, I don't think you can give a true and interesting picture of a man by making him into a stained-glass window and placing a halo round his head. The interesting thing is to show how the halo gradually appears with the acquisition of great wealth. I am not intending to apply this remark to the late Mr. Rockefeller. I know nothing about his life except that he sold oil and founded a tremendous charity. But I know that the immediate descendants of all great men are severely critical, and insist that their late distinguished relative was a saint, and nothing but a saint, and I have no reason to believe that the descendants of the late John D. Rockefeller are any less human than other people. And in any case, if he were saintly I should fail lamentably in the part; I have never been able to play nice old gentlemen convincingly.

I shall always feel that a great opportunity was missed in failing to make the Colonel House picture during his lifetime; but I don't believe any company could have been found to take the risk. . . . It may be as well to remind you that before I switched off to my Colonel House recollection, I was just finishing or had finished "The Iron Duke."

So I am still in London and Prince George is just about to marry the very beautiful and very charming Princess Marina, and I am being asked to serve on the Committee of the Prince George Wedding Fund. This was to be a wedding present to which all the Georges of the Empire might subscribe. Their Royal Highnesses had agreed to accept it on condition that the money should be devoted to the establishment of a fund to provide a Christmas treat every year for poor children and a holiday every summer for convalescent children of the poor. The co-operation of the picture houses was enlisted and with the help of Gaumont-British we made a "trailer" that was shown all over the British Isles. The only one of the committee who could be persuaded to act on the screen with me was Lord Luke. I doubt whether he would ever have made a great actor, but the reason why he had attained his present high position became obvious to me. Lord Luke has more responsibilities on his shoulders than it seems possible for any one man to bear — not the least of which is chairmanship of Bovril Ltd. As soon as he had promised to appear in the trailer, he attended rehearsals, studied his part, and stuck at the job as closely and as seriously as though his whole future career depended on his making good on the screen. When one works with a "captain of industry" it is generally fairly easy to discover why he is no longer a sergeant. He devotes himself individually to whatever matter he has in hand. When I call on Henry Ford at his office in Detroit, he always receives me as though he had nothing in the world to do but to talk to me about the theatre, or to take me to lunch in his private dining room, and explain the virtues of the five or six different kinds of bread that he is testing; or to talk about the old ballroom dances and express his delight at finding that Flo can dance the schottische with him. Big businessmen are generally good listeners. I have seldom found that they bustle or hustle or hurry. Quite different from the way we played them at the Elephant & Castle. . . .

CAST

The Iron Duke

Duke of Wellington	.	GEORGE ARLISS
Lord Arthur Hill .	.	A. E. MATTHEWS
Louis XVIII . .	.	ALLAN AYNESWORTH
Marshal Ney . .	.	EDMUND WILLARD
Duke of Richmond .	.	PETER GAWTHORNE
Talleyrand . .	.	FARREN SOUTAR
Castlereagh . .	.	GILES ISHAM
Bates . . .	.	EMLYN WILLIAMS
Uxbridge . .	.	FELIX AYLMER
Metternich . .	.	GIBB McLAUGHLIN
Webster . .	.	WALTER SONDES
King of Prussia .	.	FREDERICK LEISTER
Czar of Russia .	.	GERALD LAWRENCE
Madame . .	.	GLADYS COOPER
Duchess of Wellington .		ELLALINE TERRISS
Duchess of Richmond .		NORMA VARDEN
Lady Frances Webster .		LESLIE WAREING
Denise . . .	.	ANNIE ESMOND
Lady Frances' maid .	.	PADDIE NAISMITH

ஒ

Director . .	.	VICTOR SAVILLE
Story . . .	.	H. M. HARWOOD
Collaboration . .	.	H. M. HARWOOD AND MISS BESS MEREDYTH
Camera . . .	.	KURT COURANT
Camera exteriors .	.	LESLIE ROWSON

Chapter 15

I HAD just time to finish the trailer before taking the *Majestic* to New York in order to be in Hollywood on the date agreed in my contract for "Richelieu." Most people who are going abroad for any long period have a few hectic days before sailing. And so when you walk across the gangplank, no matter how much you love the people you are leaving behind, you heave a sigh of relief. I mean I do, and so does Flo. At least we know we have a breathing spell before we need make any more appointments. In those five or six or seven restful days that you spend crossing the Atlantic you can sometimes get to know certain people very intimately. You probably never see them again, or if you do you never meet on quite the same footing. I don't know why we should be so cordial on the water and so distant on the land. I suppose it is that when you find yourself surrounded by water, you feel trapped and decide to make the best of your fellow captives, whereas on land you can run away. The fact remains that when shipboard friends meet again in Mayfair, they dare one another to become more than a chilly acquaintance.

It happens that we have made a very few close friendships that had their beginning on the Atlantic, but then we have crossed many times. I think such instances are rare. These reflections are à propos of our finding Joseph Schenck on the *Majestic*. I had often met him, but never really knew him before. I cannot say whether he is ever going to write his autobiography; he is an original character, so perhaps he isn't, but if he should and it is half as interesting as the account he gave us of his early struggles and adventures, I strongly advise you to buy it and read it. I can hardly say we swapped picture stories because my own entrance into pictures was then comparatively recent, but I think he was interested when I told him that I saw my first moving picture before he was born. It was when I was a small boy in London; I used to like to look into a shop window in Oxford Street in which was displayed a little wheel that revolved in front of a mirror. I think the wheel was octagonal and on its outside edge it had eight little pictures of a horse in eight different poses of galloping. Each of these pictures was reflected as it passed the mirror and so with the quick revolution of the wheel there appeared the most exciting effect of a galloping horse.

Mr. Schenck assured me that it was not so many years after that, in America, of course, that he began his career in moving pictures. He was little more than a boy when he left his job in a drugstore and, in partnership with another boy, rented a disused photographic studio, and converted it into what we knew in England as a penny arcade. By that time my galloping horse had developed into a penny-in-the-slot machine — a contrivance with a handle at the side which you turned while you looked through a peephole and beheld a most animated picture, lasting as long as fifteen seconds or more. That was how Joe Schenck began. I am trusting to my memory, but I think I am quoting him correctly. From a penny showman he has become a millionaire. And there are several other executives in the picture business — millionaires — who began in just the same way. No one should begrudge them their success. They might not at first have seen any great future for the ingenious little machines, but they were showmen and were all trying to go one better than the next man in showmanship. Edison was, I suppose, the great genius watching and working on the idea (although it is claimed that an Englishman in Bath made the first practical moving picture) ; but it was the showmen who were leading it to commercial prosperity. The men who believed there was money in it are the people we have to thank for its rapid advance.

I arrived in Hollywood armed with a great many pictures of Richelieu collected from various sources — from the National Gallery, the National Portrait Gallery and some foreign galleries. My brother Fred, who seems to have keys to the most remote recesses of the British Museum, was able to unearth some little known engravings which I found interesting, if not very enlightening.

Nunnally Johnson, one of Twentieth Century's star writers, had been working on the script in Hollywood and I had devoted a good deal of time to it in London. Richelieu was by no means an easy character to put down on paper. It was very soon obvious to me that it would be wise for us to found the picture on the old play. I had no idea that there were so many people still alive who had read Bulwer-Lytton or who had seen his five-act drama "Richelieu, or the Conspiracy." But whenever I mentioned that I was going to do "Richelieu" somebody would say "Ah, Baradas, what a part!" or "That scene between Richelieu and Louis — great!" and all the old playgoers mentioned the "Magic Circle" scene.

If these flashes of memory had come only from actors I should not have been surprised, but so many of the older people who were merely theatregoers seemed equally familiar with the play! So I realized that an important section of the audience would be disappointed if we broke away entirely from Lytton's formula. When I told Mary Anderson that I was going to do Richelieu, she said "Oh, wonderful! The Magic Circle — I can see Irving now!" and to my surprise she reeled off the entire speech; I knew that she could do this with Shakespeare, but I was unprepared for Lytton; and as she finished off quite majestically with "I call down the curse of Rome," she said, "Oh, you'll be great in that scene." She said that because she likes me, — or she may even have believed it, — but of course she was quite wrong. I have never been able to rise to those great moments.

When I was studying Shylock, Dr. Furness gave me the free run of his father's library, in which one can find every kind of record of all the great Shakespearean actors. This collection of Shakespeareana tells you just how the great comedians of the past spoke their lines — every inflection, in order that you may know how they achieved their great moments. A gold mine, I thought. I turned up "The Merchant of Venice" and all the Shylocks. I studied the description of their "business" and their special and original emphasis; I declaimed the lines precisely as directed. I tried it with Kean; I tried it with

Kemble; with Irving and Booth. They all had different moments and I tried them all. I tested them in my study, on the cliffs at St. Margaret's Bay, at the bottom of the garden amongst the pine trees. They were all moments that had either held the audience spellbound or roused them to a furore of applause. When I spoke them they sounded just like me trying to be clever, and not a bit like Shylock. I got so depressed that I decided to give up Shakespeareana and rely entirely on Shakespeare.

Lytton's "Richelieu" has been played by all the great tragedians since it was first produced by Macready a hundred years ago. One would therefore have a right to suppose that it is a great play. I am not sure that it is, or ever was. I believe that a certain number of the old plays have come down to us as classics because they afforded great scope for tragedians during the periods when actors loved to declaim, and when audiences liked to hear the crystal chandeliers rattle in response. There is no doubt that Lytton's "Richelieu" has some very fine scenes and that it shows a good deal of ingenuity in construction, but I think even in its own day it must have had some very dull spots. This criticism is open to argument but no one of my associates at Twentieth Century will dispute the fact that we had a great deal of difficulty in making the play into an effective picture. It must be remembered that the morals and sensibilities of the audience are much more closely guarded in the cinema than in the theatre; for which we should be grateful because whatever opinion we may hold about pictures, we are at least spared in the cinema the intense vulgarity in dialogue and "business" that we so often have to endure in up-to-date society plays.

In the making of pictures you have to be perpetually watchful that nothing is said that can offend any religious sect. During "Richelieu" I had a Roman Catholic priest at my elbow most of the day. One of the lines that Mary Anderson remembered and repeated was: "Mark where she stands; around her form I draw the awful Circle of our Solemn Church." This was questioned by my priest and submitted to a higher authority of the Church, and finally the word "awful" had to be omitted, the contention being that it gave a wrong impression to a modern audience. But on the whole the Church gave us very little trouble; in fact, many times I found my priest most helpful. It was in the building and the writing of the story that the difficulties arose. Darryl Zanuck admitted that he was no authority on the Louis XIII period, and could not therefore permit himself to come to quick decisions with me, as he had done in previous pictures. So there was long deliberation and many changes, and at last the specialists were called in and that was the beginning of endless conferences. I might as well confess at once that I was the real stumbling block. It is perhaps unfortunate that I went fresh into the pictures after a long experience in the theatre, because the consequence is I have always seen my pictures through the theatre. This must be irritating to those writers who have grown up in the studios; what they see as effective scenes I am likely to regard as interruptions. I am intolerant of any scene that does not bear directly on the story. There are many, apart from the writers, who disagree with me as to this; who believe that the movies should be divorced or at any rate separated from the theatre as far as possible, that in spite of movies having become talkies it is still more important to satisfy the eye than the ear. I always spend several weeks on the manuscript with the assistance of Maude Howell before beginning rehearsals of any picture, in an effort to make it more like a play and less like a picture. This will explain at once why I am not popular with writers, either in London or in Hollywood. I spend too much time interfering in other people's business. But I contend that writers, and even authors, should be very patient and forbearing with the actor who has to carry the play or story on his shoulders (Chorus: "We are.").

It is one thing to write words and quite another thing to speak them. I try to convince writers that I do not alter their manuscripts necessarily because I think my changes are better, but because I think they are better for me; and if they are better for me, they are likely to be better for the picture. (Cries of "Oh! Oh!") The star on the stage or screen becomes the responsible person in the mind of the audience, just as soon as he walks on. Under all conditions he has to bear the blame. If he is really bad in the part, the audience knows it and registers accordingly. If it is a bad story the audience says, "He ought to have known better than to appear in a thing like this." If it's a half-bad story, they say, "He's not as good in this as he was in the last thing we saw him play." If the language is stilted and unreal, they say, "He doesn't seem easy, somehow; not like himself at all."

An actor may not have constructive ability, but his contact with audiences is likely to make him a good judge of how a situation should be led up to and how a point can be most effectively phrased in order to "put it over." Most actors who have become popular favorites have obvious limitations. The man who can do everything well lacks, as a rule, what is called personality — the something that makes an audience like him, remember him, recognize him when they see him again, and eventually take him to their bosom. It is precisely because of his limitations that the opinion of the actor who has made an intensive study of a part should be listened to by writers and directors with great respect. (Voice: "I suppose you mean 'patience.' ")

Sometimes the actor will be wrong. He may have failed to catch the author's idea, and his suggestions may prove destructive (Chorus: "Hear, Hear!"). But in such cases it is seldom that he is not open to correction. Although I do not attempt to disguise the fact that I am on the side of the actor, I am also in full sympathy with the writer. I do not blame a writer for regarding me with anger and contempt, or for eventually chucking up the job in despair. But he has never been an actor. He doesn't understand that when one faces an audience, it is necessary not merely to repeat the author's lines but to believe in them. Therefore if the man that the actor has to portray suddenly speaks or behaves in a way that is unbelievable in the character already established, the actor who is responsible for the portrayal of that character must in self-defense make some protest.

In an effort to make a satisfactory script of "Richelieu" new writers were brought in and went out again, and still the conferences went on. At these meetings there always sat, silent and forgotten, a girl who was taking everything down in shorthand. When the conference was over a copy of her notes was sent to each writer engaged on the script. You may remember that Mr. Zanuck's memorandum which I have quoted refers to this. The typist who records these meetings is generally experienced in the work, with ability to condense the discussion and yet keep all the essential points. Sometimes, when the specialists become excited, we get their language verbatim, which, although expressive, lacks the final polish. I offer an excerpt from one of the later conferences of "Richelieu" which may give some idea of how a story progresses from one conference to another. I should explain that the word "scene" does not mean the same thing as it would if applied to a play; it refers to the dialogue that is spoken before it becomes necessary to change the "set-up." Sometimes it is only a few lines.

Conference with Mr. Zanuck on "CARDINAL RICHELIEU"

These notes involve changes in the revised temporary script with suggestions made by Mr. Arliss.

Everything is alright through scene 28, page 22. From there go into a scene at Helene's home. It is a meeting of all the conspirators including Marie and Anne. Helene is in the background. One says: "Richelieu's power has been taken away — he cannot be a hindrance." We get over what the plot is about: with Richelieu out of the way they are going to get the King off the throne and turn the country over to Spain. At the conclusion of the meeting we show a scene of Anne about to get into her carriage. A cloaked messenger comes up to her and hands her a note. She says "All right, I'll go." FADE OUT.

FADE IN. Helene comes into a scene with Richelieu at Richelieu's home. Richelieu has the secret thing [*sic*] with Helene and then Lenore comes in. They wind up their scene

268

together and Richelieu excuses himself to go to another part of the house. Follow Richelieu into scene with Anne. She has been waiting and bawls him out about it.

FADE IN on the Jamboree. We see Helene and Lenore sneaking in. Lenore thanks Helene for bringing her to Court. Helene to Lenore: "Wait here until I pay my respects to Marie." We follow Helene up to the centre of the celebration. Follow Helene back to where she left Lenore. Lenore isn't there. WE CUT OUTSIDE to Lenore on the balcony talking to André. Lenore: "All my dreams are coming true, coming to Court and meeting you." Get over all of the stuff about the secret notes, and their previous contact.

Now CUT UPSTAIRS to Richelieu and Louis. Richelieu tells Louis about the impromptu celebration being held. "Even now Marie is sitting on your Throne. Of course, I'll go down and make my appearance — that will carry some weight. If you weren't so sick — what a great thing it would be if we walked in on it unannounced together!" This challenge gets the King out of bed and they start out together. As Louis starts to throw off the covers he cries "By God, I'll go there."

DISSOLVE TO the ballroom. Lenore is dancing with Pons . . . At the end of this scene the doors are thrown open and in comes Louis on Richelieu's arm. End the sequence the way Mr. Arliss does . . . she goes off on Richelieu's arm. This takes us up to the end of page 52.

Follow the script from pages 53 to 57.

Play scene 63, pages 57 to 61, as in the script *without* the cobbling business.

Now play the business with Richelieu and Conde. This scene ends with Richelieu saying: "All right — and I'll lead the troops out." DISSOLVE — and he's leading the troops. Come back to the house and a messenger arrives from the King and takes Lenore. André arrives and asks for Lenore and finds that she has been taken to the Palace.

Page 88 — the conspirators do not see the Army going by. A messenger arrives and says that Richelieu is leading the troops from Paris.

André joins the conspirators and says that he wants to kill Richelieu. Follow Mr. Arliss's treatment for the assassination routine.

The conspirators tell the King that Richelieu is dead. . . . Then at the climax, when they are about to give the signal, in walks Richelieu and produces the phoney document.

It is discussed that Richelieu should procure the document in the following way: he goes to Marie and takes the treaty from her by force, handling her like a chambermaid.

NOTE: Change the character of the King to conform with Mr. Arliss's suggestions.

This is a fair example, much abridged, of a conference.

Before we arrived at a final script, it became evident that something strange was happening. Zanuck was not in his office. There was no cry of "Hold everything" but there was a general slackening of work. Came the news: Mrs. Zanuck was about to have her first baby and Darryl was at home on guard. The child arrived, a boy, both doing well, and Hollywood breathed again. Joe Schenck gave a party to Darryl to celebrate this great occasion and invited the leading executives and principal writers. Although I do not belong to either class, he paid me the compliment of including me. Speeches were made and verbal bouquets were freely thrown. Nunnally Johnson, the writer, — for whom I have a great admiration, which for reasons I have indicated is, I fear, not reciprocated, — made a speech which had in it not only humor, but a great deal of affection for his close friend Zanuck. He expressed the satisfaction of all present at seeing Darryl radiant once more, and how delighted he was and how delighted everyone was at the reason for Darryl's happiness, "except perhaps Mr. Arliss, who no doubt feels that he could have done it better himself." I need not say that this was greeted with much laughter and great applause by the writers.

The number of writers on "Richelieu" had now narrowed down to two: Maude Howell and W. P. Lipscomb. Lipscomb can turn out effective dialogue quicker than anyone I know. Finally some sweeping cuts and changes were made by Zanuck and Ray Griffith, and we were off. The scenery and costumes were in my opinion unusually fine and the cast I thought well chosen.

During the filming of "Richelieu" there was a great deal of cabling and phoning from Gaumont-British in London, and finally M. E. Balcon came over to Hollywood in order to make definite arrangements for my next picture. The first choice was a new story by J. B. Priestley. I had talked this over with Mr. Priestley before I went to Hollywood, and it was now decided that if we could get the script in time, that should be my next picture. Unfortunately certain difficulties afterwards arose, and the story was never filmed. Many other possibilities were discussed before Mr. Balcon left for England. I was very anxious to do a picture about Cecil Rhodes. I suppose my interest was largely aroused by my friendship with Hays Hammond. Hammond had for years been closely associated with Rhodes in South Africa. He and I many times talked of the great opportunities to be found in a Cecil Rhodes picture, and of course Hammond was able to supply me with all sorts of intimate details that perhaps no other person then living could give with equal accuracy. Hays Hammond could have stood in much the same position, as an adviser on the Rhodes story, as that of Colonel House in a picture dealing with the Great War. M. E. Balcon shared my enthusiasm for Rhodes and so it was decided that Maude Howell should go to London to work on the story with one of the Gaumont-British writers.

Another story discussed was "The Passing of the Third Floor Back." This has often been suggested to me by various managements, but I was afraid of the central figure as a part for myself; he is so frightfully good; I was afraid the audience wouldn't believe in me. I defy anyone not to have believed in Forbes-Robertson in the play, with his glorious voice and his magnificent profile, but I have always found it very difficult to be convincingly good in the theatre.

Hans Andersen was also suggested. It is possible that some day an author will write an interesting Hans Andersen play. I have had many through my hands, but never one that I believed would hold an audience. There are many charming characters which although interesting to read about become very dull people when placed upon the stage and left to stand on their own two feet. M. E. Balcon had one very definite proposal to make and that was that I should go to Paris and see a comic film called "Rothschild." He thought that for more reasons than one an English version of this might appeal to me.

CAST

Cardinal Richelieu

Armand, Duc de Richelieu	GEORGE ARLISS
Lenore	MAUREEN O'SULLIVAN
Louis XIII . .	EDWARD ARNOLD
André de Pons . .	CESAR ROMERO
Comte Baradas . .	DOUGLAS DUMBRILLE
Gaston . . .	FRANCIS LISTER
Joseph . . .	HALLIWELL HOBBES
Queen Marie . .	VIOLET KEMBLE-COOPER
Queen Anne . .	KATHARINE ALEXANDER
Courtier . .	ROBERT HARRIGAN
Gustavus . .	LUMSDEN HARE
D'Epernon . .	KEITH KENNETH
Duke of Lorraine .	MURRAY KINNELL
Duke of Normandy	HERBERT BUNSTON
Olivares . .	LEONARD MUDIE
Soldier . . .	PAT SOMERSET
A Duke . . .	GILBERT EMERY
Innkeeper . .	LIONEL BELMORE

 oⳤ

Director . . .	ROWLAND V. LEE
Author . . .	BULWER-LYTTON
Screen play . .	W. P. LIPSCOMB, MAUDE T. HOWELL, CAMERON ROGERS
Camera . . .	PEVERELL MARLEY

Chapter 16

So once more we say good-by to our Hollywood cronies
— the Moultries, the Evanses, the Cawthorns and our
many actor friends; take our usual two little adjoining compartments on "The Chief" to Chicago, break-
fast there with Mrs. Matile and Clarence E. Richard,
the working heads of the National Anti-Vivisection
Society, of which I am president. A flying visit to Acker-
mann's to see W. Russell Button — who really should be
making a fortune drawing bogus Rowlandsons — he de-
lights me with a new one from his own hand every
Christmas. Then on by "The Twentieth Century" to
New York; a hurried call on Colonel and Mrs. House
and the Ameses; then to Cherbourg on the S. S. *Olympic*,
and so to Paris. Here we are met by Angus MacPhail,
with all the latest news from Shepherd's Bush and more
movie stories for me, collected by his department.

You will naturally think of Angus MacPhail in a kilt,
but I've never seen him in one, and I hate to think how
he'd look. He is thin and ascetic, with tastes, I am sure,
far removed from the Highland Fling. He has a brain
which is clear as crystal; he is excellent company, but
even in Paris I could not make him loose; the nearest I
came to it was the night I persuaded him to have a
second bottle of Vichy Célestin at one sitting.

Again we talked over my old friend Samuel Pepys and again we decided that there was no character nearly as good for me if we could only get the right scenario. But on considering Pepys for a picture one is always confronted with the same difficulty. Everybody knows something about Pepys' Diary but what do they know about Pepys? The fact that they know nothing would be very little drawback — might even be an advantage; but unfortunately they have formed an ineradicable conception of his character. They think of him as a comic little gentleman who can easily be led astray by the ladies, and is kept only occasionally in the straight and narrow path by the fear of his wife and his conscience. As I have already pointed out, in writing an historical part for the movies, one cannot take the risk of writing only for a well-informed minority: one must think of the masses. A good story could perhaps be built round Pepys as the savior of the navy, but my opinion is that you would have to call him by some other name or the picture audience would be disappointed. Perhaps I am prejudiced because I have never been able to get a story that shows the greatness of Pepys without destroying the preconceived ideas of the audience.

During the time we were in Paris I had a visit from Pirandello, who paid me the compliment of offering me a play he had just finished; he was willing that I should produce it either on the stage or the screen. The subject, however, was unsuited to me, and with great regret I had to decline it. Angus MacPhail now arranged for a private showing of the French "Rothschild" picture. This was the story of an old tramp. A bogus banker on the verge of bankruptcy discovers that the tramp's name is Rothschild, and proceeds to make capital out of this discovery by placing the old chap at the head of the bank. Both Flo and I thought it most amusing, and although I could never hope to approach the delightful and unctuous performance given by Harry Baur, I felt I could get away with the part from another angle. I was at first afraid that the juggling with the name of Rothschild might detract from the dignity of "The House of Rothschild," which I had so recently produced, but I was persuaded that there was no fear of this. We could not call it "Rothschild," its French title, because that would, in England and the United States, confuse it with "The House of Rothschild." So we decided to call it "The Tramp"; this title was afterwards for some reason changed to "The Guv'nor" for England and "Mr. Hobo" for America. Angus MacPhail was able to leave Paris with the definite understanding that I agreed to play an English version of this film, and that if neither of the other stories was ready, this should be my next picture.

When I got back to London, the Rhodes scenario was submitted to me, but we suddenly all woke up to the fact — which I ought to have realized from the beginning — that with all the art of the make-up department I could never look anything like Cecil Rhodes either in face or figure. However, the time spent on the story was not wasted, because the picture was afterwards made with Walter Huston.

M. E. Balcon now advised my doing the French picture at once. Milton Rosmer, the very quiet, very careful, very experienced actor, was engaged as director, and Guy Bolton set to work on the script. I had for so long been playing men of affairs that I looked forward with a good deal of interest to being a tramp. I needed a collection of the most dilapidated clothes, such as I felt would gladden the heart of any professional tramp. I knew of only one place where one could find this type of wardrobe, and that was Mike Angel's. Mike Angel's — where I used to go during my first year on the stage, those Elephant & Castle days. For a shilling or two I could buy all sorts of character stuff. But things have changed; it is no longer the Mike Angel's of my youth — no longer a wild collection of shelves yielding surprises in old waistcoats and coats dear to the heart of the character actor. Now there are departments. Now clothes are made here for men of fashion. My character clothes now repose in the "costume department." The old gentleman, old Mr. Angel, has long ago retired, and the young, bright-eyed boys that used to dart about the shop like human eels have become staid, middle-aged gentlemen.

I remember in those early days bartering with one of these bright-eyed boys for a character waistcoat. Old Mr. Angel generally saw everyone himself, but he had stepped out. I think the bright young Angel was insisting upon half a crown and I was offering a shilling (which was a good deal considering I was getting only six shillings a week salary). Old Mr. Angel had stepped in again and stood watching the struggle. And then he said, "Let him have it, Dave."

"What! For a shilling?" said the boy.

"No, for nothing," said the father. "Wrap it up and give it to Mr. Arliss. He wants it."

Such little incidents stick in one's memory. Well, it

277

seemed that Mike Angel's was still able to supply me with convincing clothes for a tramp; during the filming of the picture, one day when we were on location, this was put to the test.

To be "on location" is to be shooting scenes away from the studio — generally scenes that require distance, — fields, rivers, mountains, — scenes that are more effective shot from nature than built in the studio. We were in fields, with hayricks and a stream running through — one of those stretches of real country which are still to be found within twelve miles of Charing Cross. I was waiting for the cameras to be placed for the next scene when Maude Howell, who has an eye every-where, hurried up to tell me that there was a horrible, dirty-looking man in the next field with a cart to which was harnessed an old horse in a very bad state of shoulder-sores. It happened that we were hidden from the next field, so the horrible old man was ignorant of the fact that there were movie people about. I said to Miss Howell: "Just show me where he is; don't come with me. Leave him to me."

I am not by nature pugnacious, but Flo has taught me to arouse in myself a sense of duty where animals are concerned. I found the man on the top of a hayrick and the suffering horse below harnessed to the cart that was being loaded with hay. I shouted to the horrible man, quite forgetting that in my very careful make-up I my-self was quite indistinguishable from a very similar type of horrible man. I told him to come down and look at his horse. He looked at me, looked at his horse, looked at me again, came to the conclusion that I was drunk, and told me to go away. I was now very angry and in-

278

sisted in a magisterial way that he come down off that haystack at once. He now entirely lost his temper; that any old tramp should dare to talk to him like that — to him, who was his own master, owned the cart, owned the horse, owned the field! He let forth a stream of abuse that was really worth listening to. I saw that I was out-classed in rhetoric, so I walked away with the warning that I was at once going to telephone the police. He shouted after me certain directions which, if carried out, were intended to result in my future discomfort.

It may seem strange that it never occurred to me that he regarded me as nothing but a drunken old tramp, but when an actor gets out of the environment of his character, he is apt to forget whether he is made up for a prince or a pauper or, indeed, that he is made-up at all. The nearest telephone was in the town; my director had already been patiently waiting for me, so I had to go and play the scene before I made my police call. Well, the sequel was that by the time I had finished the scene, the owner of the horse had discovered who I was. He came after me post haste — and if ever I have to play the part of a creeping, crawling old devil, I had my lesson then. Of course, he told me it was all a mistake — that he had given strict orders that the horse was not to be used; it was his man that had done it, while his back was turned — thought the sun would do the poor old thing a bit of good, etc., etc. Well, I gave him a chance, but I had him strictly watched; the sores were properly dressed each day, and the horse was not used again until it was passed by the vet.

I was very sorry when "The Guv'nor" was finished. I had grown to enjoy my old clothes, and bad manners. And then my fellow tramp, Gene Gerrard, was such a perfect foil for me. He is one of those rare comedians who acts with you, not against you or entirely for himself; he made valuable suggestions and was quick to respond to any ideas of mine, so that our scenes together were I think always alive and rather gay. In my opinion our story was better than the original French script, better at any rate for an English audience.

After I had finished "The Guv'nor" there was a long spell of nerve-racking uncertainty and disappointment. None of the proposed stories turned out to be satisfactory, but they nearly all seemed sufficiently promising to warrant their being worked over in the hope of getting them right. I worked about as hard as I ever want to work — a great many more hours a day than when I have had something to show for it. New writers with fresh ideas were called in with no satisfactory result. It seemed impossible that with all the resources of Gaumont-British I should remain idle for lack of a story. Then I had an idea — Cagliostro. It was not exactly a brilliant idea because it had in the past brought me some disappointment. Years before I went into pictures I had tried to get a play about Cagliostro — a man full of character, with a life full of adventure. Louis Parker tried to write one for me and gave it up in despair. Other authors tried. I even tried myself, but for some reason or other the man wouldn't become a star part; you didn't believe in him. It occurred to me that although he was so difficult in a play, he might lend himself to the screen. Again the powers-that-be were enthusiastic and M. E. Balcon set a couple of very able writers to work on it. The writers were jubilant; it seemed easy. There was drama enough in his life to make half a dozen pictures; in fact a writer with imagination might almost be satisfied with what he finds in the *Encyclopædia Britannica*. That is what I thought when I was first bitten with the idea. But all the marvelous hair-raising things he did in real life, miracles that gained for him the confidence of kings and princes, seem to become just childish pranks when transferred to the stage; and much to my disappointment they were no more convincing when designed for the screen. Five or six weeks of hard labor were put into this effort. By that time everybody's confidence was shaken — everybody's but the writers', who very naturally believed that their version would have been all right if I hadn't monkeyed with it.

Then somebody got the bright idea that I should do a detective story. This did not appeal to me very strongly; not that I was averse to playing a detective, but because that sort of picture seemed to be a specialty of Hollywood both in direction and in acting. It is the thing that is likely to be done much better in America than in England. But amongst Edgar Wallace's innumerable characters is "Mr. Reeder," a different kind of detective and very English. Mr. Reeder was brought forth, and looked promising. Brian Wallace, son of Edgar Wallace, was on the writing staff of Gaumont-British and it was probably he who made the suggestion. Mr. Reeder is a type that should be the character actor's delight. He is quite unlike the average stage detective, and shows every sign of being a great favorite with the audience.

So I agreed to Mr. Reeder, and the most likely writers, including Brian Wallace, were assigned to the job. And for a considerable time they all worked furiously on it. Their script was submitted to me and I worked furiously on it. Then we had a conference and it was decided that we had all been working too furiously and that a few calm, collected writers had better be called in and allowed to work without interruption for about five or six weeks. To this I thankfully agreed; it was getting towards the end of summer and St. Margaret's had long been calling me. I had been able to make short week-end visits, Saturday afternoon to Sunday night, but no longer. I would catch the fast train to Dover, where my car would meet me, and fifteen minutes' drive would land me home.

But the week end in the summer is not a pleasant time to travel on the Southern Railway from London. Charing Cross Station at that time of year is always crowded with trippers, and most trippers are eager for autographs. The desire of one's admirers for autographs should, I suppose, be regarded as a delicate compliment. But it is not always expressed in a delicate way. I have seldom had the overwhelming experience of being mobbed — an experience which I believe often overtakes the younger generation of stars. But Charing Cross is a particularly vulnerable spot. On Saturday afternoon when I went to catch my train my autograph collectors collected in alarming numbers, and bore down upon me with that spirit of determination that makes England what it is. I had about ten minutes to wait. I couldn't retreat and leave the station because I should have lost my train. I couldn't seek refuge in the refreshment rooms, because my attackers would have no compunction in following me. So with presence of mind worthy of a great general, I thought of the Left Luggage Office. It was just behind me, and close to the platform from which I was to start. I turned to the man in charge and demanded the right to book myself as a parcel. I paid my twopence and the man took me over the counter and I was saved. This method of retreat I confidently recommend to other picture stars in railway stations.

I am afraid I cannot tell you of any exciting adventures at St. Margaret's during my visit there this time, unless — yes, we had a fire; but that was perhaps more interesting to us than it would have been to you, because we knew all the firemen by sight. They are not exactly firemen by profession; they have other occupations in the village and are firemen only when called upon to be so. You've no idea how picturesque and dashing the gardener and the postman look as firemen. They have special costumes for such occasions, and in the event of an alarm, they apparently make a quick change. This particular fire afforded great opportunity for action on the part of our brigade, because it lasted quite a long time. The reason it lasted so long was that the hose wasn't long enough to reach the fire. If the water connection had been nearer the fire or the fire had been nearer the water connection, I daresay we could have put it out with dispatch, but it wasn't, you see, so it had to burn out. It was really a scandal, and I think the council is going to look into the matter. But after all, what is there to do? Of course we could get a longer hose for future emergency, but then, on the other hand, a thing like that, a fire so far away from the water, might not happen again for years.

After about a month I am called to London for conferences. The new "Mr. Reeder" is submitted to me, and I don't like it. Further time is spent on it and eventually I come to the conclusion that this kind of detective story is not the kind of thing I can do. I decide that as far as I am concerned, I had better admit that I am beaten. It was now the end of November and we had been working on the story since August.

Just at this time messages were being received by producers from that mysterious underground source that I have already referred to, telling of an impending change in the public taste. "What They want is costume plays" came the warning. So with hope born of desperation we turned once more to Cagliostro. We dug him up hoping to find that life was not extinct. We turned him over and over, stroked him, kicked him, but there was no doubt he was as dead as a doornail. For two weeks we held a post-mortem and then sent him most irreverently to hell. We had a grand character but no story to carry him.

If, in the light of this experience, I ever give on the radio a "Fireside Talk to Writers" I shall say in simple language: "And so, my young friends, when next you write a story, be sure that you have got a story worth writing before you write it. Work out your plot on paper, from beginning to end, and then consider carefully and at length whether it is better to burn the midnight oil developing it, or, my young friends, to burn the story and save the oil."

At this moment there mercifully appeared from

somewhere a play called "The Lake of Life" by Edwin E. Greenwood, the story of which formed the basis of my next picture. I changed the title to "Hands Off," and it was again changed to "East Meets West." I liked the title "Hands Off" because my chief reason for doing the picture was that I thought it might, in a peaceful and picturesque way, express the idea that we have a right to expect honorable dealing between nations just as we look for it between individuals; that when one nation feels it has need of expansion (that time-honored excuse), instead of stealing territory from another nation it might at least consider the possibility of buying its expansion with real hard cash. I doubt whether this moral ever got over, and I have no hope that it would have had any effect on the dictators of today if it had; but at least it gave me the satisfaction of believing the picture had a plus value.

The filming of "East Meets West" remains fresh in my mind largely because of the excellent acting of the company. Lucie Mannheim gave a beautiful performance of a very difficult part. I had first seen Miss Mannheim in "Nina," in which she played a dual role; and for two acts out of three she completely deceived me — and Flo too. We thought the parts were played by two women. It was, I think, the cleverest performance of a dual role that I have ever seen. I asked M. E. Balcon if she had done anything in pictures. He told me that her only appearance on the screen was in "Thirty-Nine Steps." I had it run off for me at the studio and at once decided that she would be exactly suited to the leading part in "East Meets West." Gaumont-British made her an offer, and eventually put her under contract. She has since become a British subject and I think when her foreign accent is a little less pronounced she will be a great asset to the English stage. Ronald Ward is also going to prove that he is worthy of far more important parts than he has yet been entrusted with. I was glad to have Romney Brent with me again. When he joined me in "The Merchant of Venice" in New York, I felt sure that he was an Englishman. During rehearsal I said "What part of England do you come from?" He said, very simply, "Mexico." Since then he has established himself in England in "Three Men on a Horse." It was a great privilege to have Godfrey Tearle, whom I have always admired, not only for his acting, but for the way he has fought for the rank and file of the actors as president of the British Equity Association.

We had some outdoor work to do — location scenes; we had put them off as long as possible because they were night scenes, and we were having a particularly cold April. But we had now come to the end of our studio work and, as it was still cold, I agreed to hold up everything for a week in the hope that the weather might get less arctic. The reason for this sympathetic attention to weather conditions was that we had a crowd of colored gentlemen who had to be rather thinly clad. There would have been no postponement either in England or America on account of the actors. Actors both on the stage and screen are expected to give their lives rather than hold up the show. I can imagine the genuine astonishment of the director if an actor should say, "I think it is too cold for me to go on location tonight." It would be a joke to be repeated amidst hearty laughter. But he doesn't say it. Actors die occasionally, as a result, from pneumonia, but that does not shake the loyalty of the survivors; for too many generations they have been carrying the banner with the device "THE SHOW MUST GO ON."

By the end of the week the temperature rose and we all assembled in an open space, where a gallows was erected on one side and an entrance to the palace on the other. By the time night came, the temperature had fallen again and the colored gentlemen struck. I didn't blame them in the least; I think they were quite right. Why should they risk their lives? Acting wasn't part of their religion. They hadn't grown up in the theatre. So the actors stood about and shivered while the director assumed the character of the father of colored gentlemen and pointed out how good it was for them also to shiver in the cause of art. Finally, the Negroes decided that an extra twenty shillings a head, with the torso thrown in, was a fair price for the risk. As there were now signs of snow, I don't believe Lloyd's would have done it at the price, so the director closed with them for a pound and an extra blanket — and the show went on.

From the time I returned from Hollywood, after the filming of "Richelieu," until the final shooting of "East Meets West" about six or eight months had elapsed. During that time we had lost our friend Madge Kendal, for whom we had a great admiration. She died bravely at the age of eighty-six. Will Rogers, too, had died, the victim of an airplane crash.

CAST

The Guv'nor

The Guv'nor . . .	GEORGE ARLISS
Flit	GENE GERRARD
Barsac	FRANK CELLIER
Paul	PATRIC KNOWLES
Madeleine . . .	VIOLA KEATS
Dubois	GEORGE HAYES
Mrs. Granville . . .	HENRIETTA WATSON
Madame Barsac . .	MARY CLARE
Margot	MIGNON O'DOHERTY
Barsac's Chauffeur . .	DENNIS VAL-NORTON
Gaubert	H. R. HIGNETT
Cazin	JOHN GARSIDE
Mrs. Fenton . . .	HILDA BRUCE-POTTER
Police Inspector . .	ALEXANDER SARNER
Tramps	LEONARD SHEPHERD STAFFORD HILLIARD LESLIE FRITH STANLEY LATHBURY IVOR BARNARD
Shop Manager . . .	DENIER WARREN

୶

Director	MILTON ROSMER
Adaptation & Associate Director	MAUDE T. HOWELL
Author	PAUL LAFFITTE
Scenario	GUY BOLTON
Camera	MUTZ GREENBAUM

CAST

East Meets West

Sultan	GEORGE ARLISS
Marguerite	LUCIE MANNHEIM
Sir Henry Mallory	GODFREY TEARLE
Dr. Shagu	ROMNEY BRENT
Nezim	BALLARD BERKELEY
Carter	RONALD WARD
Lady Mallory	NORMA VARDEN
Dr. Ferguson	JOHN LAURIE
Osmin	O. B. CLARENCE
Takasato	CAMPBELL GULLAN
Goodsen	ELIOT MAKEHAM
Stanton	PETER GAWTHORNE
Abdul	RALPH TRUMAN
O'Flaherty	PAT BARR
Crowell	PETER CROFT
Suleeka	STELLA MOYA

{∾}

Director	HERBERT MASON
Associate Director	MAUDE T. HOWELL
Story & Screen Play	EDWIN GREENWOOD
Camera	O. WERNDORFF

Chapter 17

January 28th, 1936. Today George V is to be buried. A dull morning and very cold. An atmosphere of depression hanging heavily over London. Even in normal times London is a mournful place when the shops are closed on Sundays and holidays. But today, there is a quality of melancholy such as I have never felt before. It is early morning and the people in the street look strangely unreal — in dark clothes, and curiously silent. They are all moving westward.

I was born in London and have been part of all sorts and conditions of crowds. Flo and I more than forty years ago joined the stream of happy, noisy, loyal subjects out to see the illuminations on the night of the day George and Mary were married. I remember our swinging down Holborn, just going with the tide and not realizing that the crowd was getting thicker and thicker as we got nearer to the Bank of England and the Mansion House, where the big show of lights was to be seen.

I remember that soon we could no longer swing or even bend our arms as the crowd became a heavy mass that was closing inevitably about us. And I remember the gang of medical students that formed themselves into a human battering-ram to force their way through the solid wall of people. I wondered then, and I wonder now, why it is that on these occasions the medical students are the worst-behaved people in London. I became anxious for Flo, who was unused to London crowds. I looked behind and realized the hopelessness of attempting to turn back; and I remember feeling that this surging mass of human beings, now a mile deep and all intent on pushing forward, was the most awful and terrifying power I had ever seen. But on that day, if we suffered inconvenience, it was in a spirit of happiness and gaiety. The cry was "Long life and happiness to the bride and bridegroom!" Today, George was to be buried. He had been a good King. All classes had come to realize that throughout his reign he had been no mere figurehead; and all classes loved him.

I had plenty of time and opportunity to watch the crowd today. I felt rather proud of them; there was no suggestion of being "out for the day," — no feeling of "a day off," — they had come to pay final tribute to a man they loved. I should have had no special reason for feeling proud of their behavior if the crowd had been drawn merely from the West End, but when one reflects that it was made up of men and women of all classes, it is I think a sign that the British throne stands firm. I heard only one laugh during the day; that was at Hyde Park Corner. A policeman was making violent gestures in the direction of the sky. The crowd looked up and saw a man in a tree, high up, wearing a large overcoat and a soft hat; he was seated comfortably reading the morning paper and apparently oblivious of everything on earth; he looked so much at home that you felt he must live there always. How and when he got there with his large, warm overcoat and his morning paper, we shall never know. Needless to say he made no effort to respond to the policeman.

I was on my way from Maida Vale to St. James's Street, where Flo and I had two seats at Hooper's. But Flo wasn't well enough to come and she had given her place to Margaret Gore-Browne, whom I was to meet at Hooper's at nine-thirty. There were very explicit police regulations published in the newspapers; the traffic for automobiles was to be open till nine-thirty; the procession to start at ten. I left early because I like to watch people, and I like to be on time. It was seven-thirty when I left the house. In the streets it felt earlier, because of the closed shops and the silent houses. Edgware Road seemed dumb and sightless, as though in the night it had suffered a sudden stroke. There were great numbers of people in the streets; they all seemed to be speaking in whispering voices; in reality I suppose this was an illusion, but that was how it seemed to me. The only sound that came to my ears was the *clack, clack, clack* of heels on the stone pavement — always so surprisingly loud in the early morning. Gradually the motor traffic became more and more congested, until, as we reached Hyde Park Corner, the cars were just a solid mass, unable to move. It was now about eight-fifteen. I was within half a mile of St. James's Street and had more than an hour in which to get there. I rather hoped that it would take me that length of time so that I might indulge in my favorite pastime of watching people. But when fifteen, twenty, twenty-five, thirty minutes passed and we had not moved a hundred yards along Piccadilly, I began to suspect that something had gone wrong with the police regulation.

I got out of the car and threaded my way through people and traffic to the nearest policeman. He was civil, but noncommittal; he knew nothing — how long we should have to wait, or whether we should ever get to the other end of Piccadilly. I went back to my car and sat impatiently till nine-fifteen. I got out again, and elbowed my way through to a man who looked like a high official, but who turned out to be merely a uniformed member of the St. John Ambulance; he could tell me nothing. Then I pushed on to the nearest traffic policeman, who told me that he had just got orders to divert all traffic into the side streets. I knew that once I was turned off Piccadilly I could never get back, either walking or riding; I also knew that the bravest chauffeurs fear policemen. So I struggled back to my car and found it filled with a lady who had fainted on the step. I got in beside the chauffeur and told him to push straight on and take no notice of the policeman. He shook in every limb, but did it. It was just possible to pretend not to see the arm of the law, because the jam of cars was so great and we passed on the farther side of the road. We were now through to the next block; I knew we couldn't get much farther, but I was stalling for time; I hoped they might weaken and let the front part of the traffic continue down Piccadilly. But I saw now that there was no chance of this; extra traffic policemen had been added at the next corner and all cars were being diverted. I decided to desert the car, the fainted lady, and the chauffeur, and take my chance. Just as I was stepping off I saw eight gold-laced figures being escorted through the crowd in great haste. They were members of the band of the Royal Household, I think. Evidently they had been delayed in some way and were hurrying to reach a certain point in time for the procession. I saw they had to come right past my car. As they got abreast of me, I took a deep breath, and then fell into step behind them. I had on a long black overcoat which gave me a sort of military look. I pulled my hat well down and kept close at the heels of the Royal Band. Those gold-laced men were taken through the crowd, through the final cordon of police, into what suddenly seemed the great wide open spaces of Piccadilly; for now, in front of them, for half a mile, not a soul was to be seen except the line on each side of erect and im-movable soldiers and police. And where was I? I was there. To my intense surprise I was still keeping step with the Royal Band. I knew it couldn't last; but the situation fascinated me. I kept my head down and de-termined to go on while the going was good. And then, in some mysterious way which I shall never understand, the eight men in gold braid vanished. I don't know where they went to; I suppose they had reached the appointed place and had made a quick left turn, and disappeared while my eyes were on the ground. And there was I, alone.

I have never felt so alone in my life. The fact that each distant side of the road, to the right of me and to the left, was lined with silent men in uniform gave a more intense feeling of desert bareness to the middle of the road. Space, dreadful, illimitable space, through which I was passing — still walking — a solitary black spot; and before me — space — no other moving thing. What they would do to me when they took me, I didn't dare to think; but something told me that the only thing to do was to keep going. I tried to feel important; I must

294

have looked important; and as the minutes passed and I was not arrested, I almost began to think I was important. I had noticed earlier in the morning that some official-looking gentlemen when challenged by the police waved a small white card, and were allowed to pass.

I evidently have a criminal mind. I had a card in my pocket; it was the one that entitled me to my seat at Hooper's; it was about the same size as that carried by the official-looking gentlemen; so I took it out and held it in my hand; and if I saw the slightest uneasiness in the limbs of an officer on guard in the remote edges of the road, I waved it.

And so I went on and on — the only living moving thing in Piccadilly — recklessly striding over the great stretch of no man's land. Why I was allowed to go on undisturbed, what they thought I was doing there, I cannot say. I only know that I continued my walk, unmolested, until I found myself at St. James's Street outside Hooper's. But the victory was not yet mine. I was outside Hooper's; the problem was, how to get inside. I was in the road and the door was the other side of the pavement, and in between was a solid mass of people. I now summoned up all my courage and appealed to a policeman. I asked him to make a way through. He showed no surprise at seeing me in the middle of the road. I began to think I must have become invisible to the naked eye. He answered me quite normally, however. He said he was sorry, but it was more than he could do. I assured him that I only wanted to get through to that door, that I had no intention of taking anyone's place. He said, "These people have been standing here since five this morning and no power on earth can move them. You had better stay where you are." I had now pushed my hat back, and a number of friendly voices said, "Yes, George, you stay here, George. You stay with us, George." The argument was unexpectedly settled by the sudden entrance of an abnormally long arm which came from far back in the crowd. A strong right hand was at the end of the arm; it seized me by the collar, and a deep voice said, "Come on, George" and I was hauled by the neck through what was now a friendly crowd and deposited at Hooper's door.

I took my seat beside Margaret just ten minutes before the procession started. I felt ashamed to have had these experiences today. It seemed unfeeling, unsympathetic, disloyal to have gone through such musical comedy antics on such a solemn occasion. I had not meant, when I started out from Maida Vale, to defy the entire London Police Force and the British Army. It just happened.

I don't know whether or not these unexpected incidents had put me mentally out of harmony with the occasion, but for some reason, in spite of its great solemnity, the procession did not move me; I was surprised and puzzled at this, because I am easily affected, especially in the midst of a sympathetic crowd. Perhaps it seemed too set, or too public. It stretched for a mile; was it, perhaps, too long for tears? Looking back on it, I am of opinion that those who were responsible for the planning had stressed the greatness of the Empire rather than the simple grief of a nation at the passing of their King.

Chapter 18

When "East Meets West" was finished Flo and I began to feel the need of a little sunshine. We had been in London all the winter — the weeks that I had been shooting the picture, and the months during which I had been wrestling with Mr. Reeder and Cagliostro. So we packed our bags and went to Monte Carlo.

It was my first visit; we found the sunshine as we had hoped and expected, but I was quite unprepared to see so many people walking about that I thought had gone to heaven. I could not help being reminded of my friend Mrs. Patrick Campbell, who, when she was introduced in New York to an old and distinguished American actress, turned to her hostess and in her most audible stage whisper said, "I thought she was dead."

This is what Flo and I were continually saying to one another in Monte Carlo. And they all looked so happy too. I found out why. I discovered that although they had not gone to heaven, they were about halfway, in a sort of Nirvana. They had yet to be questioned by Peter at the Pearly Gates, but they had safely passed into the pleasant beyond, out of reach of the British Chancellor of the Exchequer.

Sooner than we had expected we were called back to London for my next picture. As I have said, I had signed a further contract with Gaumont-British, and had now decided on "His Lordship," a picturesque story which attracted me. There were two brothers who could easily be mistaken one for the other. In the original play the parts were played by two men, but we thought it might be an interesting stunt for me to play them as a dual role. This was an attractive idea from the actor's point of view because although the brothers were alike in face and form, they were very different in character and disposition. But as they were both men of breeding, both dressed in ordinary everyday clothes and both moving in the same society, it required a good deal of care to prevent any confusion in the minds of the audience. And as, in the development of the story, one brother had to impersonate the other, the actor is really playing three characters. When the one brother is pretending to be the other brother, it is obvious that he mustn't be exactly like his brother, because that again would confuse the audience. He must be the one brother trying to be like the other.

If I succeeded in giving this subtle variety of impersonation, I'm afraid I didn't always get credit for it. People were continually overheard saying: "It can't be the same man, because they are both on together, talking to each other." And when the brothers shook hands with one another, that was proof positive, in the minds of these doubters, that some other actor had been discovered who could look and act exactly like me. With a jealous eye on my market value, I am happy to report that these critics were mistaken. You may be interested to learn how it is done.

In a general way I do not think it fair to give away

the tricks of the trade. I would not dream of telling you, for instance, how to act like Greta Garbo, or Marlene Dietrich, or Charlie Chaplin, or Gary Cooper, because at once their means of livelihood would be lost to them; but as this doubling business is a purely mechanical trick I have no compunction in exposing it. Furthermore, as I haven't a mechanical brain I shall not be able to make it clear enough for you to understand. So it won't matter anyhow. But I will try to make it easy for you.

To start with, you have seen in play books those stage directions "Exit R" and "Exit L." This seems to establish beyond dispute that every stage has a right and a left to it. In the photographing of the scenes in which the two brothers appear together, this right and left is very definitely prescribed; the right is in fact divided from the left by a straight line down the middle of the stage. The cameraman, when he photographs the scene, can and does blot out all the right side entirely, and therefore all that is recorded on the film is what is happening on the left side, or vice versa. I hope I have made this clear, because it is important.

The scene so arranged is technically known as a "split-mat": I have a double, whose back view has to look exactly like the back view of me. This is not as easy as you may think; the press has sometimes said that my back is more expressive than my face; so there is a great deal of modeling and padding and round-shoulder-ing to be done in order to get an exact copy. The reason for this back view I will explain later; it has no bearing on the scene I am now describing, because in this, the double is not seen. The scene is now played and shot. I

play one of the brothers on one side of the split-mat —
that is, on one side of the stage — and my double plays
the other on the opposite side.

Any uninformed person watching would suppose
that the whole scene is being photographed, but as I
have confided to you, half of it is blotted out; it is only
my side of the split-mat that is being taken. All the
dialogue is spoken but only that on my side of the stage
is recorded. Now you can guess the entire process
— perhaps. The scene is repeated with me as the other
brother on the opposite side of the stage, the first side
being blotted out. This second half is taken on the same
film as the first half, the two halves making a complete
whole.

It will at once be seen, by that large section of my
readers that have keen intelligence, that once the stage
has been set and the first half photographed, nothing
but the death penalty would be sufficient punishment for
anyone who moved anything the fraction of an inch.
The position of the characters on each side of the mat
is also carefully chalked. More important still, and more
difficult to control, is the timing of the speeches. When
I have a conversation with my brother across the mat,
so to speak, his lines are spoken by my double, although
they are blotted out. So when I myself go across and play
the brother, and my double replies from the other side,
if my timing of the speeches and that of the double do
not exactly agree, there is in the final picture either an
awkward pause before a reply or else an overlapping.

For the good results we were able to get I am largely
indebted to Allan Whittaker, who was my double.
"Whitty" was resident stage-manager for Gilbert Miller

at the St. James's when I played there in "The Green Goddess." He is one of those valuable assistants who always do a great deal more than they need do, or than anyone has a right to expect of them, and are therefore seldom fully appreciated by an employer who does not come in personal contact with them.

This was his first entrance into the movies, but in a few weeks he knew more of the mechanics of the screen than I had learned in ten years. Although he has in reality a boyish form, it was his back that was made to look exactly like mine. The reason for this perfect back view is that the director may at any time show the two brothers together by shooting across the back of the double; this without the cumbersome operation of the split-mat. The mechanism of the hand-shake is not easy for me to explain. Briefly, it is the hand of the double that I shake. When the moment comes for me to shake hands, his hand appears on my side of the mat at a very definite level, and I clasp it. When I am appearing on his side of the mat, I extend my hand, my arm being on exactly the same level as the hand I clasp, and as my hand goes past the center of the mat, it is lost to the camera, and my arm becomes joined to the arm of the double already photographed.

Allan Whittaker was also my stand-in during the picture. But he was by no means typical of this class. The business of the ordinary stand-in is merely to stand. There are long periods during which the cameraman is working out his effects for the next scene. He needs the full lights and certain actors. The cameraman has no mercy; by the time he is satisfied, eggs could be fried on the exposed pink surface of many a bald-headed actor who is unlucky enough to be needed in the "set-up." As the star is likely to be in very many scenes he has to be spared these exhausting periods of preparation. The stand-in is expected to be able to stand anything. He is chosen because he has some general resemblance to the star; and his costume has to look practically the same as that worn by the star. The reason for this is that the cameraman may not be misled; that the lighting effects, once arranged, may remain unchanged when the star takes the place of the stand-in.

The stand-in for the elderly star is a pathetic figure. More often than not he is an old actor who has played everything, but has "never had his chance." And now he is nothing — a shadow. And yet he feels within him a certain sense of importance. He is dressed like the star; he believes that he looks like the star; almost unconsciously he takes on the walk, or the mannerisms of the star; he poses like him before the cameraman, and he sees himself a star. I know what is going on in his brain as he watches me play the part; he knows that if only he had the chance he could do it just as well — better. He cannot understand why I do this or that, when obviously a much better way would be — the way he would do it.

Some day an author will write a good short story about the stand-in. He will probably show him coming home to his elderly wife. There, in his lodgings, he can be a star; is a star; there he tells the old lady all the gossip of the studio; tells her what the star said to him and what he said to the star. Gets up from his supper and shows her how the star did the scene, and then how *he* would have done it. And the old lady watches him with admiration and agrees that his way is much better. And then they talk of old times when *he* was leading man, and how he was done out of the job by some designing rival. And how his failure to get on has always been due to bad luck. And how other people have got their position through influence, and what *he* would have done if only he'd had half their chances. It could be made into a nice little short story. I need not tell the writers that when they adapt it for the screen they will introduce a daughter — who does a lot of sewing at home to bring grist to the mill; and who, one day, goes to the studio, for the first time, to take her father some beef tea, and is seen by the director, who gives her the leading part, and she becomes a star, and then the old father . . .

Yes, to me, the stand-in seems a pathetic figure, because of all the great crowd engaged for the picture he is the one solitary figure that is never seen by the audience: he is dressed up, made up, placed in the center of the stage, in the limelight — and never photographed.

When we were within a week or ten days of finishing "His Lordship" there came to me a bitter blow. For the first time in my picture career I had to "hold up the show." The doctor sent me to bed. Flo and I are not very dependent on doctors. When we are asked "Who is your doctor?" we are bound to confess that we haven't got one; which shows at once that we have no social standing; all people who have any pretensions to gentility have their doctor.

Of course there is Tony, who if I am not looking well at once insists upon my baring my breast, upon which he lays two fingers of his left hand in such a position that when struck with two fingers of his right hand a hollow sound is produced. And of course there is

303

Dr. Swanberg, who does still stranger things with his fingers applied to my outside, resulting in a complete cessation of trouble within. This manual dexterity has a queer name — "shalgreen" I think it is; a very clever sleight-of-hand trick which always puzzles me. But I have no real doctor — I mean a doctor who charges you properly and gives you something for your money, things to swallow night and morning and some terribly expensive serum that has already saved hundreds of thousands of lives, a fact of which there can be no doubt because there are the statistics telling of no end of people who have been injected with it and are still alive.

If, however, you are an important person in the movies, doctors are thrust upon you. The producing company has to be insured against loss in case of your absence through illness or death, and insurance companies stake their existence on the word of the doctor. At Shepherd's Bush, the doctor representing the insurance company had his office in the studio. Before each picture I had to undergo that unpleasant procedure of being "looked over" — a looking-over which always turned out to be a very complete examination. I had been pronounced sound in wind and limb when I started the picture, but later ran into one of those influenza seizures which I struggled against for some days, but which gradually developed with high fever and all complete; so the insurance people decided that the less expensive alternative was to delay the shooting and keep me alive.

It is not until you become an imminent liability to an insurance company that you find out what a really important person you are; you don't merely have a doctor, you have consultations. The morning after I had been sent home, rows of doctors filed into my rather small bedroom; it seemed like rows to me in my somewhat fevered state; in reality I don't think there were more than three at a time. At the head of the procession came the studio insurance doctor, whom I have already mentioned; then a doctor sent I believe by Gaumont-British; and finally the underwriters' doctor, whom I seem to remember as a rather lugubrious-looking man; Flo insisted upon calling him the undertaker's doctor, and it really did seem to me, when the three of them, after looking gravely at me, glided into my adjoining bathroom and closed the door for a secret conference, that the time they took was far too long to be devoted to discussing my symptoms, and that they must be talking over the funeral arrangements. These rather depressing consultations continued until Dr. Swanberg took a hand (in fact both hands), when I soon became well enough to be taken to St. Margaret's, where, of course, I rapidly got well. But it was three weeks from the time I left the studio to the day I got back to work; and I was a good deal relieved when I finished the picture without any further interruption.

My contract called for still another picture, but as there was no story ready for me, and as my physical condition was now looked upon with suspicion, it was decided that I had better take a holiday until next spring — 1937. I do not wish you to think that I agreed at once to this long vacation. I should not like my capacity for doing nothing to be fully realized by my faithful supporters. I had never had such a long holiday before, and deep down in my secret soul I knew that, if only I could

305

stifle my conscience, I should enjoy it. Flo insisted upon my going to St. Margaret's and staying there for at least six months. I was glad she did that, because it gave me an opportunity of making a stern resistance which I knew would be overruled. So we went to the heavenly seclusion of the cottage. It must not be supposed, however, that we could remain entirely unmolested. There were innumerable plays to read. Maude Howell was busy at the studio, going through possible stories for my next picture, and occasional conferences were required. Then I was called to the studio for an "added scene" to "His Lordship," a scene decided upon after the preview. These added scenes and retakes, which bring the cast together again long after everyone believes the picture to be finished, are rather ghostly occasions. It is difficult to recapture a character at a moment's notice when once you have said good-by to it, and allowed the spirit to go free. The members of the cast, too, whom you knew so well, now seem strange to you, except that you feel you have met them all before somewhere in the dim past.

Then there were more pleasant functions that drew us away from our retreat. When Grace and Edwin Hubble came from Pasadena, Edwin in a blaze of glory to give the Rhodes Memorial Lectures at the invitation of Oxford University — that was worth leaving St. Margaret's for. And our visit to Rhodes House before Edwin's lecture, — just the Hubbles and the Gore-Brownes and ourselves as the guests of Mr. and Mrs. Allen, who were so exceedingly kind and considerate, — that was something to remember. It amused me to watch Edwin trying to efface himself. I believe if he were not compelled to burst forth into public notice by the spontaneous combustion of his own achievements, he would be content to stay in Pasadena and just talk over the stars with Grace (who, he insists, knows as much about astronomy as he does) and remain unknown to the world. At the end of his lecture he was congratulated by all the great hooded and begowned professors, and when finally he broke away and I was able to express to him my great pleasure at the ovation that these important scientists had given him, he assured me that all they said was: "How marvelous of you to get George Arliss here with you. Congratulations! It's made you very popular with the students." By which you will realize that Edwin has quite my Uncle Charlie's sense of humor. Of course we had to take him and Grace to Broadway and introduce them to their illustrious compatriot Mary Anderson, whose son, Tony, is a professor at Cambridge, — of Prehistoric Archæology I think, — so Mamie is fully alive to the importance of any honor bestowed by the universities.

My theatrical friends naturally couldn't understand any actor of experience taking a long holiday that was not forced upon him. Great inducements were held out to me to do a London season. I should probably have allowed myself to be persuaded to make some revivals, but Flo put her foot down. I can be firm, but when Flo insists upon my not working, I am inclined to be weak.

I am not sure but what that perfect rest which we speak of in connection with St. Margaret's is rather a delusion. There is something doing the whole time. Distant sales to be attended; important debates with Flo as to where we are going to put the things, now that we have bought them; bridge with the Victor Smiths; bridge with the Vincent Sheeans — Vincent Sheean, that obscure and penniless author who married the beautiful Diana Forbes-Robertson, and, just as we who loved her were all getting ready to say "What a shame!" disappoints us by becoming very well-known and very well-off and very much liked by all of us. Plays quite good bridge too.

Sometimes Flo has to go and open a fête; there seem to be almost as many fêtes in the county of Kent as there are apple trees. And then there are our American week-end visitors, — the Montagues from Boston, the Millikens from New York, — Mrs. Milliken was Elsie Leslie, the original Little Lord Fauntleroy, and my first Clarissa in "Disraeli" when the play was produced in 1911. Sometimes there is Jeannette Gardner from St. Louis — a close friendship that started as a steamship acquaintanceship, one of the exceptions that I mentioned, when Mr. Gardner was Governor of Missouri and Jeannette was First Lady. That was twenty years ago. She is the loveliest white-haired lady that I have ever known. When we meet in London, or New York or Paris, Flo lets me walk out with Jeannette because it makes people talk, and Flo loves a bit of scandal.

Then, however fine the weather is, I have to go to London to the R.A.D.A. Council Meeting — that is, the Royal Academy of Dramatic Art, and later to a tremendous dinner when Kenneth Barnes, the Principal, goes and gets knighted and becomes Sir Kenneth — anybody with a name like that had to be knighted. Then Gordon Selfridge entertains some great American businessman and gives one of those Anglo-American dinners. And I sit next to H. G. Wells and we talk about wine and food and not a word about art, literature or the drama — which is a great relief to both of us. Gordon Selfridge is an ardent theatregoer and has shown me many little courtesies and kindnesses ever since 1923 when I played "The Green Goddess" in London. Then there is a reception at the American Embassy. And of course we make no attempt to resist the appeal of our much valued friends the Duchess of Hamilton and Miss Lind-af-Hageby when they ask us to open the Bazaar of the Animal Defence and Anti-Vivisection Society in St. James's Place. Flo and I have always been stanch Anti-Vivisectionists. Miss Lind is the founder of the society and one of the most convincing orators that it has ever been my good fortune to hear. The Duchess has that surprising capacity of being able to devote her entire life to the cause and yet never fail to be by the side of any one of her numerous family in case of emergency; and these emergencies appear to be frequent, because, whether the family need advice or first aid, they all seem to call for Mother.

So it will be seen that we were not allowed actually to vegetate at St. Margaret's. Furthermore it seemed as though I had selected a restless period through which to take my quiet holiday. An uneasiness was developing in Shepherd's Bush; it looked like another abdication; this time by the Ostrer Brothers. A farewell cocktail party was given to M. E. Balcon, who was leaving because the control of the Gaumont-British had passed into somebody else's hands. This at any rate was what I understood. I do not vouch for any of the information I got at this time except that there was what is known as a "shake-up" in the Gaumont-British Company. It turned out to be a very severe shake-up. A shake-up with the top of the shaker removed, so to speak; for by the time the shake-up was finished, there was nothing left inside. The studios were empty and Gaumont-British had ceased producing. Of course they had to complete certain contracts, one of which was mine. I had one more picture to make. Eventually I was passed over to a subsidiary company — the Gainsborough Pictures.

At the moment, however, it was fairly easy to see that there was a good deal of shaking-down to be done before conditions became really restful for me; so, as it was getting cold at St. Margaret's, Flo and I decided to go to Monte Carlo till called for. When we arrived there, we found many friends — Margaret Miller and Mrs. Anley, both very beautiful, both bridge experts and both very gentle with us when we displayed our ignorance; and Hamilton Revelle (who looks about forty and who played a leading part with me in "The Devil" in 1908), ready and willing to show us all the beauty spots within a fifty-mile radius; and Lady Sherston-Baker, eager to teach us an infallible system at the tables, and to give us certainties for the races; and of course all the lively dead ones that I've already alluded to. I now discovered that although you may flee from London, — though you may be leading the gay life at Monte Carlo, — you cannot escape the accusing finger of the underwriter. Gainsborough Pictures was evidently taking the first step in preparation for my next picture. Came a letter directing me to go to a certain address in Monte Carlo where a physician would look me over and report on me. This was not a pleasant interlude in the gay life. Who knows, a Monte Carlo doctor might find distressing symptoms that English doctors, when they looked me over, had overlooked. I am sure Dr. Mitchell was expecting an interesting patient and was rather shocked when I walked into his office looking very healthy. However, I had been sent to him for inspection, so he unwrapped me, looked inside me, weighed me, measured me, wrapped me up again and sent me away with a twelve months' guarantee, or whatever doctors give to underwriters.

About this time Rufus LeMaire arrived in London from Hollywood and began to telephone me. Rufus always telephoned, irrespective of time, space or expense. And when Rufus once starts telephoning there is no more peace. So Flo and I bowed to the inevitable and I went back to work — to Islington.

It does seem extraordinary to find a studio at Islington. I thought Shepherd's Bush as a district to choose for making pictures was unbelievable; but Islington is the limit. Once inside the studio, however, I was greatly surprised. There is a pleasant feeling of domesticity — as of a completely furnished house very well run. Edward Black was a further surprise. He is so entirely unlike a movie boss: he doesn't seem to interfere with anyone. It is only by degrees you find out that he has everything under his hand and that he really directs the movements of every department. He is very like a mere businessman, one who believes that it is of no use to lay in a stock of goods that can never produce any return; and that the making of canned pictures should be controlled with the same care as the preparation of any other canned goods intended for public consumption. Unless I am much mistaken, Edward Black is going to show us how pictures made in England can be made to pay.

I have spared you the details of the number of plays and stories that I had read and declined, and of the amount of research work carried on at the studio during the days that I spent in riotous living in Monte Carlo. Suffice it to say that we eventually decided on "Dr. Syn." It had no plus value but it was entertaining and one of Russell Thorndike's best-sellers. It had for me a special appeal because the story was laid in my beloved Kent.

You might think that the insurance people would have been content with my report from Monte Carlo, but evidently they didn't think it possible that anyone could be as healthy as Dr. Mitchell pronounced me, so the "undertaker's doctor" had it all done to me again. He also refused to allow Herbert Mason to direct because Mrs. Herbert Mason had German measles. It is quite obvious that you can't get anything out of an insurance company without suffering for it. So Roy Neil took Herbert Mason's place as director and we finally started to shoot "Dr. Syn."

CAST

His Lordship

Richard Fraser Lorimer, Lord Duncaster	GEORGE ARLISS
Bill Howard . . .	ROMILLY LUNGE
Vera Norton . .	RENEE RAY
Gertrude, Lady Duncaster . . .	JESSIE WINTER
Ibrahim . . .	JOHN FORD
Barak	ALLAN JEAYES
Nahal	LAWRENCE ANDERSON
Artist	BERNARD VEREFIELD
Prime Minister . .	JOHN TURNBULL
Abdullah . . .	BASIL GILL
Selim	ALEXANDER SARNER
Servant . . .	ALAN MOWBRAY
Native Guard . .	HENRY MORRILL

༜

Director . . .	HERBERT MASON
Author . . .	NEIL GRANT
Screen Play . . .	L. DuGARDE PEACH AND MAUDE T. HOWELL
Camera . . .	E. KRAMPF

CAST

Dr. Syn

Dr. Syn	GEORGE ARLISS
Imogene	MARGARET LOCKWOOD
Denis Crabtree . . .	JOHN LODER
Captain	ROY EMERTON
Jerry	GRAHAM MOFFATT
Rast	FREDERICK BURTWELL
Mipps	GEORGE MERRITT
Squire Sir Anthony Crab-tree	ATHOLE STEWART
Dr. Pepper	WILSON COLEMAN
Bo'sun	WALLY PATCH
Mulatto	MEINHART MEINER
Mrs. Waggetts . . .	MURIEL GEORGE
Townsman of Rye . .	ALAN TROTTER

ༀ

Director	ROY NEIL
Author	RUSSELL THORNDIKE
Screen Play . . .	ROGER BURFORD
Associate Director . .	MAUDE T. HOWELL
Camera	JACK FOX

Chapter 19

I THINK I have pointed out that when once work begins in the studio, nothing that happens in the outside
world is of any relative importance. But however much
you love your art and however much you may be in
Islington you cannot remain entirely unaware of a
Coronation taking place in Westminster Abbey.

May 12th, 1937. I don't know whether there is any
country in the world as loyal as England. Anyone who
was in London on this Coronation Day would, I think,
be led to doubt it. The courage of this younger brother
in shouldering the responsibilities thrust upon him, and
the attractive personality of the little Scotch lady who
was to be Queen, at once gained the admiration and affection of the British people. London was hemmed in
with towering flagstaffs and grandstands, all flaming
with crimson and gold; and with stands that were not
so grand; and with shabby stands that were cheaper
because nothing could be seen from them. It was a
public holiday and everyone was out for a wild and
hilarious time.

I was a very superior person on that day. I had a
seat in the Abbey; and I had my photograph taken at
six-fifteen in the morning — that alone is an experi-

ence of which very few people can boast, even movie actors. The precise reason for the several gentlemen arriving at our house with their apparatus at 6 A.M. and taking my portrait and going away again, I can't remember; whether it was a spontaneous effort by the public press, or a deep-laid plan of the private press agent for Gainsborough Pictures, I cannot say. I think it was probably Edward Black. I never saw the photo but I am sure I must have made a picture any mother would be proud of — in my stockings and knickerbockers — that is, my breeches you know, and buckled shoes and sword.

I don't wish to brag, but I assure you it takes a good actor to dress up in his own bedroom and look like anything at six in the morning; what you have to do is to forget time and think only of the occasion. As I buckled on my sword at five-thirty, and prepared to say farewell to my wife, I remembered that I had seen magnificent steel engravings of cavaliers doing this, and I felt important. Flo had had an invitation from Bill Adams, bearing the address "Buckingham Palace" (no less), but she decided to stay at home with Sadie Thompson. Nevertheless, Flo loves royalty; I don't know anybody anywhere more loyal than Flo; but she also has a very great belief in sandwiches when she is sending me off on any prolonged expedition. I had to be in my seat in the Abbey by 8 A.M.; the ceremony would not be over till two to two-thirty, and we had been warned that there would be delay in leaving. Of course no food could be got there. In America there would probably have been a welcoming hot dog stand within reach. But this was Westminster Abbey, into which no dog, hot or cold,

316

dead or alive, even if consumed on the premises, would ever be allowed to enter.

Before leaving my bedroom, I glanced at my reflection in the mirror — very stately! And when Flo brought me some sandwiches wrapped in grease-proof paper, I was quite ashamed of her. Here was I, all in black velvet and glittering steel buttons — and Flo holding out a sandwich package to me. I flushed. Flo observed this emotion, and said severely, "Never mind. You take it." I hesitated. Flo said: "You'll be glad enough of them later on. Take them with you and eat them." It was evident that Flo had not grasped the solemnity of the occasion. I said (perhaps a trifle loftily) : "But suppose the King — " "Never mind the King. You eat them when you're hungry." There are certain tones, conveying a command, which Sadie Thompson and I have learned to obey without further resistance.

But really, you know, how is one to carry a package of sandwiches? Where is one to put it? You recall those court costumes, the tight-fitting breeches, and tight waistcoat, and the coat made with that uncomfortable degree of tightness that tailors, for some unaccountable reason, call "snug." Even the handkerchief has to be carried up the sleeve to avoid corrupting the curves. Without admitting my argument against the sandwiches to be insuperable, Flo had to allow that it was sound. Then with that quick deliberation that has so often rescued me in times of crisis, she said, "The Cloak." I had quite forgotten that of course I was wearing a cloak. That settled it; particularly as the cloak was as ample as the coat was snug; it was one of those cloaks with a hood to it that you dress up in when you go to receive an Honorary Degree. The question as to which spot on the cloak to fix the sandwiches to was at once settled by Flo who produced a large safety-pin and pinned the package in the hood. This was really an inspiration; the hood formed a pocket and was big enough to take food for a family of three if necessary; mine was a fairly large packet of sandwiches but it could lie there undisturbed.

So now I had had my photograph taken and the men had gone and my car was at the door, and I had everything — my white kid gloves, my hat under my arm; as a matter of fact I was quite at home in my costume, having worn it hundreds of times in various plays. I had probably worn court costume many more times than any of the real people who appeared in their regalia only on state occasions. I was therefore not afraid of tripping over my sword or any such undignified and humorous performance. After I had put on my cloak, and Flo had given me a reassuring wave, which meant "The sandwiches don't show a bit," I lay back in my car with easy grace. The traffic regulations required that we stick on the car window a large sign, provided for the purpose, to show that we were bound for the Abbey. My card of invitation gave a plan of a specific route to be followed, and this route was open only to carriages going to the Abbey. Every road in London is familiar to me, but these streets seemed strange this morning. Not yet seven o'clock; a stream of carriages carrying men and women, all the nobility of Great Britain, in their magnificent robes of crimson and ermine, tiaras and coronets. I am bound to confess that the nobility were not sitting back with easy grace;

their coronets were bobbing about; nobody was looking very happy or good-tempered, having been up since goodness knows when. I was a lone figure in a black cloak, but all the carriages around me were a blaze of color and literally groaning under the weight of regal paraphernalia and family trees. The streets through which we passed were bare of pedestrians, because everyone was taking up a position on the route to be followed by the royal procession, which was not our route; so except for the moving carriages with their precious burdens, the road was strangely quiet. We had to go through the West End; past the houses of the rich; now and then there were little groups of servants from below stairs, straining their eyes to see inside the carriages, but looking weary and rather dispirited on finding that the figures in one car looked exactly like the figures in the next, that all the lords looked alike today. And this is where I made history. In two hundred years' time, historians like Godfrey will record that I, on the day of the Coronation of George VI — that I got the first cheer from the British populace; not the Prime Minister, not the Lord Chancellor, not the premier duke of the realm, but I! The groups of servants at their area railings, or gathered together at the corner of the street, were eager for diversion. The Prime Minister, the Lord Chamberlain, the premier duke of the realm had no doubt all rolled by unrecognized in their royal disguises. I have already mentioned that I was gracefully sitting back in my car: suddenly I was impelled by some unseen agency to lean forward; the maids and the men grouped round the area steps, who had been long waiting for something to thrill them but had given up hope, at once came to life; here, in the midst of all this dross, was a movie actor! Could it be? — Yes, it was — No it ain't — It is, though — "Good old George Arliss! Well I'm blowed!" And there came a cheer that shook the British aristocracy to its very foundations. I was very much surprised at this outburst. I really did not foresee it or make a bid for it, but, it having come once, I tried it again, and continued to play up for it until we arrived at the Abbey. It brightened the corners for my faithful subjects and for me.

I have never before seen a Protestant place of worship look really gay, but Westminster Abbey, on this day, had an air of actual festivity. Just how it was done I don't remember, but by the skillful arrangement of flags and colored materials the place was entirely relieved of that chilly atmosphere that you have to endure when you are invited to a wedding at the Abbey. I am not going to attempt to give an account of the ceremony, which is perhaps just as well, because from where I sat I couldn't see it. As a matter of fact the proportion of places from which the actual ceremony could be seen was very limited, and those places were quite rightly allotted to the elite. But I could see the entire procession as it swept along the aisle. I have said that the peers and peeresses looked uneasy in their carriages, but they certainly pulled themselves together for the ceremony. The women looked charming and graceful and carried their robes as though they wore them every day.

I should be forgiven for looking at this whole pageant through the eye of the theatre, but knowing the difficulties of carrying unaccustomed costumes, I was bound to admire the way our British nobility held themselves. I confess I was sorry that the peers ever had to wear their coronets; they arrive and walk up the aisle without them, but during the ceremony, at a given moment, they all have to put them on and wear them for the procession which follows the Coronation. There were very few who were able to maintain their dignified appearance when once they had put on these headpieces. The King and Queen with their crowns got away with it with flying colors, but the peers were not equally successful. As they walked up the aisle bareheaded they looked like noble lords. Coming back they nearly all looked like amateur actors — and you know how funny they can look as kings and courtiers.

I am afraid that honesty compels me to recount a slight incident which to some extent robbed me of my own accustomed dignity. My seat was in a balcony; there was a tier above me and a tier below — quite a long way below, well below the level of my feet. Immediately in front of me, in the row below, was the largest and heaviest man I have ever seen outside a show. It didn't matter to me how large he was, because I was so far above that my view was quite unobscured even when we got on our feet to applaud, which everyone did when a member of the Royal Family passed in the procession; but I couldn't help noticing how large he was.

The first procession, that preceding the arrival of the King and Queen, was the thrilling one, because then we were seeing everyone, and all the magnificent coloring, for the first time. I sat with my sword properly bestowed, having taken off my cloak and placed it across my knees. There was a quiet little man on my right, covered with most amazing orders, and a thin, ascetic-looking man on my left with no orders at all. We had risen several times as members of the Royal Family passed, and each time I got up I had to clap my hands and prevent my cloak from falling down both at the same time. Then came Queen Mary, who was easily the star turn. She looked not merely beautiful (in blue and silver), but an ideal Queen; and with her the two little Princesses; the elder one with all the consciousness of her coming responsibilities, the younger one intent on remembering the directions that had been given her before she left home which were, obviously, "Keep up with your sister, and for goodness' sake don't turn your toes in." We all stood up; I applauded wildly; the fact that on two occasions I had had the privilege of a short conversation with Her Majesty gave me a feeling of close personal acquaintanceship with her. You have only to meet very important people twice to feel that you know them intimately — so long as they remain important. Everybody was standing and everybody was applauding. But through the applause I heard an odd, incongruous noise that sounded like *"Plomp"* and I was conscious that something had happened in the region of my cloak. I looked down and there, in the middle of the seat, very temporarily vacated by the large gentleman below, was my packet of sandwiches. A great revulsion of feeling swept over me. Those sandwiches, which I had once treated with contempt, I suddenly cared for tremendously. I already felt the pangs of hunger. And there they were, well out of my reach, and threatened with destruction. With everybody applauding Queen Mary I couldn't lean over and hit the man on the shoulder and say, "Excuse me, don't sit on my sandwiches." Besides, Queen Mary was a friend of mine; it would be disrespectful. But the applause was weakening; Queen Mary was passing by. Thirty seconds more and it would be too late; once he sat on my sandwiches, all would be over. If the people in the balcony behind me had known what was passing in my mind they would have thought I had decided on suicide, for I suddenly took a high dive and disappeared from sight. Nobody screamed. All eyes must have been, mercifully, on Queen Mary. I had taken a terrific chance and had trusted to luck; with one hand I held on to the balcony, and, head downwards and with superhuman stretching, I rescued my sandwiches. A second after, the fat man sat down, unaware that he had nearly been the cause of a Tragic Incident in Westminster Abbey. In the presence of Royalty I suppose the body becomes supple, for in that second I had been able to swing myself back to normalcy. A thrilling scene that would have been the making of a movie, and nobody had seen it! Although in that second I had safely reversed my body to a sitting position, I had had no time to hide the fruits of my daring. Greaseproof paper is no disguise for sandwiches: I caught the eye of the man on my right and in it I saw the lust for food; I turned away from him quickly, lest I should weaken, and caught the eye of the man on my left as it rested on my grease-proof paper. I realized that resistance was useless and I shared with them my elusive sandwiches. They evidently had no Flo to tend the inner man.

Between 2 and 2:30 P.M. the ceremony was over: the King and Queen had left, the tension was broken, and there was a general relaxed feeling, particularly in the region of the stomach. I think mine were the only sandwiches in the Abbey — and blessed sandwiches they were — and now that the show was over there was nothing for anyone to think about but food. Through a megaphone a commanding voice gave forth instructions that nobody was to leave until the number of his section was called. When you arrived at the Abbey your car was sent to a parking place bearing the number of your section. When the ceremony was over your section was told to leave as soon as your turn came and the cars bearing the number of that section were called by telephone. This looked to me like a long job. There was an usher for every section — tremendous toffs the ushers were, each one the scion of a noble house — so I asked ours what time he thought our cars would be called; he said he was afraid it might be five o'clock or so. Three hours to sit there doing nothing, and all the excitement over! I asked if it wasn't possible for us to go without our cars. He said he was afraid not; he was afraid nobody would be allowed to go without his car. For the next half-hour everybody in the Abbey remained glued to his seat. Then the megaphone announced that those peers and peeresses who were due to lunch — somewhere, I think it was the House of Lords — would now leave. A number of happy lords and ladies rose. It seemed to me that this clearing business was being badly managed. I should have been willing to obey the rules, but I objected to being the victim of bad management. Besides, my third of the sandwiches was wearing off. I sulked. I thought, "Suppose I had a maiden aunt who depended on me to make her a cup of tea every afternoon at four; why should I

324

have to sit here, knowing that she is pining for me?" I got up and spoke once more to the usher. I said, "Suppose a man — " (I had evidently worked myself up into a hypothetical condition) "Suppose a man had important business, wouldn't he be allowed to go?" The usher said he was afraid not. I said, "Suppose a gentleman fainted, is there no place to which they might carry him and revive him?" He said he was afraid he didn't know, but there might be. I went back and collected my hat and my cloak (the safety-pin was still firmly attached — the sandwiches had slipped out at the side). The men on the right and left of me asked me longingly where I was going. I said I felt faint, which they didn't believe. I had to pass the usher; he asked me where I was going. I said I felt faint, which he didn't believe, but he had no proof and he couldn't leave his post. So I passed through the door and down some steps, and was, as I had hoped, in time to join the peers and peeresses. I could not look like a peer, because my inky cloak betrayed me, but I meant to get out. We all trailed along a temporary covered-way made of canvas; at the end of the covered-way the lords' cars were arriving, each one called by name and each lord bundled in — an interminable business. It had now started to rain, and the canvas flapped; when it flapped, it flapped open, and through one of these openings I darted out. There wasn't a taxi to be had and it was now pouring with rain; but what did I care? I had had a wonderful time, but I was tired of Abbeys and welcomed the streets. I walked to Victoria and took a station cab, and was home by a quarter to four — just in time to get my

325

hypothetical aunt her cup of tea. My chauffeur got his call at the parking place at eight-fifteen. I complained to Flo about the behavior of the sandwiches; she said, "Well, why didn't you eat them before they fell out?" Flo has a very practical mind.

Chapter 20

"DR. SYN" was finished without further interruption. And that is my last picture up to the time of going to press. Maude Howell went back to her native California, for a much needed rest; she had worked with me without a break for more than two years. I said good-by with much regret to the friends I had made in the Islington studio, including Edward Black, who had always been patient with me and considerate; to my director, Roy Neil, and to all those in the executive departments. . . . Some day I should like to give an expensive dinner, in honor of all the writers that have written for me since I came into pictures — that is, during the past ten years — and make it up with them. I should like to assure them that had I been a reader and not an actor I should have had great admiration for their work and should have passed it without change. Indeed, had it been for any other actor I should perhaps have seen no reason to alter it. I should like to give this expensive dinner and invite the writers. But would they come?

Looking through my ten years in the studios, certain disjointed thoughts come to me in connection with the general development of pictures.

It was not so very long ago that the films and the

legitimate theatre appealed each to its own separate audience. The theatre audience shuddered at the word "cinema" and almost swooned at the term "movies." The movie audience regarded the theatre as slow and old-fashioned. The two audiences are now almost entirely merged into one. This has come about largely because the talking pictures are becoming more and more closely allied to the legitimate theatre owing to the continuous improvement in production made by the great studios. It seems almost inconceivable that talking pictures as a popular entertainment have existed for little more than ten years. Is it any wonder that there are still certain crudities and that we have not yet developed the perfect article?

The silent picture was really a more consistent production than the talking picture of today. Its complete silence removed it from any actual competition with the legitimate theatre, and it allowed in some ways greater scope for the ingenuity of the director. You may remember that scraps of dialogue — "titles" they were called — had to be thrown on the screen to explain the plot or to clarify the meaning of the emotions being expressed by the actors. A good director always endeavored to have as few of these titles as possible because they halted the action of the story, inasmuch as time had to be allowed for the audience to read them. The director was therefore always seeking some way, a look, a gesture, or a piece of business, by which the actor could give information to the audience without words.

One has only to watch the facial expression of the inimitable Charlie Chaplin to see how much can be conveyed by a glance, by the sagging of the shoulders or the movement of a hand — more eloquent than any words. These methods of condensation have had their influence not only on the talking pictures but also on the legitimate theatre, and on the audience of today. The long-drawn-out dialogue that can be found in many society plays of thirty or forty years ago, between the butler and the maid, is considered almost unendurable by present-day audiences. That was a means of conveying information that came with the disallowing of the soliloquy. In my opinion, there is much to be said in favor of the soliloquy. In half a dozen lines the hero can explain as he gazes at the old homestead that it is twenty years since he saw it last, during which time his dear old father and mother have passed away, leaving the property etc. — and the way is cleared for the vital development of the story to follow. The pictures, however, have quickened the perception of the people who go to the theatre, and today the audience will catch in a few words explanations that with the passing of the soliloquy had to be hammered in by heavy dialogue. If the screen has quickened the perception of the audience, it may also have had its influence on the actor.

On the stage, I mean in the legitimate theatre, the acting dominates, or should dominate, the scene. On the screen the human and mechanical effort must blend to perfection. The lights must strike the exact spot, almost to the fraction of an inch; the microphone must be so placed that you may get perfect registration, and everything must work together with the greatest precision. Words must come clearly and without hesitation. On the stage, an actor may cover a fault with some piece of business; a momentary lapse of memory may

329

pass unobserved by an audience. But the camera does not permit any such straying from the path of virtue. The slightest slip is at once registered by that all-seeing eye. It is of no use for the actor to pretend it was a natural pause — the camera has caught that fleeting expression of agony in his eye which at once exposes him as a delinquent. And the camera has no secrets from the audience. On the stage, an actor can assume deep thought and walk across the stage and do some clever piece of business while he waits for the prompter to give him the word. But he can't do that sort of thing on the screen; the lights are placed for him to do a specific thing in a given spot, and if he fails to do exactly what the camera expects of him, he is found out. Sometimes, when the actor is giving a perfect performance, a fly comes gaily into the picture and settles on the actor's nose. On the stage a fly can often be brushed away unnoticed, but on the screen it immediately assumes the importance of a new character in the play. Again, all may be well with the actor, but at the end of a scene it is found that the camera was not running with perfect precision. Then the camera and the actor may behave perfectly, but the microphone for some unaccountable reason is displaying temperament.

Once when I was making a picture a fly settled on the microphone and ruined the scene. In the event of any one of these misfortunes the entire scene must be taken again. The stage actor in his early days of picture-making tears his hair when he finds that after he has given a particularly good performance of a scene, something was wrong with the mechanics, and that he has to do it all over again. But as time goes on he accepts these conditions without a murmur. No pains are spared to get perfect results from the camera. Three or four years ago a number of cameras would be used, placed so that each one took a different angle, and so, with one performance of a scene, as many as four different aspects were photographed. But as the increasing importance of lighting effects became recognized, it was seen that the lights which were good for one angle were likely to be badly placed for another. So now the scene is usually repeated by the actor many times in order that each angle may be specially lighted to get the full value of the picture. Then there is the necessity of taking the scenes at various distances. There is what is known as the long-shot — used to establish the full scene, or to give scope for broad action. There is the medium-shot, which allows a group of people to be seen more intimately, and closer shots for two people. Then we get to the close-up, which is used to emphasize important reactions on the characters. There are moving shots, which allow the actors to be seen walking and talking. You will notice that in two-shots — that is, the shot that shows two people — the camera shifts from the face of one character to the face of the other. The audience is given a fair and satisfactory view of each figure as its turn comes to speak or to register facial expression. So the whole scene is taken twice; first with the camera focused throughout on the one character, and then repeated with the camera focused on the other. The film of both these shots is eventually manipulated by the cutter, whose business it is to select the right moment to switch from one character to the other — to cut back to a long shot or to accentuate a

331

point by a close-up in order to gain the best results.

The cutter is in a very responsible position. It can hardly be said that he can make a bad picture appear good, but he can destroy a good scene by lack of appreciation of its possibilities or a full understanding of its meaning. All pictures are made too long to start with. The average length, when shown on the screen, is an hour and twenty minutes. Some pictures, if shown before cutting, would run twice that time. I believe the majority are fully half-an-hour too long when they are first put together. The responsibility for cutting is shared by the director and the cutter, and often some higher officials of the studio take a hand, but as a rule it is left very much to the professional cutter, who is often amazingly clever in eliminating unnecessary scenes. It is generally admitted that any scene that can be taken out, without interfering with the story, *should* be taken out if its elimination does not influence its production value.

Speed is the watchword of most makers of pictures: speed and action — that is what the cutter has to work for. If he's a bad workman he often cuts out scenes that should be left in. When we see films that throw us into a state of mental confusion as to where the characters are, or how they suddenly got there, and why, we may be reasonably sure that it is the fault of the cutter. Speed at any price is what he is after. I am bound to say that the other extreme is almost as maddening.

Up to a few years ago the English producers were very rightly criticized by America for being too leisurely. Just as the American talkies suffered at first by the direction of those who had grown up in the silent pictures, so the English talkies were often impaired by being directed by stage managers whose experience had been gained entirely in the legitimate theatre. On the stage the actor has to be got on and off; that is a necessary condition to which the audience adjusts itself. The actor can say good-by to his hostess, walk up to some piece of furniture where he has placed his hat and gloves, walk over to the door, open it, and shut the door after him, and the audience remains perfectly patient. But on the screen such action would seem interminable; so when the actor in the movies says good-by to his hostess and he leaves the picture, the camera remains a moment on the hostess, and then switches to the departing guest at the door as he is leaving. Everything in the picture must be speeded-up. We see a man writing a telegram to his father, and immediately cut to the father receiving it.

In my first days in the talking pictures I begged them not to make close-ups of me and not to break up a scene by switching from one character to another, and not to cut a well-written scene, even though it was long. I pointed out to them that now we had the spoken word on the screen the audience necessarily had to listen, and that if they would listen to a good scene in the theatre, there was no reason why they should not listen to it on the screen; that if there was literature for the theatre there should be the same literature for the screen. Their answer to me was, "They'll never stand it." My argument appeared to me a fairly good one, but with my riper experience I have to admit that it was not as good as it seemed. The same audience that will listen to a long scene, without action, in the theatre, becomes restless in the cinema.

I wish I could believe that we shall be able to see on the screen the plays of Shakespeare spoken as they are spoken on the stage, with all their magnificent soliloquies, or the old comedies in their delightful original state. But I do not believe we shall, and if you ask me why, I am afraid I shall have to answer, "They'll never stand it." I have frequently asked myself why they won't stand it, and I have come to the conclusion that it has nothing to do with any lack of intelligence on the part of the audience. I think it is a purely physical condition.

Why is it that long dialogues which we listen to with interest on the stage seem interminable on the screen? The only reason that I can find is that in the theatre, although our attention is mainly upon the actors, our vision is taking in a wide stage on which we see perhaps a window with a view of a beautiful garden beyond — color, furniture, or other background. Our eyes perhaps stray to a door, through which we expect another character to appear; at any rate, we are seeing an entire room or an entire stage on which the characters are placed. On the screen during this same dialogue our vision is concentrated on two figures only; we are watching, without any scenic distraction, just these two figures — first one and then the other is forced upon us, until there comes a natural desire for relief from the intense concentration. This theory is more or less borne out by the fact that all pauses in speech, such as are used for giving point or effect to lines or situations, seem twice as long on the screen as they do on the stage; for the screen they have to be closed up to about one half. This, again, I can only suppose is because in long dialogues the camera picks out the character and to a large extent eliminates his

334

setting. The physical conditions of the picture palaces make this accentuation of the characters advisable, if not necessary. The auditorium is frequently so vast that, if we did not have some close-ups, the audience would lose to a great extent the facial expression of the actor.

If we are compelled to admit that we can never have on the screen the full literary value of a great dramatist, as we have it in the theatre, it brings us to the consideration of whether the screen has been a good thing for the drama — or the reverse. To arrive at a fair conclusion on this question we must once more examine the state of the theatre in relation to the contemporary drama at the time that the silent pictures made a bid for competition. At that time I did not know the American stage, but I knew all the London and provincial theatres of England. The West End theatres of London were producing plays by the best British and foreign authors. But in the East End and on the Surrey side and in almost every provincial town the entertainment for the most part was just pure blood-and-thunder, machine-made plays performed by machine-made actors. At the Elephant & Castle Theatre we put on a different drama each week. There was a dramatist attached to the theatre who was engaged all the year round at a weekly salary. He got thirty shillings a week, and was expected to doctor up old plays and to turn out a new and original one for Bank Holidays and other special occasions. For each original play he wrote he got, I believe, an extra two-pounds-ten an act. The thirty shillings a week was to keep him alive, and the extra two-pounds-ten an act was a special reward for original inspiration. Needless to say, his original plays were always in five acts. They were quite good of their kind. Many of them were really worth more than he got for them. But they were not elevating. They did nothing for the theatre but keep it at a low level of intelligence.

I do not wish to suggest that the theatre should necessarily elevate, but I am strongly of opinion that it should not debase. It was this type of play that was being performed week after week, with few exceptions, in hundreds of theatres in the provinces. These plays were seldom vulgar; they were, in fact, distressingly moral, but were always artificial.

There was invariably the type of villain for whom I have already admitted my admiration, and of course there was always the protecting hero. I played one of these heroes in a drama called "Just in Time" — an apt but too descriptive title. I was always just in time to save the lady. The audiences in these provincial theatres were in a measure part of the entertainment, and they thoroughly enjoyed their share. They knew just when they were expected to applaud and when to laugh, and they responded with great loyalty. They knew their cues because the actor practically pointed them out. When my part was handed to me, for instance, in "Just in Time," I saw that innumerable speeches were underlined with red ink. I asked what that meant, and was told by my manager that those were rounds of applause. The actor told the audience when he wished them to applaud by giving an upward or downward inflection at the end of a speech — not subtly, but boldly and blatantly; a further method of giving them their cue was by an unmistakable gesture of the arms, or by the banging of the fist. The actor never failed to get a round of applause on his exit if he opened the door by striking it vigorously with his forearm and going off quickly. This was easy of accomplishment because there were no handles on the doors in our scenery: they opened by being pushed, and remained open until they were gently coaxed back by an invisible stage hand from without.

I have gone into these details because what I have described is, without exaggeration, the type of entertainment that was being offered by the theatre all over Great Britain — outside the West End of London. There were some exceptions, but this was the backbone of the English provincial stage.

Then came the silent picture. It supplied all the blood and all the thunder of the theatrical entertainment. It brought a new atmosphere — the open spaces of Western America, and cowboy adventures. It at once appealed to the taste of an audience that had never asked for subtlety and never got it. No effort was made by the old theatre managers to compete with the invasion. Large and comfortable picture houses were built and lower prices charged for admission, but the old temples of the drama still remained dirty and neglected, and gradually the spoken drama of the English provinces was almost entirely silenced. The living theatres in the smaller towns were swept away, and even large cities that had for years supported three or four theatres offered nothing but pictures. That was what the silent pictures did for the theatre. Then came the talkies with their million-dollar productions, and that seemed like the death blow to the British stage. But the unexpected happened. The human element began to exert itself. Groups of people throughout the country

337

became hungry for the legitimate theatre. As there was none within reach, they formed themselves into amateur theatrical societies and gave their own performances. This revival of interest gave courage to professional actors, and by degrees innumerable repertory companies were established and began to strive for something better. Unknown authors found an outlet for their work, and young actors were able to gain experience.

That is what happened in England. The effect of the pictures in America was almost identical: the disappearance of the blood-and-thunder theatres; the passing of the "ten-twenty-thirties," — the ascendancy of the pictures, — the killing of the road shows; the desire for a return of the living theatre and the gradual rise of independent companies. The theatre can never die.

If the subject matter of plays today has closer relationship to human life than it had twenty years ago, I believe it is due to the fact that the movies took over the blood-and-thunder and compelled the theatre to cater for a public that was ready to welcome something less conventional.

It is only right that having paid for your seat in the cinema, you should be critical of the pictures offered you. But also it is only fair that you should consider the difficulties of the producers. You sometimes come away from the cinema feeling very resentful and saying, "A wasted evening." But do you stop to consider the enormous number of stories that have to be invented and written in the course of a year to supply the demands of the millions of movie-goers? Compare

338

this output with the number of plays that are required to supply the regular theatre. Cinemas demand continual change: they must be fed regularly or cease to exist. Producers agree to supply a given number of pictures during the year, and they have to live up to their contract. Frankly, it is impossible to find a sufficient number of good stories. Any star will admit that he often has to accept something second-rate because it has not been possible to find anything within the required time that he considers really worth doing. The producer can only do his best with what he can get. Stories have to be written; even if they grew on trees, I doubt whether the plantation could have matured as quickly as the crop of movie-houses has grown.

I believe that the people who are most contemptuous of the movies are those who most seldom go to see them. If one really made a critical examination of the pictures which are produced, one would, I think, be surprised to find how many good ones there are. The difficulty is that the desire for pictures as entertainment has grown too rapidly. It has taken the place of many of the home occupations that once used to engage the rising generation. I do not know how many families today gather round their mother's knee to hear Charles Dickens read aloud; not many, I think. Wool mats are no longer made, and I know very few girls who are learning to play the piano. But in a year there are hundreds of millions of admissions paid to the British and American cinemas alone. I do not offer any opinion as to whether this change is good or bad for the youth of today, but it is one of the factors that has necessitated the output

339

of more pictures than it is possible to produce without sometimes descending to a lower level than is desirable.

People who like me have said that my pictures are always "worth while." I do not make this claim. For reasons I have explained, I have sometimes had to accept what I believed to be in the second class. I claim, however, that I have always given the greatest care to the consideration of form in my stories — what I may describe as a beginning, a middle, and an end. My conviction has always been that, although an author should be aware of the intelligence of his audience, he should nevertheless tell them exactly what he means to convey, and not resort to the slovenly method of leaving them to guess. If he knows what he means, let him say it. I resent those dramatists who make a reputation for cleverness by writing of deep subjects and never getting below the surface; who suggest a great reserve of intelligence by asking questions and never answering them.

Having, in this book, taken you into my confidence, I hope you will not, in future, be too severe about the films. Be gentle with us. Remember that we are all doing our best and trying very hard to please you. A great amount of thought and labor has gone into every picture you see. If that effort has been misdirected, it is our misfortune and not our fault.

I am looking for a story that I believe to be worth doing, and one that I think will please you. How long it will take me to find it, I cannot say. But if you do not hear of me for a year or two, don't all say: "He must be dead." I may be resting; I may be loafing. I may have taken Flo to China — Flo has always wanted to go to China.

Or I may be at St. Margaret's, at the bottom of the garden, amongst the pines, thinking.

THE END

Index

343

Arliss, George —(*Continued*)
duction value, 127–131; on expenses, 130–131; on actors' salaries, 131–132; returns to New York, 134–135; 136; on picking casts, 137–142; incidents during filming of "The Millionaire," 142–143; on writing memoirs, 143–146; on treatment of stars, 144–145; trip to Carlsbad Caverns and Grand Canyon, 148–152; meets the Kelloggs, 150; establishes rights to "Alexander Hamilton," 153–154; receives medal for "Disraeli," 156; receives award from American Academy of Arts and Letters, 156–157; acceptance speech, 157–160; 162; contemplates return to stage, 163; returns to England (1931), 163; at St. Margaret's, 164; on dogs, 165–169; on domestic details, 171–176; and use of lipreader to play on screen, 177–178; on movie conferences, 181; describes Darryl Zanuck, 182–188; on propaganda, 189; fan mail, 189–191; 192; between pictures, 193–196; "the public's the thing," 197–199; returns to England, 200; on Voltaire, 204–205; and Ben Silvey, 211–214; 216–219; on 1933 bank holiday, 220; on earthquakes in California, 221; returns to England on *Bremen*, 223; protests from Jews, 223–225; on vicissitudes of acting, 226–229; on Hollywood business methods, 229–231; decides in favor of "The Iron Duke," 240; letters from Mrs. Muriel A. Goodchild, 241–243; misses criticisms of Zanuck and Howell, 244; describes people in London, 245–250; at Gaumont-British, 236–259; at Colonel E. M. House, 251–256; correspondence with House, 253, 254–255; serves on Prince George Wedding Fund, 257; returns to United States to make "Richelieu," 260; and Joseph Schenck, 261–262; on method of studying "Shylock," 263–264; on actors' abilities, 266–267; President of National Anti-Vivisection Society, 274; arrives in Paris, 274; receives

visit from Pirandello, 275–276; procures wardrobe from Mike Angel, 277–278; and incident with farmer, 278–279; discusses playing "Mr. Reeder," 281–282; on autograph hunters, 282–283; fire at St. Margaret's, 283; on death of George V, 290–296; leaves for Monte Carlo, 297; on impersonation, 298–300; on doctors, 303–305; vacation at St. Margaret's, 305–316; at Coronation of George VI, 315–326; reflections on ten years in the studio, 327–341

Arliss, Mrs. George (Flo), 4, 32; as Lady Beaconsfield, 64; vacation at Mt. Tauquitz, 64; leaves for England, 78; at opening of "Old English," 89; 136; trip to Carlsbad Caverns, 148–149; 219; 234; and sandwiches for George VI's coronation, 317–318, 322–323

Arnold, Edward, 273
Astor, Mary, 196, 218
Aylmer, Felix, 259
Aynesworth, Allan, 259

Balcon, M. E., 238, 271, 272, 276, 280, 285, 309
Barker, Granville, 112
Barnard, Ivor, 288
Barnes, Sir Kenneth, 308
Barr, Pat, 289
Baur, Harry, 276
Beamish, Richard, 11, 13–16; 20–24, 27, 81; welcomes Arliss to New York, 134–135; 232
Beecher, Janet, 226, 235
Beery, Noah, 136, 143
Bell, James, 219
Bell, Mr. and Mrs., of Bel Air, 65
Bellew, Kyrle, 77
Belmore, Lionel, 162, 273
Bennett, Joan, 78
Berkeley, Ballard, 289
Biggers, Earl Derr, 119–120; 136
Bigham, Sir Trevor and Lady, 148
Birmingham, Alan, 219
Black, Edward, 312, 327
Boles, Captain, 151
Bolton, Guy, 276, 288

345

Forbes, Ralph, 58
Ford, Henry, 257-258
Ford, John, 313
"Forsyte Saga, The," 239
Fox, Jack, 314
Franklin, Edgar, 216
Frith, Leslie, 288

GAINSBOROUGH PICTURES STUDIOS, 310
Galsworthy, John, 82, 85-86, 97
Galsworthy, Mrs. John, 84-85
Garbo, Greta, 299
Gardner, Shayle, 77
Garner, Lee, 77
Garside, John, 288
Gateson, Marjorie, 201, 219
Gaudio, Tony, 217
Gaumont-British, 231-232, 236-258, 271-272; "shake-up" in, 309-310
Gawthorne, Peter, 259, 289
George V, death of H. M., 290
George VI, coronation of H. M., 315-326
Gerrard, Gene, 288
Gibbs, George, 204, 217
Gill, Basil, 313
Gillmore, Frank, 156-157; makes acceptance speech, 157-160
Goetz, William, 234
Goodchild, Muriel A., letters to Arliss, 241-243
Goodman, Jules Eckert, 192
Goodwin, Henrietta, 97
Gore-Browne, Margaret, 148, 292
Green, Al, director, 53-54, 58, 64, 77, 87, 97
"Green Goddess, The," 27, 37-39, 53; cast of, 58; 98, 118, 120, 132
Green, Paul, 217
Greenbaum, Mutz, 288
Greenwood, Edwin E., 285, 289
Griffies, Ethel, 97
Griffith, Ray, 185, 234, 271
Gullan, Campbell, 244, 289
"Guv'nor, The," see "Mr. Hobo"

HALE, LOUISE CLOSSER, 192
Hambourg, Jan, 243
Hamilton, Duchess of, 310
Hamilton, Hale, 218

Hamlin, Mary, 146, 152, 162
Hammond, John Hays, 194-195, 271
Hardy, Sam, 136
Hare, Lumsden, 234, 273
Harolde, Rolf, 162
Harrigan, Robert, 273
Harrison, Frederick, 132
Harvey, Paul, 234
Harwood, H. M., 243, 259
Hayes, George, 288
Hays, Will, 148
Hazen, Mr., 15-17, 20-25
Heggie, O. P., 219
Heidfelt, Mr., 61
Heming, Violet, 180, 192
Henderson, Ray, press agent, 71-72; death of, 73
Henry, Charlotte, 235
Herbert, Holmes, 234
Hicks, Mrs. Seymour (later Lady Hicks), 250
Hignet, H. R., 288
Hilliard, Stafford, 288
"His Lordship," 297-306; holdup on, 303; cast of, 313
Hobbes, Halliwell, 273
Hollywood, life in, xi; description of, 29-36; cost of living in, 51-52
Hopper, Hedda, 192
House, Colonel E. M., 251-256, 274
"House of Rothschild, The," 164, 200, 222-225; cast of, 234
Howell, Maude T., stage manager, 47, 58, 87, 97, 122, 138, 147, 162, 180, 192, 201, 216-219, 226, 234, 266, 271, 273, 278, 288-289, 306, 313-314, 327
Hubbard, Lucien, 185
Hubble, Mr. and Mrs. Edwin, 146-147, 306-307
Hurst, Brandon, 234
Huston, Walter, 276
Huxley, Aldous, 195

IBSEN, HENRIK, 108
"Iron Duke, The," 241-259; cast of, 259
Irving, Henry, 180, 264
Isham, Giles, 259

JAMESON, DR., 194
Janney, Leon, 97

346

347

349